Exploiting the Amstrad PCW9512

Exploiting The Amstrad PCW9512

John Campbell
&
Marion Pye

NEW·TECH

Newtech
An imprint of Butterworth-Heinemann Ltd
Linacre House, Jordan Hill, Oxford OX2 8DP

◉ PART OF REED INTERNATIONAL BOOKS

OXFORD LONDON BOSTON
MUNICH NEW DELHI SINGAPORE SYDNEY
TOKYO TORONTO WELLINGTON

First published 1991
Reprinted 1991

© John Campbell and Marion Pye 1991

All rights reserved. No part of this publication
may be reproduced in any material form (including
photocopying or storing in any medium by electronic
means and whether or not transiently or incidentally
to some other use of this publication) without the
written permission of the copyright holder except in
accordance with the provisions of the Copyright,
Designs and Patents Act 1988 or under the terms of a
licence issued by the Copyright Licensing Agency Ltd,
90 Tottenham Court Road, London W1P 9HE, England.
Applications for the copyright holder's written permission
to reproduce any part of this publication should be addressed
to the publishers.

British Library Cataloging in Publication Data
A CIP record for this book is available from
the British Library.

ISBN 0 7506 0075 6

Printed and bound in Great Britain by
Biddles Ltd, Guildford and King's Lynn

Contents

Chapter One - A Specimen Chapter To Introduce This Book
1-1 Some Opening Words	1
1-2 How This Book Works	4

Part One LocoScript
NOTES FOR LocoScript LEARNER DRIVERS Introduction	9
NOTES FOR LocoScript LEARNER DRIVERS Starting Up LocoScript	10
NOTES FOR LocoScript LEARNER DRIVERS Closing Down LocoScript	13
NOTES FOR LocoScript LEARNER DRIVERS About The Disc Drive(s)	14

Chapter Two - Creating Documents
2-1 Introduction	19
2-2 Keying In Text	20
2-3 Editing - Getting Rid Of Unwanted Text	23
2-4 Editing - Inserting Letters And Words	27
2-5 Creating Short Documents - e.g. letters & memos	29
2-6 Creating Longer Documents - Report/Thesis/Book	32

Chapter Three - Printing & Editing
3-1 Introduction	39
3-2 Printing a Document	40
3-3 Printing Part of a Document	44
3-4 Inserting Blocks of Text into a Document	46
3-5 Finding a Word (or Words) in the Text	49
3-6 Finding and Substituting Words	52
3-7 Handling Blocks of Text	55

Chapter Four - Controlling The Layout Of Documents
4-1 Introduction	63
4-2 Using The 'SET' And 'CLEAR' Menus	64
4-3 Changing The Margins For The Whole Text	68
4-4 Changing The Margins For Part Of The Text	69
4-5 Setting Tabs	71
4-6 Indenting Text Temporarily	73
4-7 Using Margins And Tabs In A Document	74
4-8 Creating And Using Stock Layouts	77
4-9 Controlling The Page Length	79

Contents

4-10 Changing The Character And Line Spacing	81
4-11 Justifying Text To Both Margins	83
4-12 Centring And Right Aligning Lines	87
4-13 Creating A New Standard Template	89

Chapter Five - Enhancing The Printed Page

5-1 Introduction	97
5-2 Printing Words Underlined	98
5-3 Printing Words In Bolder Type	101
5-4 Paper Sizes And Types	104
5-5 Using Other Printers (with LocoScript)	107
5-6 Changing A Print Wheel	111
5-7 Changing A Ribbon Cartridge	113

Chapter Six - Mailmerge With LocoMail

6-1 Some Background	117
6-2 Creating A Master Letter	119
6-3 Printing A Master Letter (FILL)	123
6-4 The Master (MERGE) Document	125
6-5 Creating A Merge Data File	128
6-6 Implementing A Mailshot Run	134
6-6 Implementing A Mailshot Run	135

Chapter Seven - Checking Your Spelling With LocoSpell

7-1 Introduction	139
7-2 Checking Your Spelling	141

Part Two General Applications

INTRODUCTION What The Rest Of This Book Covers	145

Chapter Eight - General 'Housekeeping' With CP/M

8-1 Introduction	149
8-2 Discs And Drives	150
8-3 Some Tips On Looking After Your Files	151
8-4 Resetting (Rebooting) The PCW	153
8-5 Finding Out What Is On A Disc	155
8-6 Checking The Space Left On A Disc	158
8-7 Making A Duplicate Copy Of A Disc	160

Contents

8-8 Copying A Disc From 8000 Format	163
8-9 Booting Automatically Into A Program	166
8-10 Creating A (data) Disc	169
8-11 Naming And Storing Your Document FILES	172
8-12 Matching Up File Names ('masks')	174
8-13 Making A Duplicate Copy Of A File	176
8-14 Getting Rid Of Unwanted 'Files'	178
8-15 Renaming A Document File	180
8-16 Some General Points About CP/M Commands	181
8-17 Personalising Your System	183
8-18 Setting Up Special Function Keys	184
8-19 Protecting Your Files	188
8-20 Setting Passwords	190
8-21 Installing & Using Commercial Software	191

Chapter Nine - Storing Information With LocoFile & dBase II

9-1 A Word About Databases In General	195
9-2 An Introduction To LocoFile	197
9-3 Installing LocoFile	198
9-4 Running LocoFile	202
9-5 Finding A Particular Record.	205
9-6 Changing The Index Key	206
9-7 Making Changes To A Datafile	208
9-8 Getting Rid Of Unwanted Records	212
9-9 Using LocoFile	214
9-10 Changing The Index	220
9-11 Extracting Items	224
9-12 Setting Up Your Own Datafile	226
9-13 Setting Up A Pattern Card	228
9-14 Exchanging Datafiles With LocoMail	230
9-15 An Introduction to dBase II	233
9-16 Using dBase II On The PCW	234
9-17 Working With The dBase Welcome Program	235
9-18 Creating A Brand New Database	237
9-19 Adding Records To Your New Database File	239
9-20 Examining The Records In A File - BROWSE	241
9-20 Examining The Records In A File - DISPLAY	243

iii

Contents

9-21 Sorting The Records In A File	245
9-22 Programming With dBase	246

Chapter Ten - Working With Numbers – SuperCalc 2

10-1 A Word About Spreadsheets In General	249
10-2 Starting up SuperCalc - The Screen Display	250
10-3 Putting Information Onto The Spreadsheet	252
10-4 Commands - Saving Your Work	256
10-5 Commands - Cancelling And Quitting	258
10-6 Starting Up And Loading A File	259
10-7 Getting Rid Of Unwanted Items - Blank	261
10-7 Getting Rid Of Unwanted Items - Delete	262
10-8 Printing A Copy Of The Spreadsheet	263
10-9 Inserting Extra Rows And Columns	264
10-10 Replicating Entries	265
10-11 Some Closing Words	266

Chapter Eleven - Integrated Software mini Office Professional

11-1 Introduction	269
11-2 Getting mini Office Started	270
11-3 Word Processing	273
11-4 The Word Processor Menu	281
11-5 The Word Processor Menu - Printing	283
11-6 Spell Checker And Thesaurus	285
11-7 Database Module	287
11-8 Processing Data	293
11-9 Printing The Results	294
11-10 Using Database Files For Mailmerging	296
11-11 Spreadsheet Module	297
11-12 Graphics Module	301
11-13 Communications Module	302
11-14 Disc Utilities	303

Some Closing Words

Applications We Have Not Explored	307

Index

Chapter One
A Specimen Chapter To Introduce This Book

SECTION 1-1
Some Opening Words

The purpose of this chapter is simply to get you used to the way this book is laid out and how it works.

The purpose of the *book* is a bit more complex. What we have tried to do is to give all users of the PCW9512 a pretty good insight into how they might use their machines for far more than just word processing with LocoScript.

It is our guess that the PCW9512 is so popular because it is a simple and attractive package and it doesn't cost an arm and a leg. It is the sort of package which appeals to people in small businesses who are trying to make their minds up whether to go for computing or not, and its price makes it quite feasible to risk an experiment. Then again, there are many people who have bought the machine for use at home - perhaps to get away from hand written letters. So PCWs pop up all over the place.

Many of them are owned and driven by people who are completely new to computing and, at first, they are quite happy to stick to using their machine as a word processor - a sort of 'super typewriter'. After about eight months or so many PCW drivers have conquered their initial apprehension about using a computer and they begin to realise that their PCW is not just a word processor, it is in fact a full blown general purpose computer.

It may not be *state of the art*, and it probably never was *at the leading edge of technology* (we thought we'd get the clichés and the 'hyper-speak' out of the way early on), but it is still a powerful and useful tool; one that anyone can use to do any of the jobs you'd expect a computer to do - assuming you can get the software (the computer programs) to do it.

So, about eight months after they take delivery of their very first computer, a good proportion of PCW owners begin to look around for other kinds of software. But to do what exactly? What *applications programs* are available for the PCW?

SECTION 1-1
Some Opening Words

Well, that is what this book explores. Broadly speaking, it has two parts: the first is about using the PCW as a word processor with LocoScript. The second part examines a range of other applications programs you can use on your PCW. In these pages you will find information about:

- LocoScript
- LocoMail
- LocoSpell
- CP/M
- LocoFile
- dBase ll
- SuperCalc^2
- mini Office Professional

Actually, while we were planning the book, we found ourselves in a bit of a quandary. We have no idea how much you already know about LocoScript. If you have had your machine for a matter of days, then you probably won't know much about it, but if you have had your machine for several months, then you will know about it. So what do we do? Do we include information about LocoScript or not?

We have decided on a belt and braces approach and we have included quite a lot of information about LocoScript. Our reasoning goes like this: If you, the reader, are new to your PCW then you will probably need some help with LocoScript and you'll find it here. If, on the other hand, you have been using the PCW for some time, you will probably have developed your own ways of doing things - some good, some bad - so you could probably benefit from a sort of revision of the topic - particularly as we might have found some wrinkles which you haven't.

SECTION 1-1
Some Opening Words

So, if you are new to the PCW, treat the first chapters as an easy introduction to LocoScript. If you have been using LocoScript for a while, or if you've read the *Step By Step* book *'Using The Amstrad PCW9512'*, treat the first few chapters as a reminder of things you may have forgotten, or not yet had a chance to try.

The LocoScript sections of *this* book (*Exploiting* the PCW) cover many of the points in the original book (*Using* the PCW) - we're talking about the same subject, so that's inevitable, but it does not go into the sort of fine detail about basics as we did in the 'Using the PCW' book. So, if you really are completely new to computing and you're not even sure how to switch the computer on and off, or what a disc drive is for and the like, then you may need to work through that book as well.

So, the first part of the book can be either new information, or a chance to revise and review your understanding of LocoScript. The second part deals with the most popular general applications for computers: Firstly, *databases* - in which we describe LocoFile and dBase II and secondly a *spreadsheet*; in this case SuperCalc^2. Then we take a look at an *integrated package* - mini Office - which has modules for word processing, database, spreadsheet, graphics and communications (between computers).

Computers have many more applications, but these are the main ones and they are the ones you are most likely to move towards.

SECTION 1-2
How This Book Works

As you might expect from a book in the *'Step By Step'* series, we try to describe, step-by-step, how to get results with the machine and the various software packages. And we assume that you'll be trying things out on your own computer as we go along.

Where we are providing background information, or where we are describing how the PCW should respond after you have carried out an activity, then the paragraphs are laid out just like this one.

Where we are describing how to carry out a procedure, in *'do-this'* paragraphs:

1   You will find them laid out like this.

2   In do-this paragraphs we shall be asking you to tap a key, or key in a command. The keys you should strike will appear in boldface. Most often, we shall use **UPPER CASE BOLD** to show you what to key in (even in those cases where you can use upper or lower case letters). But sometimes - mostly when we are giving examples - we shall use lower case letters, just to reinforce the point that you don't *have* to use capitals for most of the commands. E.g. We might ask you to key in,

   dir a:[RETURN].

3   Where you see a word enclosed in square brackets, [RETURN], or [ALT], or [EXIT], or even [Z] we shall be referring to an individual key on the keyboard. When it appears in bold, as in,

   dir a:[RETURN]

it means that you should tap the key in question. So, this example reads, *'Key in the letters "dir" then a space, then "a:", followed immediately by (tapping) the big key marked "RETURN" to complete this step of the process.'*

SECTION 1-2
How This Book Works

Occasionally, when a command has several outcomes, or where the software offers you more than one option, you will find paragraphs laid out like these:

- Each of these 'bullet points' will describe one of the options open to you
- They are very useful for teasing out the separate strands of a complicated looking screen, for example
- So, we use bullet points when we want to work through a list

Every page in the book is headed up like this one, so you can:

- Keep track of where you are
- Find information quickly
- Recognise when you have reached the end of an activity

Quite often you will find that a single procedure involves two or three separate stages. In those cases, when you have finished one stage the *do-this* paragraph numbering starts from 1 for the first action in the new stage; so don't think we've lost count, or run out of fingers if you suddenly see the number 1 half way through a longish section.

The book is split up into separate chapters - each one covering how to get particular results with a given software package. And each chapter is split up into sections which deal with a set procedure. We have tried to get all the important information into the book, but more importantly we have tried to make it easy for you to get the information back out again. We hope we have succeeded.

John Campbell & Marion Pye

Tillington, 1990.

■ NOTES FOR LocoScript LEARNER DRIVERS
Introduction

Remember, if you are completely new to the PCW9512 and to computing, you will probably benefit from reading the companion book in the *Step By Step* series, *'Using The Amstrad PCW9512'* by John Campbell. It assumes no prior knowledge of computers whatsoever, whereas this book is really pitched at users who have had their PCW for a short time. Consequently we skip most of the basic details which are covered in *'Using The Amstrad PCW9512'*.

But just in case the book shops are closed and you want to get going, we begin this section with a few hints for the first timer, covered in the type of detail you will find in *'Using The Amstrad PCW9512'*.

■ NOTES FOR LocoScript LEARNER DRIVERS
Starting Up LocoScript

1 Plug the machine in to the mains. Turn the mains switch on and then turn the machine on with the push button at the rear of the monitor.

Note: You should always work with a *copy* of the master disc for any software you use. If you don't know how to make a copy, refer to section 9-7 of this book. Make a copy, keep the original master somewhere safe and work with the copy.

2 Take the disc labelled 'LocoScript 2' out of its clear plastic case and put it in the disc drive slot (the left hand one if you have two drive slots). Make sure that side 1 of the disc is uppermost.

3 After a few moments you should see the light on the drive glow, and you should hear the disc drive whirring. If nothing seems to happen for some time, try tapping the long **[SPACEBAR]** on the keyboard just once.

You should see a pattern of horizontal lines start to appear on your screen. If the screen flashes, or if the PCW beeps at you hysterically, you have put the wrong disc in the drive - or perhaps the right disc but upside down.

4 Put the correct disc in (with side 1 uppermost) and tap the **[SPACEBAR]**.

You will have to wait for a few moments while the PCW 'reads' the LocoScript software and loads a copy of it into its memory (the original is still on the disc and is not changed at all).

■ NOTES FOR LocoScript LEARNER DRIVERS
Starting Up LocoScript

You will know when the software is loaded because the screen will display a pattern of boxes and columns with names in them. The top three lines will display in reverse video (black on white rather than white on black like the rest of the screen).

This is LocoScript's *'disc management'* display - which seems very intimidating at first, but it is not that complicated once you understand the basic principles of the display.

Firstly all but the top three lines of the screen are taken up by details about the disc drives you have available - this is simply for information purposes and needn't worry you just yet.

The top three lines (in reverse video) are concerned with LocoScript itself. Those three lines will stay on screen at all times when you are using LocoScript, though the information on them will change to reflect what you are doing at the time.

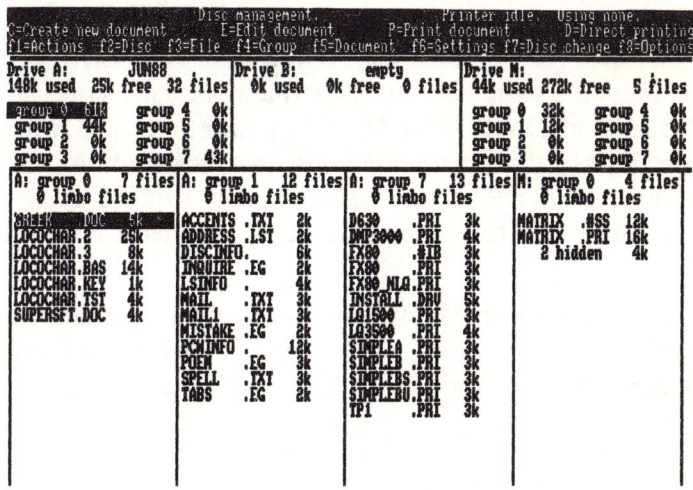

Fig. 1: *Disc Management* screen.

■ NOTES FOR LocoScript LEARNER DRIVERS
Starting Up LocoScript

The top LocoScript information line reminds you of what you are doing, the other two lines provide you with a list of tasks that you can carry out from this point in the program.

Note: We have found that the best way to picture the function of this screen is to imagine you have walked into a building through the main doors and you have found yourself in a hallway with lots of other doors leading off - each one labelled with a different task (C to Create a new document, E to Edit an existing document and so on). You can take any one of those doors now, but you must come back to this point before you can change tasks or leave LocoScript via the main doors again, and if you don't leave via the main doors, you may destroy the work you have done. So this *Disc Management screen* is very important to you, when you start up, when you change tasks *and* when you close down.

Note: The screen display just below the three bright lines gives you information about three disc drives. Drive A: is the one that holds the LocoScript disc (the left hand slot if you have two) Drive B: is the second drive on a twin drive machine (the right hand slot) and drive M: is the *Memory Drive*. Drive M: is very easy to use and it responds far more quickly than either A: or B:, but beware.!! As its name implies drive M: is not really a disc drive - it is simply a part of the PCW's memory that has been set aside to work as if it *were* a disc drive!!

When you switch the PCW off, its memory is emptied and you lose whatever was in it. So think of the memory drive as a **temporary** lodging place for your work.

■ NOTES FOR LocoScript LEARNER DRIVERS
Closing Down LocoScript

When you are ready to close down, get back to the *Disc Management* screen (LocoScript will tell you how).

If you have been working on the memory drive (drive M:) make sure you have a **permanent** copy of all the documents you want to keep (by copying the document 'files' onto a disc).

When you have finished and you are satisfied that you have safety copies of everything you need, remove the disc(s) and switch off the machine.

Note: It is good practice to check that the drive slots are empty *before* switching the PCW on or off.

■ NOTES FOR LocoScript LEARNER DRIVERS
About The Disc Drive(s)

1 Switch your machine on and start up with a copy of your LocoScript master disc. Wait until the PCW displays the disc management screen.

The disc management screen displays two main types of information: The top three lines (in reverse video - i.e. black letters on white rather than white letters on black) are to do with the way LocoScript works. The rest of the screen gives you information about the disc drives on your machine.

The information about your disc drives is in turn broken into two types: The oblong boxes, just below the LocoScript information, tell you about the disc drives themselves. And the columns of information which take up the rest of the screen, are the names of *Files* (or *documents*) held on the disc drives.

Every PCW has at least two drives: A: and M:

The **A:** drive is the physical disc drive - the slot - on the **front left of the main unit** (if you have another drive slot on the **front right** of the unit this is drive B:). Drive M: is not actually a disc drive - it is a part of the PCW's memory which has been set aside to respond as if it were a disc drive.

Memory Drive - Drive (M:)

Because it is electronic rather than mechanical, the memory drive (drive M:) works much faster than an actual disc drive and that is the main advantage of having it. But beware! When you switch the PCW off you lose everything in its memory circuits - including the memory drive! So if you want to keep a copy of your work you *must* put that copy on one of your discs, before you switch off.

NOTES FOR LocoScript LEARNER DRIVERS
About The Disc Drive(s)

When you **Create** a new document file, you have to start by deciding where on your discs you intend to keep that file while you are working on it. When you want to **edit** a file which already exists you have to start by selecting the file you want to work with. You do both these jobs by moving the bright bars you can see on the screen. So how do you do that?

2   Find the **Cursor Control keys** - the four keys marked with arrows in the pad of keys at the right hand end of your keyboard. Tap the **[DOWN ARROW]** key just once.

The bright bar in the first column moves down one line to highlight the second filename in the list. But notice that the bright bar in the first oblong box has not moved.

3   Now hold down a **[SHIFT]** key and tap **[DOWN ARROW]** twice.

This time the bright bar in the first oblong box does move down and at the same time the bright bar in the columns area moves two columns to the right. Why is that? The upper of the bright bars highlights the name of a **group** of files, while the lower bright bar highlights the name of a file **within the highlighted group.** (If you look at the name at the top of the column you will see that it is the same as the name being highlighted in the oblong box.)

The **upper** bright bar is your **groups** cursor. The **lower** bright bar is you **files** cursor.

Note: The groups cursor is still in the box headed 'Drive A:' but also notice that there is a box for Drive B: (whether you have one fitted or not) and there is a box for Drive M:.

15

NOTES FOR LocoScript LEARNER DRIVERS
About The Disc Drive(s)

4 Hold down a [SHIFT] key, keep an eye on the screen and tap [RIGHT ARROW] twice. (four times if you have twin drives).

Your groups cursor moves to drive M:.

5 Hold down a [SHIFT] key and tap [UP ARROW] once then tap [LEFT ARROW] twice (four times if you have twin drives) and release the [SHIFT] key. When the screen settles down again, tap the [DOWN ARROW] (unshifted) and move the files cursor onto a file called '**DISCINFO**'.[1]

6 To select this file for editing, tap the letter [E].

A flag menu appears, asking you to confirm that you do want to edit the file of a particular name in group 1 on drive A:.

7 If this is what we want to do, tap the [ENTER] key to confirm and LocoScript will load the file, ready for you to work on.

8 Have a look at the file and then work through the *close down* procedure we discussed a few pages back from here.

---

1 *If you have a version of LocoScript other than version 2, you will have to choose another file to edit. Select one which does not have the suffix '.???'*

Chapter Two
Creating Documents

SECTION 2-1
Introduction

You can create a 'document' with LocoScript in a number of ways. The most simple and direct is to select the *'Create a Document'* option from LocoScript's opening menu, give the document a name and then key-in the text. For longer documents, for example a report or book, you can easily bring together text and data from a variety of sources. In this chapter we shall look at the different methods and examine the ways in which we can use LocoScript to improve the layout and organisation of the finished product.

Once we have created a document, we shall need to know how to move around it quickly and how to locate particular items. How to move between pages, from one page to another specified page and one section to another are important aspects of document creation that we shall consider here.

SECTION 2-2
Keying In Text

You key in text much as you would if you were using a typewriter. The keys give lower case letters, numbers or symbols which can be altered by holding down one of the [SHIFT] keys or setting [SHIFT LOCK] on.

The main difference, however, between a word processor and a typewriter is in the way you can move around your text and alter or edit it before committing it to paper. One of the best ways to find out about these is to work through a series of examples which are designed to incorporate those facilities you will most commonly need.

1 Switch your machine on and start up with a **copy** of your LocoScript Start of Day disc. Wait until LocoScript displays the *'Disc Management'* screen. Hold down a [SHIFT] key then tap the [RIGHT ARROW] twice (four times if you have twin drives) and the [DOWN ARROW] once, to move the groups cursor into *'Group 1'* on drive M:. Tap [C] to create a **new** document.

LocoScript displays the name *'DOCUMENT.000'* for this new file, and tells you that you are in Group 1 on drive M:. You will need to give your files names that relate to what they contain (see the section headed, *'Naming And Storing Your Document Files'*).

2 Key in the file name, **EXAMPLE1.TXT** (it does not matter whether you use capitals or lower case letters, LocoScript will convert them to capitals automatically). Then tap the [ENTER] key.

After a short while, you will see the LocoScript blank page display.

SECTION 2-2
Keying In Text

3 Key in the following paragraph, but **do not** press the 'carriage return' (the **[RETURN]** key) at all and do not key in the quotation marks. Keep an eye on the screen as you type the words in, and do not worry if you make mistakes.

'The book called, "Exploiting The Amstrad PCW9512" will help you prepare professional looking documents and keep detailed business records.'

4 Now, tap the **[RETURN]** key twice, and key in:

'The book assumes some prior knowledge of computers, but will take you quickly through the basics and on to the detailed refinements.'

5 Tap **[RETURN]** and then tap the **[EXIT]** key to get this screen:

Fig. 2: The EXIT from editing flag menu.

21

SECTION 2-2
Keying In Text

The flag menu (see the illustration on the previous page) offers you four options. All except the second one will get you back to the *'Disc Management'* screen, but in different ways. The first option will **save** a copy of the file before returning to the disc management screen, the second one will **save** a copy of the file but **remain** in the document. The third one will **save** a copy of your work and then **print** it. And the fourth one will **abandon** your work without saving a copy first.

6 Tap the letter **[S]** then the letter **[P]**. Put some paper in the printer - lining-up the left hand side with the **third** rib on the printer casing. Tap the **[ENTER]** key. If the cursor is flashing at the left of the LocoScript control area, tap the **[EXIT]** key.

A flag menu shows you some of the printer selections. You can change these if you want to. For now, just tap **[ENTER]** to accept the standard settings.

A second flag menu confirms certain things about the printed output and then asks you to confirm that it should proceed.

7 Tap the **[ENTER]** key to proceed.

As the printing starts, you get a warning that the file you have created will be saved on drive M: and reminding you to make a permanent copy before switching your computer off (see *'About The Disc Drive(s)'* in the notes for LocoScript Learner Drivers).

8 Acknowledge the warning by tapping the **[ENTER]** key.

LocoScript saves a copy of your work, returns to the disc management screen and then seems to stop. But if you look in the column for drive M: Group 1 files you will see one there called **EXAMPLE1.TXT**.

SECTION 2-3
Editing - Getting Rid Of Unwanted Text

No matter how good you are at driving a keyboard, you will eventually make a mistake of some kind. On a typewriter, that might mean starting all over again, but with LocoScript all you have to do is remove the mistake and then key-in the text correctly. The following exercises take you through the various ways you can **delete** text and move the cursor through text.

1 Switch your machine on and start up with a **copy** of your LocoScript Start of Day disc. Wait until LocoScript displays the disc management screen, move you file cursor onto the filename *'DISCINFO'* in Group 1 on the A: drive. We shall copy an existing file onto drive M: so that we can work on it without making any permanent changes to the original.

2 Tap **[f3/f4]** and then tap **[ENTER]** to confirm that you want to copy the file. Move your groups cursor onto Group 1 on the memory drive (drive M:). Tap **[ENTER]** twice to make the copy. Now, tap **[E]** to edit this file, then **[ENTER]** to confirm your choice.

Note: If your copy of the file 'DISCINFO' has been edited before, the exercises might not work precisely as we describe here. Please make allowances for this or get an un-edited copy of the file. We shall not be saving any of the changes we make, so you will not damage the file while you are trying things out.

3 I want you to make a change in the second paragraph. Move the cursor down to the fifth line of that paragraph (using the **[DOWN ARROW]** key) and across to the word *'quite'* (use **[SHIFT]** and the **[WORD/CHAR]** key).

23

SECTION 2-3
Editing - Getting Rid Of Unwanted Text

4 With your cursor on the start of the word, tap the **[DEL->]** key (above the **[RETURN]** key) **six** times to **DEL**ete the word **and the space after it**. Now move your cursor to the word *'work'* near the end of paragraph three, and tap the **[<-DEL]** key **four times** to DELete the word *'can'* and the space after it.

Notice that as you moved down to paragraph three, the words in paragraph two adjusted themselves to take account of the space left by the removal of the word *'quite'*.

5 If you want to *'relay'* (short for re-lay-out, i.e. lay the paragraph out again) a paragraph while you are still in it, try this: Move the cursor to the beginning of line two in paragraph three. Delete the word *'together'* and the space after it using the **[DEL->]** key. Now tap the **[UNIT/PARA]** key.

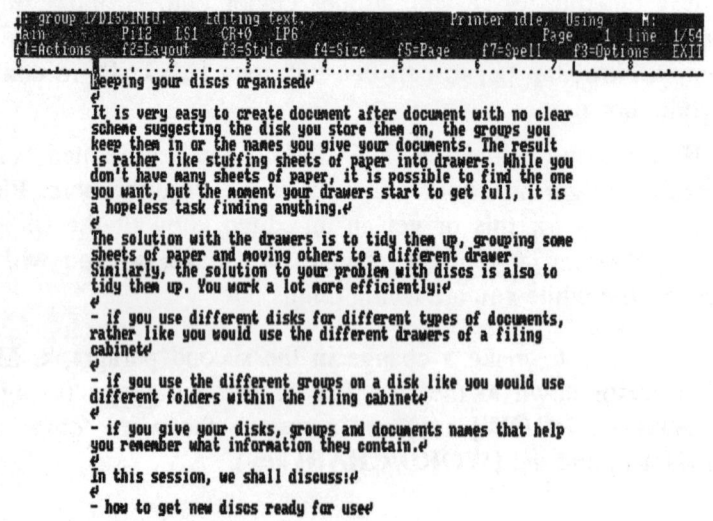

Fig. 3: The amended text.

SECTION 2-3
Editing - Getting Rid Of Unwanted Text

Note: As the cursor moves through the text LocoScript ensures that the text conforms to the page layout. **This is a general rule.**

7   Tap **[ALT]** and **[DOC/PAGE]** to get back to the start of the page.

If we wish to remove a larger section of text there is another way to do it.

1   Tap the **[CUT]** key (in the top row of the pad of keys at the right of the keyboard). LocoScript flashes up a reminder of what to do next. Hold down a **[SHIFT]** key and tap **[WORD/CHAR] five** times.

You will see that all the text from where you pressed **[CUT]** to the present position of the cursor is highlighted.

2   Now tap **[CUT]** again.

If you look closely you will see that LocoScript has 'cut' or deleted everything that had been highlighted *including* the carriage return symbols.

3   Tap **[DOC/PAGE]**. When the cursor reaches the start of page two, hold down the **[ALT]** key and tap **[UNIT/PARA]** three times. The cursor moves up to the start of the third paragraph from the bottom of the page.

4   Tap **[CUT]** and then **[UNIT/PARA]** twice. Then tap **[CUT]** again and watch as LocoScript deletes the text you have marked line by line and at the same time 'pulls' all the other text up to fill the gap that would otherwise have been left there.

SECTION 2-3
Editing - Getting Rid Of Unwanted Text

The broad line across the screen represents the end of the page. What we have done here is to pull text from page two and put it on page one. You may not want that to happen, so refer to section 4-9 *'Controlling The Page Length'* for details of how to 'force' a page break to occur just where you want.

5 Move the cursor down to the fourth line of the paragraph which begins *'Earlier in this tutorial'* - by using the **[UNIT/PARA]** key. Find the words *'information, specified by its capacity'*, then move across to the *'I'* of *'If it has been'*. Tap **[CUT]**, then move the cursor down two lines (notice the highlighting) and finally, move the cursor left to the space after the full stop and before the word *'If'*. Then tap **[CUT]** again and watch the screen.

Once again we have made a mess of our layout, but we can soon put it right.

6 Tap the **[UNIT/PARA]** key and watch the screen.

So LocoScript enables you to delete text one character at a time and it enables you to cut words, lines, paragraphs, or pages in one go.

7 Abandon the file in memory by tapping **[EXIT]** then the letter **[A]** then tapping **[ENTER]**. The disc copy of the file will be unchanged.

SECTION 2-4
Editing - Inserting Letters And Words

1   Switch your machine on and start up with a *copy* of your LocoScript Start of Day disc. Wait until LocoScript displays the disc management screen.

2   Move the cursor onto the filename *'DISCINFO'* in group 1 on the A: drive. Tap **[f3/f4]** and then tap **[ENTER]** to confirm that you want to copy the file. Move your groups cursor onto Group 1 on the memory drive (drive M:). Tap **[ENTER]** twice to make the copy.

3   Now, tap **[E]** to edit this file, then tap **[ENTER]** to confirm your choice.

The first line of text in this file seems to be intended as a sub-heading, but it looks just the same as the rest of the text. We need to make it stand out more.

1   Tap the **[SHIFT LOCK]** key (you should see the little red light come on). Now, key in the words: **'WORKING WITH LOCOSCRIPT:'** followed by two spaces.

You will see the first line of the text move down to make room for the words you keyed in. It looks as if your text is on a different line from the original.

2   Tap the **[UNIT/PARA]** key and watch what happens.

The layout adjusts itself. The space was created temporarily to give you room to work in.

3   Move the cursor down one line and across to the first word *'you'* in that line (use **[SHIFT]** and **[WORD/CHAR]**). Now key in the words, **or drive** followed by a space. Watch the screen closely as you tap **[UNIT/PARA]** again.

27

SECTION 2-4
Editing - Inserting Letters And Words

So you can see that you can insert letters and words as you wish. In a later section, *'Inserting Blocks Of Text Into A Document'*, we shall see how to insert much larger pieces of text. But we have some more groundwork to do before that, so:

4   Abandon the file in memory by tapping **[EXIT]** then the letter **[A]** then tapping **[ENTER]**. The disc copy of the file will be unchanged.

SECTION 2-5
Creating Short Documents - e.g. letters & memos

Documents can be created by keying in text or copying in text already stored on the computer. This section deals mainly with keying in text but includes a short phrase already stored in your copy of LocoScript.

1 Switch your machine on and start up with a **copy** of your LocoScript Start of Day disc. Wait until LocoScript displays the disc management screen.

2 We are going to create a short document in drive M:, so move your files cursor into the M: Group 1 column and tap **[C]**.

You would not normally put your document files on this disc - you would create a separate data disc - but we shall work on the same disc here because we cannot be certain that you have in fact created a separate data disc (see your computer's *'User Instructions'* for details).

LocoScript will offer you the file name *'DOCUMENT.000'*, so the first thing to do is to think of a more useful name for the file.

3 Overtype the existing file name with: **EXAMPLE2.TXT**.

If you hit a wrong key, just use the [<-DEL] key to delete the mistake and key it in again. It does not matter whether you key in the letters in upper or lower case. LocoScript will automatically display capitals on the screen.

4 Tap the **[ENTER]** key to open the new file and to get the 'blank' page display.

You will see that this page display has margins set at column 10 and at column 72, so the printed text will have a maximum width of 6.2 inches if you print out at 10 characters per inch (cpi.) and it will have a maximum width of just over 5 inches if you print out at 12 cpi. (see *'Printing A Document'* in the next chapter).

SECTION 2-5
Creating Short Documents - e.g. letters & memos

You can create a document by keying in new text or pasting in text already stored by LocoScript. We shall use both methods here to show how this can be done.

Note: LocoScript holds a series of blocks or phrases which you insert into documents by tapping the [PASTE] key followed by a letter of the alphabet. See section 3-7, *'Handling Blocks Of Text'* for more information.

5 For this exercise I want you to key in the text which appears on the next page. If you hit a wrong key, just use the **[<-DEL]** key to delete the mistake and key it in again. In your own time, have a go at creating the document. The words in **bold** print and in square brackets tell you which keys to hit and when.

6 When you have checked your work and corrected any mistakes, tap the **[EXIT]** key and then tap the letter **[S]** and the letter **[P]** (watch the highlighting bar on the menu). Put a sheet of paper in the printer, then tap **[ENTER]**.

You will notice the cursor flashing at the left of the LocoScript control area.

7 Tap the **[EXIT]** key to continue.

LocoScript saves the work you have done and then displays a flag menu which describes what it is about to do. For now, just tap **[ENTER]** to accept the standard print procedure, and tap **[ENTER]** again to accept the standard print settings.

LocoScript reminds you that you are working in memory drive, drive M:.

8 Tap **[ENTER]** once more to acknowledge the memory warning. When the printer has finished, remove the paper and have a look at your finished work.

■ SECTION 2-5
Creating Short Documents - e.g. letters & memos

MEMORANDUM[**RETURN**]

[**RETURN**]

TO: Department Heads[**RETURN**]

FROM: Managing Director[**RETURN**]

DATE: 20th September 1990[**RETURN**]

[**RETURN**]

I have just taken delivery of a new computer with LocoScript, LocoMail and LocoFile software and I am taking this opportunity of letting you know that I now propose to word-process my own documents, leaving the office staff time to deal with correspondence and enquiries.[**RETURN**]

[**RETURN**]

I had a few initial problems getting to grips with the keys.[**RETURN**]

[**PASTE Z**]

[**RETURN**]

There are many other uses for Locomotive software, as you will discover, and I look forward to receiving your comments and some statement from you of how your department might benefit.[**RETURN**]

Fig 4:   A memo for you to create (see previous page).

■ SECTION 2-6
Creating Longer Documents - Report/Thesis/Book

Longer documents can be keyed in directly, but are often assembled from smaller documents as we shall see here. A report or thesis or book is different from a letter or memorandum in two main ways: Firstly, the size of the finished document and secondly, the fact that the layout conventions are much more open to individual interpretation. So we need a page layout which gives us maximum freedom.

We shall also be handling much larger amounts of text so we shall need some help with organising and referencing sections, varying layout/style and coping with oversize files. To introduce some of these facilities we shall work with one of the documents supplied with your copy of LocoScript.

1 Switch your machine on and start up with a **copy** of your LocoScript Start of Day disc. Wait until LocoScript displays the disc management screen.

2 Move your files cursor onto the *A: MANUSCRP* column and tap **[C]**. A flag menu appears, offering you a very unhelpful file name. Tap the **[->]** key to move the cursor in the first line of the flag menu to the space after the dot in the file name. Key in two of your initials and then tap **[DEL->]** to delete the spare character. (It does not matter whether you use capitals or not, LocoScript will convert to capitals anyway.) Tap **[ENTER]** to open a new file on drive M: and get the blank page display.

You will see that this page display has margins set at column 10 and at column 72, so the printed text will have a maximum width of 6.2 inches if you print out at 10 characters per inch (cpi.) and it will have a maximum width of just over 5 inches if you print out at 12 cpi. (see *'Printing A Document'* in the next chapter). Notice also that five tabs have been defined for this page layout.

SECTION 2-6
Creating Longer Documents - Report/Thesis/Book

3 Tap the **[f1/f2]** key. Accept the *'Document set-up'* option by tapping the **[ENTER]** key.

The display you get on screen now looks a bit of a muddle at first. You need to note firstly that it mentions **'headers'** and **'footers'** and it refers to odd and even pages. Headers and footers are sections of text which will be printed at the head and the foot of each page in the document and you can arrange things so the headers and footers on even numbered pages are different from those on odd numbered pages.

So, you can specify four different sections of text. The on-screen display shows you what those four sections of text are now. You will edit this layout to suit yourself.

4 Hold down a **[SHIFT]** key and tap the **[EXCH/FIND]** key. Key in the words **'Book Title'**. Move the cursor down one line on the menu and key in the name of the file you are creating **DOCUMENT.(your initials)[ENTER]**. Then follow the screen instructions to make the replacements.

You can also ask LocoScript to number the pages, and select where the number should appear. In this example, the page number has been set to appear at the right hand side of the page footer on odd numbered pages and to the left on even numbered pages. (See the sections on using the set and clear menus in Chapter 4 for more details.)

Now when you print the finished document the footer and page number will be printed too.

5 Tap **[EXIT]** followed by **[ENTER]** to return to the Edit.

We shall remove the explanatory text from the screen and then load in some text to our document.

■ SECTION 2-6
Creating Longer Documents - Report/Thesis/Book

6 Tap the **[CUT]** key followed by the **[DOC/PAGE]** key, followed by **[CUT]** again and the page will clear. Now tap the **[f1/f2]** key, select *'Insert text'* and tap **[ENTER]**.

7 Move the cursor onto the *'LSINFO'* file in Group 1 on drive A: and tap **[ENTER]**. Tap **[ENTER]** again to confirm your selection and the text loads into your document.

One facility which is very useful when working with large documents is the ability to move to another, specified, page directly. This is a very simple operation, so try it now to move back to the beginning of your document.

1 Tap the **[f5]** (PAGE) key and a flag menu appears.

2 Key in the number **[1]** and **[ENTER]**. A message on screen confirms the page you wish to move to and monitors progress.

To make use of the layout facilities available to us in our new document, we can indent the items marked with hyphens half way down the first page for added emphasis.

1 Move the cursor down to the first hyphen and tap the **[TAB]** key once. Tap the **[RELAY]** key and repeat for the remaining three items.

SECTION 2-6
Creating Longer Documents - Report/Thesis/Book

In addition to referencing and numbering the document pages and using different layouts for emphasis, you may also find it useful to **mark sections** within your text. This can be invaluable if you need to find a section quickly in order to move it, change it's layout, or create a new file because you are running short of memory.

1 Move your text cursor down to the beginning of the paragraph which begins *'Because you will want'*, tap **[<-DEL]** to delete the carriage return and key in **[+] [UT]**. (The + or 'set' key is at the bottom left of your keyboard.) Switch on the word processing codes **[SHIFT f7/f8][+][ENTER]** and you will see the word *'(UniT)'* has appeared.

2 Move the text cursor down to *'LocoScript also organises'* and repeat to place a marker there.

Now, in addition to moving quickly from page to page (using the [DOC/PAGE] key), you can move quickly from section to section, using the UNIT key. (UNIT is [SHIFT] + [UNIT/PARA].)

3 To move up to the *beginning* of that section, hold down the **[ALT]** key (to reverse the action) and tap the **[UNIT]** key ([SHIFT] + [UNIT/PARA]).

■ **SECTION 2-6**
Creating Longer Documents - Report/Thesis/Book

Now that we have identified a section of our document, we can highlight it quickly if we need to move, delete, copy or edit it.

1 To show this, tap the **[COPY]** key followed by **[UNIT]** and watch as the section is highlighted. Now tap the **[CUT]** key followed by **[UNIT]** and watch the section disappear.

Note: You can CUT, COPY or CANcel a block if you wish. (These facilities are dealt with in more detail in *'Handling Blocks Of Text'* in the next chapter.)

2 When the screen settles down, tap the **[EXIT]** key and then tap the letter **[S]** and the letter **[P]**.

3 Put a sheet of paper in the printer (see *'Printing A Document'* if you are not sure how). Then tap **[ENTER]**. You will notice the cursor flashing at the left of the LocoScript control area. Tap the **[EXIT]** key to continue.

LocoScript saves the work you have done and then displays a flag menu which describes what it is about to do.

4 For now, just tap **[ENTER]** to accept the standard print procedure and tap **[ENTER]** again to accept the standard print settings.

5 **Wait for the printer to print the footer for the page!** When the printer has finished, remove the paper and have a look at your finished work.

Chapter Three
Printing & Editing

SECTION 3-1
Introduction

Once a document has been compiled, it is a relatively straightforward process to produce a printed copy. We saw in the previous chapter how to save and print a whole document at the end of an editing session. This chapter deals with printing a document from the menu screen and printing out a single page or pages of a longer document.

LocoScript has a FIND and a FIND/EXCHANGE function which allows you to search quickly through a document and make amendments to particular words or groups of characters. In this chapter we shall also see some of the many ways in which this can be useful. In addition, LocoScript has the ability to identify, copy, move and delete sections of text, using a few *'dedicated'* keys, [CUT], [COPY] and [PASTE]. The last section deals with the use of these and with the creation of standard *Phrases* which you can store on your copy of LocoScript, for future use.

SECTION 3-2
Printing a Document

LocoScript has two main printing procedures. If you have worked through either of the last two sections in the previous chapter you will have seen the first: Saving your work and then immediately printing **the file you have just created or edited**. The second print procedure is very similar, but much more flexible in that you can print **any document you like**. In this section we shall be looking at the second procedure.

LocoScript has a set of standard printing settings - which you can alter if you want to. We shall be examining the main changes you might want to make, but first we shall look at the standard printing process.

1 Switch your machine on and start up with a **copy** of your LocoScript Start of Day disc. Wait until LocoScript displays the disc management screen. If your machine is already switched on, put the copy of your LocoScript Start of Day disc in drive A: and hold down **[SHIFT]** and **[EXTRA]** with your left hand and then tap **[EXIT]** with your right hand.

2 Start by moving your files cursor onto the document we want to print. In this case, move the files cursor onto *INQUIRE.EG* in A: Group 1 and tap the letter **[P]** (for print).

The flag menu (see the illustration on the next page) tells you that LocoScript is about to print the document it describes, in high quality print and it will produce one copy of the complete document. So this menu describes **what** LocoScript is about to print.

If you have a standard daisywheel printer and no other, you have no option but to accept the high quality setting. But if you install a dot matrix printer into your system, you will be able to select either **draft** (higher speed) printouts, or **high quality**.

SECTION 3-2
Printing a Document

3 Move the highlighting bar down the menu to the *'Number of copies'* line, and tap the number **[2]**. Then tap **[ENTER]** to confirm this setting and tap **[ENTER]** again to tell LocoScript to go ahead.

The next flag menu tells you **how** LocoScript is about to print your document.

4 Put a sheet of your standard typing paper in the printer - if you do not know how to do it, see the next page.

5 First, check that the printer's *tractor feed* (for continuous stationery) is **not** fitted. (If it is fitted, remove it by unclipping the front edge and then lift and 'hinge' the unit backward, so the two hooks at the back of the unit clear their locating holes.) Fit the *paper tray*.

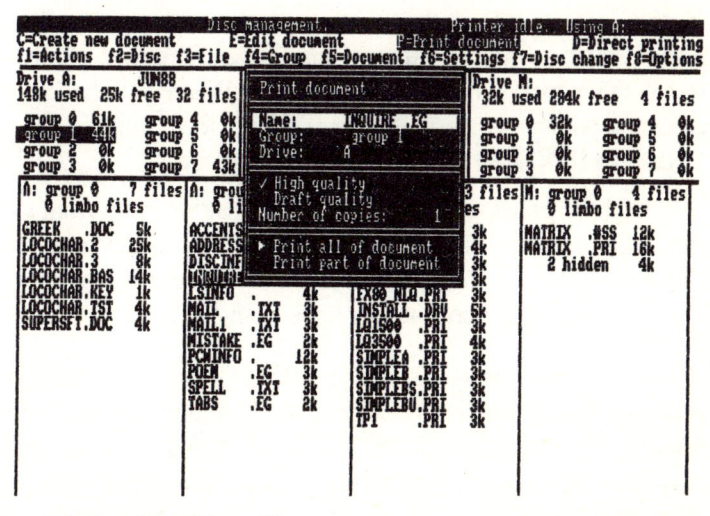

Fig. 1: Printing *Flag Menu* (1).

41

SECTION 3-2
Printing a Document

6 Take a sheet of your typing paper and slip it gently between the casing of the printer and the back surface of the printer PLATEN (the black rubber roller). Line-up the left hand edge of the paper with the third rib on the printer casing.

Toward the right hand end of the platen - you will see two levers. The one to the rear of the platen is the *paper release lever*, the one just in front of the platen is the *paper load lever*.

7 Move the paper load lever toward the front of the printer to its **fullest** extent. This lever has two positions and you should move it through the first 'stop' to the second. Then let it return about a third of the way back to the first 'stop'.

The printer will now feed your paper in, leaving it in position ready for you to start printing.

8 If you want to adjust the position of the paper, move the paper release lever toward the front of the printer. This will allow you to move the paper into the right position. When you have finished adjusting your paper, reset the paper release lever **and** the paper load lever. Tap **[ENTER]** to tell LocoScript to proceed.

When you load the printer LocoScript assumes that you may want to make a number of adjustments to the printer, so it automatically goes into its *Printer Control State* (or *Mode*). If you look at the three bright lines at the top of the screen you will see that they have changed.

10 For our purposes now, just tap the **[EXIT]** key to escape from the printer control state and start the print out. Wait until the printer finishes printing the first copy. Then load your second sheet of paper (as described above) and tap **[EXIT]** again. Take your second copy from the printer. That is all there is to printing out on your standard settings.

SECTION 3-2
Printing a Document

The next few pages examine one of the variations you can make to the standard printing process. Please remember that this book is not meant to replace your *'User Instructions Manual'*. It does **not** cover every possible eventuality - it is designed to provide you with a source of **quick** reference to those facilities you are most likely to use.

Try tapping the key labelled **[PTR]** to put the computer into **printer control mode**. If you look at the bottom line of the LocoScript control area you will see a list of the changes you can make from here.

Call up each of the function key menus in turn, have a look at the options and then tap **[CAN]** to cancel the menu. Tap **[EXIT]** when you have finished.

Note: That the F1 Actions Menu has an *'Abandon Printing'* option if you change your mind and do not wish to proceed with printing.

SECTION 3-3
Printing Part of a Document

1 Switch your machine on and start up with a *copy* of your LocoScript Start of Day disc. Wait until LocoScript displays the disc management screen. If your machine is already switched on, put the copy of your LocoScript disc in drive A: and hold down **[SHIFT]** and **[EXTRA]** and then tap **[EXIT]**.

2 Move your files cursor onto the file called 'PCWINFO1' in A: Group 1. Tap **[P]** to print this file. When you see the flag menu, move the highlighting bar down to the *'Print part of document'* line. (Notice that the arrowhead moves down with the bar.) Tap **[ENTER]**.

The new flag menu tells you the name of the file and it tells you that the first page is numbered *'1'* and the last page is numbered *'3'*. It is also set to print out from page 1 to page 3 inclusive.

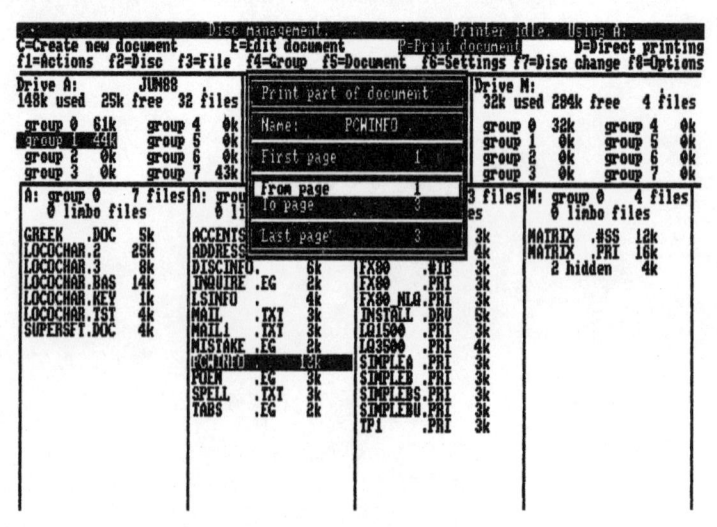

Fig. 2:   Print *Flag Menu* (2).

SECTION 3-3
Printing Part of a Document

We shall print page 2 only.

3 Check that *'From page'* is highlighted and key in the number **[2]**. Tap **[ENTER]** to confirm that setting. Move the highlighting bar down one line and key in the number **[2]** again. Tap **[ENTER]** to confirm **this** setting and tap **[ENTER]** again twice to proceed.

4 Put a sheet of your standard typing paper in the printer. Check with the previous section, *'Printing A Document'* if you are not sure how to prepare your printer for printing.

5 Then, just tap the **[EXIT]** key to escape from the printer control state and proceed with printing page 2 of the document.

SECTION 3-4
Inserting Blocks of Text into a Document

1 Switch your machine on and start up with a *copy* of your LocoScript Start of Day disc. Wait until LocoScript displays the disc management screen. Move your groups cursor down one and then across to 'Group 1' on the M: drive. Tap the letter **[C]** and then **[ENTER]** to create a new document with the name that LocoScript suggests.

The blank page display tells you that LocoScript is waiting for your 'input'. In this section we shall construct a document with the absolute minimum of typing.

2 Tap the **[f1/f2]** key. The third item on the flag menu is *'Insert text'* which is what we want to do. Select *'Insert text'* (either by tapping the letter **[I]** or by moving the highlighting bar) then tap the **[ENTER]** key.

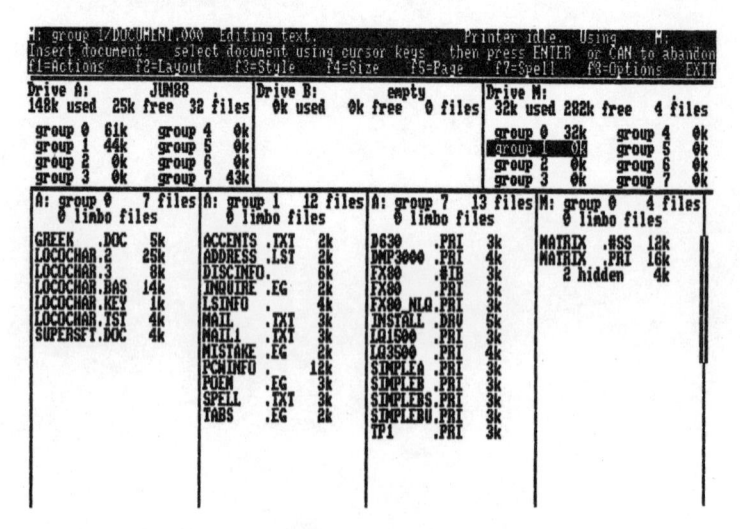

Fig. 3: *Disc Management* screen - Inserting Text.

■ SECTION 3-4
Inserting Blocks of Text into a Document

LocoScript displays what looks like the normal disc management screen, but if you look at the top line of the control area you will see it says: *'Editing text'*.

3   Move the groups cursor onto 'Group 1' on the A: drive. When the screen settles, move the file cursor onto the file called *'MISTAKE.EG'* to select that file as the one to be inserted into our empty document.

If you were to Edit the file *'MISTAKE.EG'* you would see that it is fourteen lines long and it is set up with margins at the 10th and the 50th character positions, i.e. the text is not more than 40 characters wide. Watch what happens as you insert it into **this** document.

4   Tap the **[ENTER]** key twice to confirm your selection.

LocoScript reads the disc and loads a copy of *'MISTAKE.EG'* into the page on screen. (The copy on the disc is still there, unchanged.)

Ignore the spelling for the moment, but notice that the file takes up only 12 lines here. That is because LocoScript automatically adjusted the text to fit the layout for your new file. (Here the text has a maximum width of 62 characters.)

5   Tap the **[RETURN]** key a couple of times and now insert another (longer) document. Tap **[f1/f2]**. Tap the letter **[I]** followed by the **[ENTER]** key.

Notice that the groups cursor is on drive M: again and not where you left it when you selected the file to be inserted.

6   Move the groups cursor back onto 'Group 1' on the A: drive. Then move the file cursor onto the file *'DISCINFO'*. Tap **[ENTER]** twice to select and read the file into your document.

SECTION 3-4
Inserting Blocks of Text into a Document

You have created a new document more than 2 pages in length and yet you have keyed in no text at all. Of course, **someone** had to type the text in the first place, but even so you can see the value of being able to read in text. It means you will only have to type, say, a standard paragraph for a quotation, once. And you can use it over and over again. See also the section headed, *'Handling Blocks Of Text'* for some other aspects of this same principle.

7 Abandon the file in memory by tapping **[EXIT]** then the letter **[A]** then tapping **[ENTER]**.

SECTION 3-5
Finding a Word (or Words) in the Text

The ability to FIND certain sections of the text is one that has many uses. Once you know how to do it - and once you realise how easy it is - you will devise your own procedures. We'll start by making a copy of a file so we have something to experiment with.

1 Switch your machine on and start up with a *copy* of your LocoScript Start of Day disc. Wait until LocoScript displays the disc management screen.

2 Move your files cursor to the right and then down until it settles on the file *'PCWINFO1'* in Group 1 on the A: drive. Tap **[f3/f4]** and then tap **[ENTER]** to confirm that you want to copy the file.

3 Move your groups cursor onto 'Group 1' on the memory drive (drive M:). Tap **[ENTER]** twice to make the copy. Now, tap **[E]** to edit this file, then tap **[ENTER]** to confirm your choice.

We'll use this file for our 'Find' experiments.

1 Once you have the text on screen, tap the key labelled **[EXCH/FIND]** (in the second row of the pad of keys at the right hand end of your keyboard).

The flag menu (see next page) is asking you to key in the text you want to find and it is also offering you some alternative ways of carrying out the search. LocoScript assumes that you want it to ignore the 'case' of the text - i.e. you do not mind if it looks for the text in capitals or in lower case. It assumes that you do not want it to look just for 'whole words' - i.e. if the text you key in occurs within a larger word it will point that out for you. It assumes that you will not be using 'wild cards' - i.e. that you will not be using a specific character to represent another (see below) and it assumes you will want to continue with the search.

SECTION 3-5
Finding a Word (or Words) in the Text

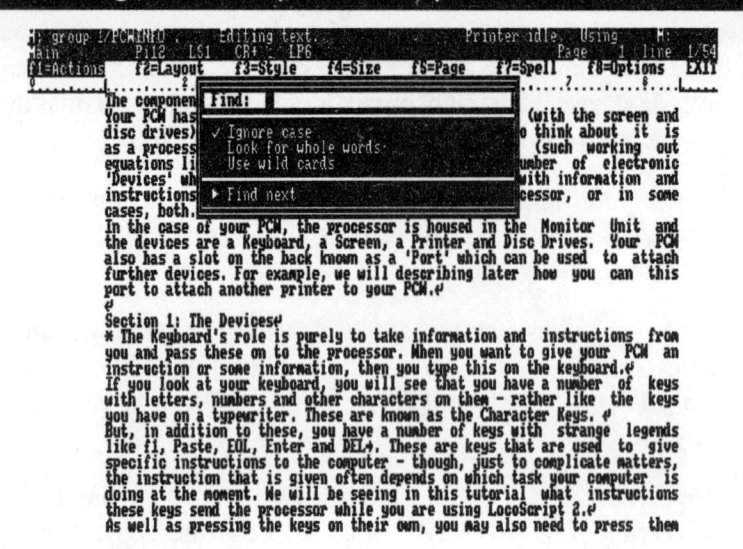

Fig. 4: The 'Find' Flag Menu.

The best way to find out what the last paragraph on the previous page means, is to work through some examples.

1 Key in the word **'key'**, and tap the **[ENTER]** key to continue with the search.

LocoScript searches through all the text on screen, then scrolls the text up until it finds the first occurrence of our text in the word *'Keyboard'*. Notice it starts with a capital 'K', but the text we supplied for the search did not. It is also part of a longer word.

2 Tap **[EXCH/FIND]** again and tap the **[ENTER]** key to repeat the search. Carry on through the document if you wish and when you have finished your search, hold down **[ALT]** and a **[SHIFT]** key and then tap **[DOC/PAGE]** to get back to the start of the file.

SECTION 3-5
Finding a Word (or Words) in the Text

A search always goes forward from the position of the cursor, so on short documents like this it is a good idea to start the search from the beginning of the file.

1   Tap **[EXCH/FIND]**, delete the text we keyed in for the previous search with the **[DEL->]** key. Now key this in: **'comput?'**. (N.B. the '?' symbol is the 'wild card' symbol we mentioned just now.) Now move the black bar on the menu down to the line which says *'Use wild cards'* and then tap the *Set Key* (the key marked **[+]** at the bottom left of the keyboard). The tick against the option, shows it is set **on**.

2   Tap the **[ENTER]** key to continue with the search.

LocoScript has found the word *'computing'*. This matches our 'mask' for the search - which was, *'comput-something'*.

3   Tap **[EXCH/FIND]** again, followed by **[ENTER]**.

This time LocoScript has found the word *'computer'* which, of course still matches our mask.

If you want to delete your text a sentence at a time (See also *'Getting Rid Of Unwanted Text'*), you can speed up the process by using the *Find* procedure and the *Cut* procedure in combination, like this.

1   Hold down **[ALT]** and **[SHIFT]** and tap **[DOC/PAGE]** (to get back to the start of the file for our example). Tap the **[CUT]** key. Now tap **[EXCH/FIND]**. Delete the text in the top line of the flag menu and then key in a '.' (fullstop or period). Watch the screen and tap **[ENTER]**. Now tap **[CUT]** again. Use **[DEL->]** to tidy up.

2   Now abandon the file with **[EXIT]**, **[A]**, **[ENTER]**.

SECTION 3-6
Finding and Substituting Words

The ability to find and replace certain sections of the text is one that has many uses. Here too we shall start by making a copy of a file to experiment with and then open the copy file.

1 Switch your machine on and start up with a *copy* of your LocoScript Start of Day disc. Wait until LocoScript displays the disc management screen.

2 Move your files cursor to the right and then down until it settles on the file *'PCWINFO1'* in group 1 on the A: drive. Tap **[f3/f4]** and then tap **[ENTER]** to confirm that you want to copy the file.

3 Move your groups cursor onto 'Group 1' on the memory drive (drive M:). Tap **[ENTER]** twice to make the copy.

4 Now, tap **[E]** to edit this file, then tap **[ENTER]** to confirm your choice. Once the text is on screen, hold down a **[SHIFT]** key and tap the key labelled **[EXCH/FIND]** (in the second row of the pad of keys at the right hand end of your keyboard).

The flag menu, illustrated on the next page is asking you to key in the text you want to find and what you want to replace it with. It is also offering you some alternative ways of carrying out the search and exchange procedure (see the previous section).

1 Key in the word to *find* as: **'LocoScript'**, then move the highlighting bar down a line on the menu (with the **[DOWN ARROW]**) and then key in the replacement word **'LOCOSCRIPT'**. (In this instance we are just changing lower to upper case for emphasis, but the same procedure would apply if we were changing the word altogether.)

SECTION 3-6
Finding and Substituting Words

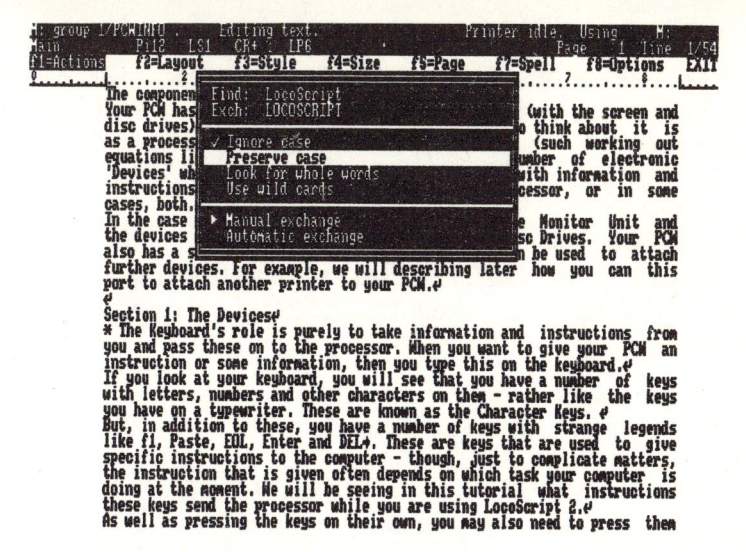

Fig. 5: The *'Find and Exchange'* Flag Menu.

2 The flag menu assumes we want to preserve case, but in this instance we do not, so move the highlighting bar down to *'Preserve case'* and tap the CLEAR Key (marked **[-]**) at the lower left corner of your keyboard. In the bottom section of the flag menu you will see that LocoScript has assumed that you want to make a *'Manual exchange'*, rather than an *'Automatic exchange'*.

3 Tap **[ENTER]** to accept this setting and begin the procedure.

A flag menu gives you three options now. If you tap the *SET Key* (marked **[+]**) LocoScript will make the exchange. If you were to tap the *Clear Key*, LocoScript would not make an exchange, but simply move on to find the next occurrence. If you were to tap the **[CAN]** key LocoScript would cancel (abandon) the activity.

SECTION 3-6
Finding and Substituting Words

4   Tap the *Set Key* (**[+]**) to make the exchange.

Notice that while the *'Match Found'* flag is on the screen, you lose the text cursor, so it is impossible to tell where the match is. Wait for a few seconds until the flag menu disappears and the text cursor reappears, then tap the key you want.

5   Carry on making the changes until you get to the end of the file. Then hold down **[ALT]** and one of the **[SHIFT]** keys and at the same time tap the key labelled **[DOC/PAGE]** to get back to the start of the document.

Now let's get LocoScript to change **every** occurrence of **LOCOSCRIPT** (in capitals) to **LocoScript** (in its original form).

1   Hold down a **[SHIFT]** key and tap **[EXCH/FIND]**. Use **[DEL->]** to get rid of the word *'LocoScript'* then key in **'LOCOSCRIPT'**. Now move down a line with the **[DOWN ARROW]** key and change *'LOCOSCRIPT'* to **'LocoScript'**.

2   This time we want an automatic exchange, so move the highlighting bar down to the bottom of the flag menu and notice that as the bar moves from *'Manual exchange'* to *'Automatic exchange'* the arrowhead moves with the bar. Tap the **[ENTER]** key and watch as LocoScript makes the changes.

3   Abandon the file in memory by tapping **[EXIT]** then the letter **[A]** then tapping **[ENTER]**. The disc copy of the file will be unchanged.

A note of caution about automatic exchanges: *If, for example, you wanted to change the word 'disc' to 'disk' (the American version) and you asked for the change to be made automatically, 'discuss' would become 'diskuss' unless you tell LocoScript to look for whole words only!*

SECTION 3-7
Handling Blocks of Text

1 Switch your machine on and start up with a *copy* of your LocoScript Start of Day disc. Wait until LocoScript displays the disc management screen.

On many occasions you will want to make changes to quite large sections (i.e. *blocks*) of text. LocoScript equips you to do three things with such blocks: You can either *copy* a block, *move* a block, or you can *delete* a block. The procedure you follow is essentially the same for each activity, but with minor but critical changes in the basic procedure for each activity. You carry out *'block'* activities with the three keys in the top row of the keypad at the right hand end of the keyboard.

The following examples will illustrate each of the procedures. Let's start by making a copy of the file so we can play about with it.

2 Begin by moving your files cursor to the file name *'PCWINFO1'* in Group 1 in drive A:. Tap the **[f3/f4]** key and tap **[ENTER]** to copy the file. When prompted, move the groups cursor to Group 1 on the memory drive (M:) and tap **[ENTER]** twice to make the copy. Tap **[E]** and then **[ENTER]** to edit this file.

Before you can work with a block you have to tell LocoScript what you intend to do and which parts of the text comprise the block you will be manipulating. If you intend to delete the block, you would **start** by tapping the *CUT* key, but if you were intending to copy or move the block you would start by tapping the *COPY* key.

1 Tap the **[COPY]** key.

A flag menu reminds you to mark the text and prompts you to tap the *[CUT]* key if you want to remove the text from the page.

SECTION 3-7
Handling Blocks of Text

If you want to leave it on the page, but take a copy of it to duplicate elsewhere then you would press *Copy* again.

2   Watch the screen and tap the **[DOC/PAGE]** key.

As the cursor moves to the start of the next page, it marks the text for you. We shall move that text elsewhere - which means we shall need to *Cut* it from here and *Paste* it in somewhere else.

3   Now tap **[CUT]** and then in response to the prompt, give this block the number '1' by tapping the number **[1]** key in the top row of your keyboard. The marked text slides away, **but you still have a copy of it.**

4   Tap the **[f1/f2]** key, then key in **[S]** and **[B]** (show blocks) and tap **[ENTER]**.

Against the number 1 in the list you will see the first few characters of the block you have saved.

5   Tap the **[CAN]** key to cancel the flag display. Now, tap the **[DOC/PAGE]** key twice to move to the end of your document and then tap the **[PASTE]** key, followed by the number **[1]** to paste your block into this new position.

Once you have saved a block in memory like this it will stay there until you RESET your computer, so you can call it up over and over again if you want to.

6   Go back to the beginning of your document **[ALT] [SHIFT]**, **[DOC/PAGE]**, tap **[PASTE]** and the number **[1]** again.

SECTION 3-7
Handling Blocks of Text

To summarise so far: if you have decided to either move or copy (duplicate) a block of text, *start* by tapping the *[COPY]* key. Mark the text and give the block a number, then move the cursor to the point in the text where you want the block inserted and then paste it into position.

To delete a block is a more simple, though similar, process.

1 Tap the **[CUT]** key. Now tap **[ALT] [SHIFT]** and **[DOC/PAGE]**. (This time you are not asked to provide a number, because you are cutting and discarding text.) Now tap **[CUT]** again and watch the text slide away.

So you have seen the essential points about working with blocks of text, but LocoScript also allows you to call up standard *'Phrases'* and paste them in. How are they different? The principal difference is that phrases are loaded into memory when you start up your system, so they are available all the time. But you also use and save them differently.

2 Tap the **[PASTE]** key and then key in the letter **[Z]**.

LocoScript goes to its **phrases library** and reads in the (longish) phrase it knows as *'phrase Z'*. So what other phrases are available to you now?

3 Tap the **[f1/f2]** key and then tap the letter **[S]** to highlight *'Show phrases'*, then tap **[ENTER]**.

These are the phrases which have already been set up for you. The line of arrows at the bottom of the flag display means tap the *down arrow* to see more. As you have seen, you can call up any of these phrases simply by tapping the *Paste* key and then tapping the relevant letter key.

SECTION 3-7
Handling Blocks of Text

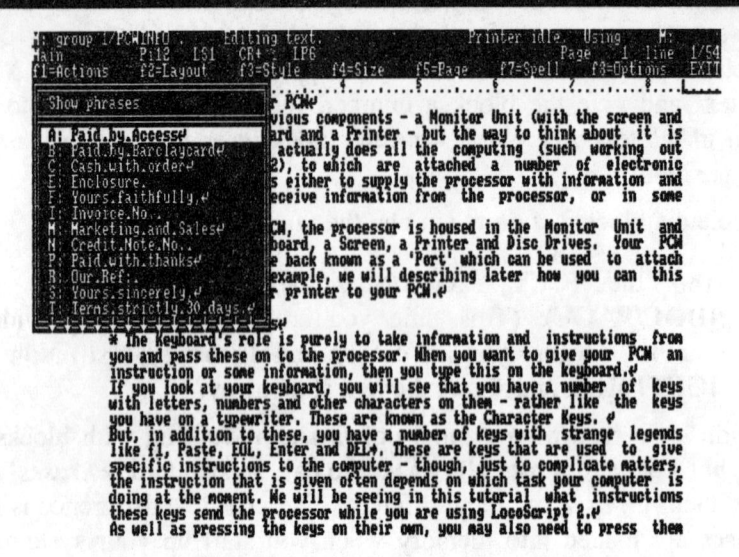

Fig. 6: The Phrases Display.

4 Tap [CAN] to cancel the phrases display.

You may want to create a phrase for use while you are working in a particular document, to save you having to key it in repeatedly. This is similar to inserting blocks, except that you have a maximum of 1000 characters available in each phrase. The LocoScript *'User Guide'* will give details of all the possibilities, but if you wish to create and save a phrase for use in a particular group, this is how you do it.

1 Go back to the beginning of the document [ALT, SHIFT, DOC/PAGE], tap [COPY], move the cursor across to the end of the line *'The components of your PCW'*, tap [COPY] again, followed by the letter [H]. (This is a phrase *'name'* that LocoScript has not used.)

SECTION 3-7
Handling Blocks of Text

You can now insert this phrase as many times as you wish into your document by repeating *Paste H*, wherever you position your cursor. Once you have returned to the disc management screen, you can save this phrase for future use.

2   For now, abandon the file in memory by tapping **[EXIT]** then the letter **[A]** then tapping **[ENTER]**. The disc copy of the file will be unchanged.

The phrase you have created will remain in memory until you switch off or reset your machine.

To save the phrase for future use *in the current group,*

1   Tap **[f1]**, select *'Save phrases'*.

2   Tap **[ENTER]**. A flag menu shows the name *'PHRASES.STD'* so tap **[ENTER]** to confirm.

Now, each time you load this LocoScript disc and open a document in this group, the standard phrase you have saved will be available to you.

Note: You should currently be working on drive M:, so you will need to move the cursor to drive A: if you want to save the phrases permanently.

59

Chapter Four
Controlling The Layout Of Documents

SECTION 4-1
Introduction

In Chapters 2 and 3 we saw how to create a document and, by simple editing, how to prepare it for printing. In this chapter we shall look at the ways in which LocoScript allows you to control the layout and printing characteristics of your documents to a very sophisticated level. Although we shall be examining some very detailed refinements, they are all quite simple to operate and we shall look at each stage a step at a time.

SECTION 4-2
Using The 'SET' And 'CLEAR' Menus

If you have worked through the procedures in the previous two chapters you will have seen that you have a great deal of control over the way your document will be laid out on the page. But, so far, you have seen only one way of achieving the end result you want - by working through a series of flag menus in each procedure.

LocoScript offers you another, much quicker way of achieving many of the same results. The flag menus you have seen, in many cases, are there to provide you with ways of switching LocoScript controls on and off, that is, they enable you to *set* and *clear* LocoScript controls. In many instances, the **SET** and **CLEAR** Keys offer you an alternative and quicker way of doing the same jobs.

1 To start our exploration, switch your machine on and start up with a *copy* of your LocoScript Start of Day disc. Wait until LocoScript displays the disc management screen.

2 Highlight the file *'LSINFO'* in the *'A: group 1'* group of files. Tap **[E]** and **[ENTER]** to call that file onto your screen.

3 Now tap the **SET KEY** at the extreme bottom left of the keyboard - marked **[+]**, and wait for a moment.

The cursor disappears from the text and at the same time a long flag menu unfurls from the ruler line (see the next page). This is the **SET MENU**. If you look at the bottom of the menu you will see a row of arrows which tells you that there are more options on offer. Notice, that at the moment the bottom line of the menu reads 'SiC'.

4 Hold down a **[SHIFT]** key and tap the **[DOWN ARROW]**.

The bottom line of the menu now reads '- hard hyphen' and the previous bottom line (SiC) is now about a third of the way up. Notice also that there is now a row of arrows at the top of the menu.

SECTION 4-2
Using The 'SET' And 'CLEAR' Menus

5   Hold down a **[SHIFT]** key and tap **[UP ARROW]** to move back to the top of the menu. Move the black bar down a line, onto the *'CEntre'* option. Keep an eye on the top line of the text and tap **[ENTER]**.

Remember, your **text cursor** was on the top line of the text before you tapped the SET key. Now that you have selected *'CEntre'* from the SET menu, the top line of text has jumped to the centre of the page as the menu disappears from the screen.

6   Tap the **[< DEL]** key and watch what happens.

The text returns to its previous position, because you have deleted the LocoScript control code which caused the text to be centred. So it is usually possible to cancel the effect of a control code by simply deleting the code itself.

There is another way to achieve the same effect, using 'Keystrokes'. Key in the following sequence of keys as quickly as you can.

7   Tap: **[+]** (the SET key) **[C] [E]** and then look at the top line of your text.

You have achieved exactly the same end result as you did by working through the menu. This means that, once you have got used to the various codes, the **SET** key provides you with a very quick way of controlling and enhancing your text. (We shall see other examples of this feature later in this chapter, and elsewhere.)

■ SECTION 4-2
Using The 'SET' And 'CLEAR' Menus

1 Tap the [+] key and have a good look at the menu.

The key letters for the various codes are the ones in capitals. That's how LocoScript differentiates between codes which start with the same letter. For example, to change the Line Spacing to 2:

2 Key in [L] [S] [2] [ENTER].

Now let's have a look at something else.

1 Tap the **CLEAR KEY**, marked [-] (next to the SET key). Again, wait for a moment.

After a short delay, the CLEAR Menu, illustrated on the next page, appears.

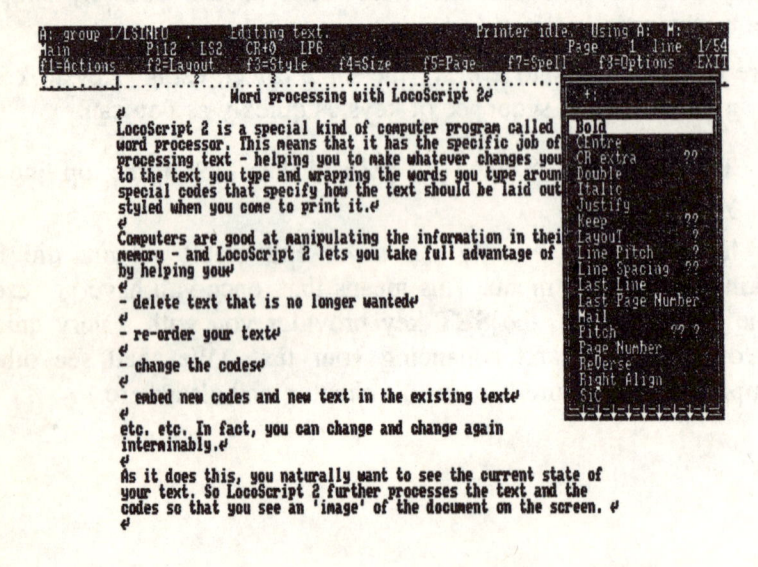

Fig. 1:   The SET Menu.

SECTION 4-2
Using The 'SET' And 'CLEAR' Menus

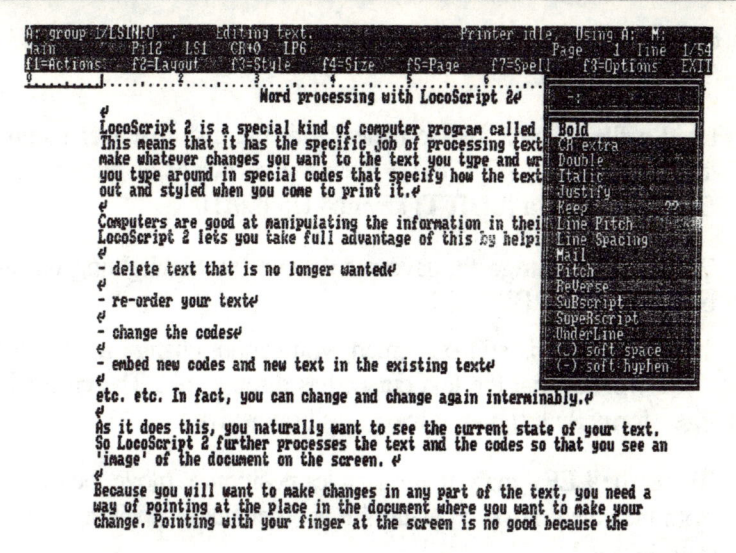

Fig. 2:   The CLEAR Menu.

The **[+]** key enabled you to switch things on, so it is logical that the **[-]** key should switch them off again. Why, then, is the CLEAR Menu so much shorter than the SET Menu?

If you think about it, the answer is simple. Firstly, some of the controls on the SET Menu such as the C**E**ntre option, operate for one line only. Others, like Layou**T**, for example, you switch off by switching another Layou**T** on. Yet others, are 'global' commands which are used only once in a document e.g. **L**ast **P**age Number. Factors like these whittle down the list to the one you have on screen now.

The key point remains, though: *You use the [+] key to SET certain attributes ON and you use the [-] key to CLEAR certain settings from the text.*

11   Tap the **[CAN]** key, then **[EXIT] [A][ENTER]** to abandon this file.

■ **SECTION 4-3**
Changing The Margins For The Whole Text

1   Switch your machine on and start up with a *copy* of your LocoScript Start of Day disc.

2   Load a file of your choice (select it at the disc manager menu and then tap **[E]** and **[ENTER]**). Leave your cursor at the start of the file. Hold down a **[SHIFT]** key and tap **[f2/f1]**.

3   We want to **change** the layout so move the highlighting bar down one line and tap **[ENTER]**.

Even though the text is still on screen, you cannot change it. If you look closely you will see that the text cursor has disappeared. The cursor in the **ruler line** - formerly a **'ghost cursor'** - is now active.

4   To set the LEFT margin at character position 5, move the cursor left with the cursor arrow keys until it is on character position 5.

5   Now tap **[f2/f1]**. Make sure that the option to: 'Set Left Margin' is highlighted and tap **[ENTER]**.

6   To set the RIGHT margin at character position 60, move the cursor to character position 60. Tap **[f2/f1]**. Highlight the 'Set Right Margin' option and tap **[ENTER]** and then tap **[EXIT]** to finish.

7   Hold down a **[SHIFT]** key and tap **[DOC/PAGE]** to reset the whole document to the new margins.

8   Tap **[EXIT]** if you have finished editing. Select the option you want from the menu and then tap **[ENTER]** to confirm your choice.

Don't forget that if you have saved your document on the M: drive, you will have to copy it onto one of your floppy discs if you want a permanent copy.

SECTION 4-4
Changing The Margins For Part Of The Text

1   Switch your machine on and start up with a *copy* of your LocoScript Start of Day disc.

2   Load a file of your choice (select it at the disc manager menu and then tap **[E]** and **[ENTER]**). Move your cursor to the start of the text you want to lay out differently from the rest. Hold down a **[SHIFT]** key and tap **[f2/f1]**.

3   We want the text to be in a **New** layout, so make sure that this option is highlighted and tap **[ENTER]**.

Even though the text is still on screen, you cannot change it. The text cursor has disappeared and the cursor in the **ruler line** - formerly a **'ghost cursor'** - is now active.

4   To set the LEFT margin at character position 20, move the cursor to character position 20 on the **ruler line**.

5   Now tap **[f2/f1]**. Make sure that the option to: 'Set Left Margin' is highlighted and tap **[ENTER]**.

6   To set the RIGHT margin at character position 50, move the cursor to character position 50 on the ruler line. Tap **[f2/f1]**, highlight the 'Set Right Margin' option and tap **[ENTER]** and then tap **[EXIT]** to finish entering the details for your new layout.

You may find that your text seems to have moved across a little. Why?

7   Hold down a **[SHIFT]** key and tap the **[f8/f7]** key. Tap the **[+]** (SET) key and then tap **[ENTER]** to show the state of the (word processing) codes on the screen.

You will see that LocoScript has inserted the code '(LayouT)' into the text.

SECTION 4-4
Changing The Margins For Part Of The Text

8 Now move your cursor down to the place in the text where you want this 'new' layout to end. Notice that the layout changes as you move through the text.

9 Hold down a **[SHIFT]** key and tap **[f2/f1]**, tap **[ENTER]** to set a new layout, then reset the margins, using the same procedure as above. Then tap **[EXIT]** to finish entering this 'new' layout.

10 Move your cursor through the document to reset it to the new margins.

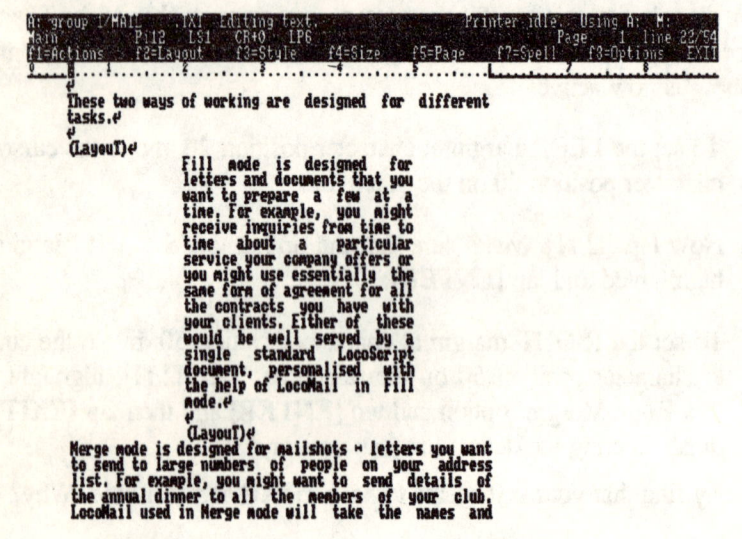

Fig. 3:   New Layout.

11 Tap **[EXIT]** if you have finished editing. Select the option you want from the EXIT menu and then tap **[ENTER]**.

Remember to save the file on a floppy disc if you want a permanent copy.

■ SECTION 4-5
Setting Tabs

1 Switch your machine on and start up with a *copy* of your LocoScript Start of Day disc.

2 Load a file of your choice (select it at the disc manager menu and then tap **[E]** and **[ENTER]**). Move your cursor to the start of the text you want to lay out differently from the rest. Hold down a **[SHIFT]** key and tap **[f2/f1]**.

3 We want to alter the layout by putting tabs in so, hold down a **[SHIFT]** key and tap **[f2/f1]**. Highlight the option to *Change Layout* and then tap **[ENTER]**.

The LocoScript control area changes and the top line reminds you that you are editing the layout settings. Notice 'f3=Tabs' in the bottom row of the control area.

4 Tap the **[f4/f3]** key. As you may already have tabs set, let us begin by making sure that you start with a clean sheet. Move the bar down the menu to the 'Clear All Tabs' option.

Before you execute that instruction, just notice that you can set four different types of tab from this menu. I want to show you another quicker way though.

5 Tap the **[ENTER]** key to clear your tabs.

Note that you are still editing the layout. Now we can look at the quick way of setting tabs.

1 Move your ruler line cursor to where you want the first tab to be - say, on character position 5. Now tap the SET key **[+]** once.

A right pointing arrow appears in the ruler line. This marks where you have set a normal or **simple tab**.

71

■ SECTION 4-5
Setting Tabs

2 Without moving the cursor, tap the **[+]** key again. The right pointing arrow turns into a left pointing arrow. You have now put in a **right tab**.

3 Tap **[+]** once more, and the left pointing arrow changes to one which points right **and** left. This signifies a **centre tab**.

4 Tap **[+]** one last time. The black blob indicates that you have set a **decimal tab** here.

A *simple tab* behaves just like the tab on a typewriter - i.e. the cursor jumps straight to the tab column ready for you to key in text. The text moves to the **right** as you key it in. With a *right tab* the text moves to the **left** as you key it in. With a *centre tab* the text ranges itself to the **right and left** of the tab column as you key it in. The *decimal tab* acts like a combination of a left tab and a right tab. You would normally use a decimal tab to line up columns of numbers. As you start to key the number in, the individual numbers move to the **left** *until* you key in a decimal point - they then move to the **right**.

5 Put in the tabs you want, using the procedure on the previous page.

6 When you have finished, tap the **[EXIT]** key to finish editing the layout and to return to editing your text.

You will see your tab settings in the ruler line.

7 Tap **[EXIT]** if you have finished editing. Select the option you want from the EXIT menu and then tap **[ENTER]**.

Remember to save the file on a floppy disc if you want a permanent copy.

■ SECTION 4-6
Indenting Text Temporarily

When you are creating a document which presents complex information you will help your readers if you can show which bits of the information are subordinate to others. One of the best ways to do this is to **indent** the subordinate text. You *could* do this by changing the margins, but there is a better way.

1 Switch your machine on and start up with a *copy* of your LocoScript master disc. Wait until LocoScript displays the disc management screen. Load a file of your choice (select it at the disc manager menu and then tap **[E]** and **[ENTER]**).

This procedure assumes that you have tabs set for this document. If you have not done so, set them now (see the section *'Setting Tabs'*).

2 Move the cursor down to the start of a paragraph which you want to indent. (If you are keying in text and you want to indent the NEXT paragraph move to the line on which the paragraph will start.)

3 Hold down the **[ALT]** key and tap **[TAB]**.

The symbol on screen (like a tab symbol with a bar on the tail) indicates that a temporary indent has been set here. If you are keying in new text, just go ahead. If you are working on an existing document:

4 Tap the **[UNIT/PARA]** key and watch LocoScript re-lay the paragraph to one tab setting. Now hold down **[ALT]** and this time tap the **[TAB]** key TWICE.

5 Now tap the **[UNIT/PARA]** key again to re-lay this paragraph, this time to two tab stops. Tap the **[UNIT/PARA]** key once more and you will see that the next paragraph is unaffected.

So you can see that indenting text temporarily is really very quick and simple.

SECTION 4-7
Using Margins And Tabs In A Document

Being able to vary margins easily can be very useful for indenting paragraphs for emphasis, or to draw attention to a particular type of information. You can key the original text in quickly, without having to worry about layout and then quickly set the new layout when you have keyed in all the text. There is one particular occasion, however, when using different margins and simple, right, centre and decimal tabs together can be indispensable, and that is when you are keying in tables.

To set up the layout for a table, first position the cursor at the point in the text where the table is to appear. You will not need an extra carriage return at this point, because setting up the new layout automatically inserts one for you.

1 With the cursor at the position you wish your table to start, tap [SHIFT] [f1/f2] and the LayouT flag menu appears. Tap [Enter] to select [New Layout].

The first of the LocoScript information lines tells you that you are *'Editing layout'* and the screen cursor has disappeared. The name of the current layout is shown in the second of the LocoScript information lines. The last line now has the LayouT menu.

2 Using the right arrow key, move the ruler cursor to position 15, tap the [f1/f2] key and select [Set Left Margin]. Move the ruler cursor across to position 65 and select [Set Right Margin].

3 To set the tabs for the table, tap [f3/f4] and select [Clear All Tabs] to remove any already set. Move the ruler cursor to position 28 using the arrow key and tap [f3/f4] again. This time, select [Set Simple Tab] by tapping [Enter].

■ SECTION 4-7
Using Margins And Tabs In A Document

4 Repeat this last stage at position 40, but this time select **[Set Decimal Tab]** by moving the selection bar down with the arrow key and tapping **[Enter]**. Then repeat to select **[Set Centre Tab]** at position 50 and finally **[Set Right Tab]** at position 64.

In each case, you position the ruler cursor on the appropriate point across the page, tap **[f3/f4]** and select the tab you want from the menu.

5 You are now ready to enter the data for your table. Tap **[Exit]** to return to your document and key in the following table. Tap the tab key to move from one column to the next on each line. Tap **[Return]** to move down at the end of each line.

```
Item          Ref.No.     Price    Qty        Cost
Staple Gun    SG442       £15.70   1          £15.70
Pens          PB602       £0.70    50         £35.00
Staples       ST555       £1       1 box      £1.00
Copy Paper    CP123W      £3.77    2 boxes    £7.54

                          Total               £60.24
```

You may want to use this new layout elsewhere in your document, so rather than go through the process of setting the margins and tabs again, you can identify this new layout for further use.

1 Hold down a **[SHIFT]** key and tap **[f7/f8]**. Tap the **[+]** Set key followed by **[ENTER]** and the *(LayouT)* code appears. Move the cursor back to the code at the beginning of the table you have just keyed in. Hold down **[SHIFT]** and tap **[f1/f2]** and select **[New Layout]**.

SECTION 4-7
Using Margins And Tabs In A Document

2 Tap **[F7/f8]**. The name of the current layout appears, so tap the [-] Clear key and key in the new name e.g. *'Table'*, followed by **[Enter]**. Tap **[EXIT]** to return to your document.

You can now save this new layout and copy it as a block to other parts of your document, as described in the section *'Handling Blocks of Text'* in chapter 3. To save it for use with other documents you will need create a Stock layout as described in the next section. The text between the two tables will have the 'Table' layout, so to change it back to 'Main' layout, call up Stock layout from the New layout menu by tapping [f5/f6] [Enter] or [+] LT1. Move the cursor down through the block of text and LocoScript will re-lay it.

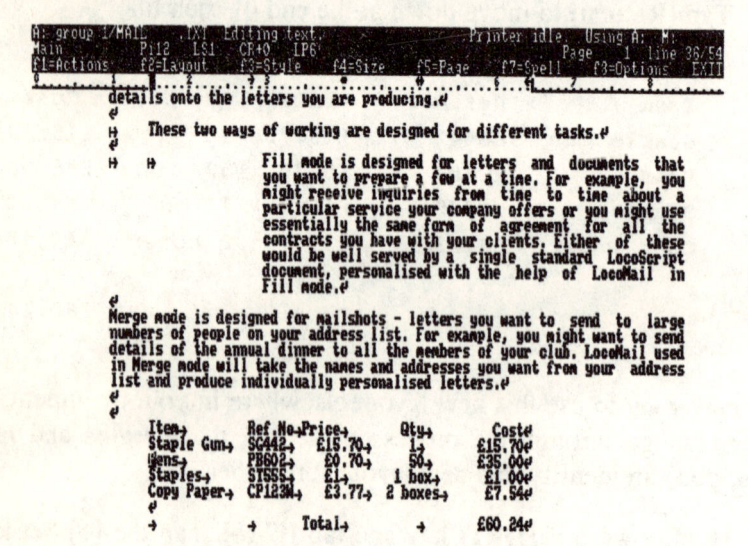

```
A: group 1/MAIL    .TXT Editing text.              Printer idle. Using A: M:
Main         Pi12   LS1   CR+0   LP6               Page   1  line 36/54
f1=Actions   f2=Layout   f3=Style   f4=Size   f5=Page   f7=Spell   f8=Options   EXIT

details onto the letters you are producing.

    These two ways of working are designed for different tasks.

              Fill mode is designed for letters and documents that
              you want to prepare a few at a time. For example, you
              might receive inquiries from time to time about a
              particular service your company offers or you might use
              essentially the same form of agreement for all the
              contracts you have with your clients. Either of these
              would be well served by a single standard LocoScript
              document, personalised with the help of LocoMail in
              Fill mode.

    Merge mode is designed for mailshots - letters you want to send to large
    numbers of people on your address list. For example, you might want to send
    details of the annual dinner to all the members of your club. LocoMail used
    in Merge mode will take the names and addresses you want from your address
    list and produce individually personalised letters.

    Item      Ref.No  Price      Qty         Cost
    Staple Gun SC442  £15.70     1           £15.70
    Pens       PB602  £0.70      50          £35.00
    Staples    ST555  £1         1 box       £1.00
    Copy Paper CP123N £3.77      2 boxes     £7.54

              Total                          £60.24
```

Fig. 4:   Tabs and Tables.

11 Tap **[EXIT]** if you have finished editing. Select the option you want from the EXIT menu and then tap **[ENTER]**.

SECTION 4-8
Creating And Using Stock Layouts

If you wish to set up a new layout and keep it for future use, other than in a single document you are currently working in, you can change one of the LocoScript *Stock Layouts*, rename it to remind you what it is for and then save it in its new form in the list of Stock Layouts. This is useful if you regularly use tables or indented paragraphs in your documents.

1 Switch your machine on and start up with a *copy* of your LocoScript Start of Day disc. Wait until LocoScript displays the disc management screen. Load a file called *INQUIRE.EG* (select it at the disc management screen and then tap **[E]** and **[ENTER]**).

There is a table shown on page 119 of your LocoScript User Guide. We shall set the layout up for this table as follows, but this time I'll get you to change one of the Stock Layouts so that our new layout can be kept for future use.

2 To create a layout which you can keep for future use, tap **[f1/f2][ENTER]** for Document Set Up, then **[f1/f2]** again and select *'Change Stock Layout'*. Now select *'Layout 3'* and you return to the Document Set up screen, but notice you are still *'Editing a Layout'*.

3 First Clear All Tabs, then set a Simple Tab at position 30, set a Right Tab at position 50, set a Centre Tab at position 60 and set a Decimal Tab at position 70.

4 Rename the layout as before, then tap **[EXIT]**, select *Exit* from the Change Stock layouts flag menu, followed by **[EXIT] [ENTER]** to return to your document.

■ SECTION 4-8
Creating And Using Stock Layouts

5 Move the cursor down to the end of the document using the **[DOC/PAGE]** key and tap **[+][LT][3]** to select your new layout. You are now ready to key in the table.

Note: When you are selecting a stock layout, the layout code does not add a carriage return as was the case when using a new layout described in the previous section.

SECTION 4-9
Controlling The Page Length

You need to be able to control the page length for a document in two ways: Firstly you must be able to end a page and start a new one whenever you want (e.g. when you want to end one section and begin the next on the next page). Secondly, you will want to specify that a certain document will be printed on a particular length of paper (i.e. so many lines per page). The first way is known as **forcing a page break**.

1 Switch your machine on and start up with a *copy* of your LocoScript Start of Day disc. Wait until LocoScript displays the disc management screen. Load a file of your choice (select it at the disc management screen and then tap **[E]** and **[ENTER]**).

2 Move your cursor down the page until you get to where you want LocoScript to start a new page. Hold down **[ALT]** and tap **[RETURN]** - and that is it! You have forced a new page.

Notice that the PCW has put the broad 'end of page' line across the screen.

The second procedure, *'Page Length Setup'*, involves changing the way that the document has been set up.

1 With the document displayed on screen, tap **[f2/f1]** then select *'Document setup'* and tap **[ENTER]**. Look in the LocoScript control area and you will see - on the bottom line - that F5 is for Page functions. Tap **[f6/f5]**.

LocoScript displays a flag menu with 5 'page' options (plus the option to Exit). Explore these on your own later. The one we want now is the one which enables us to select the type of paper which this document will use.

SECTION 4-9
Controlling The Page Length

2 Ensure that the *'Paper type'* option is highlighted and tap **[ENTER]**.

The flag menu which appears, shows you which type of paper is selected now (the one with the tick against it), it tells you whether the printing will be portrait or landscape (the paper lengthways or sideways in the printer) and the bottom section allows you either to use the paper type which has been specified, or take a look at its dimensions.

3 Move the black bar onto one of the paper types which does not have a tick against it and then tap the SET **[+]** key to move the tick mark. Tap **[ENTER]** and then select **[EXIT]**. Tap **[EXIT]** followed by **[ENTER]** again to get back to your editing.

What you have actually done here is to specify that the document you are editing will be printed out on a particular type of paper. LocoScript will automatically work out the number of lines on the page if you select one of its standard library of paper types. If you intend to use an unusual paper size you can enter the details of that paper type into LocoScript, to add it to the library.

Note: You can store the details of 10 different paper types. (See 'Session 19' in your LocoScript User Guide.)

SECTION 4-10
Changing The Character And Line Spacing

From time to time you may want to change the print wheel on your printer and print out with a different spacing (e.g. 12 cpi instead of 10), or you may want to select a different line spacing (e.g. double spaced for a draft manuscript). There are two ways to make such changes. We shall deal with the first here, see *'Using The 'SET' And 'CLEAR' Menus'* for the second.

1 Switch your machine on and start up with a *copy* of your LocoScript master disc. Wait until LocoScript displays the disc management screen. Load a file of your choice (select it at the disc manager menu and then tap **[E]** and **[ENTER]**).

2 Hold down a **[SHIFT]** key and tap **[f4/f3]**.

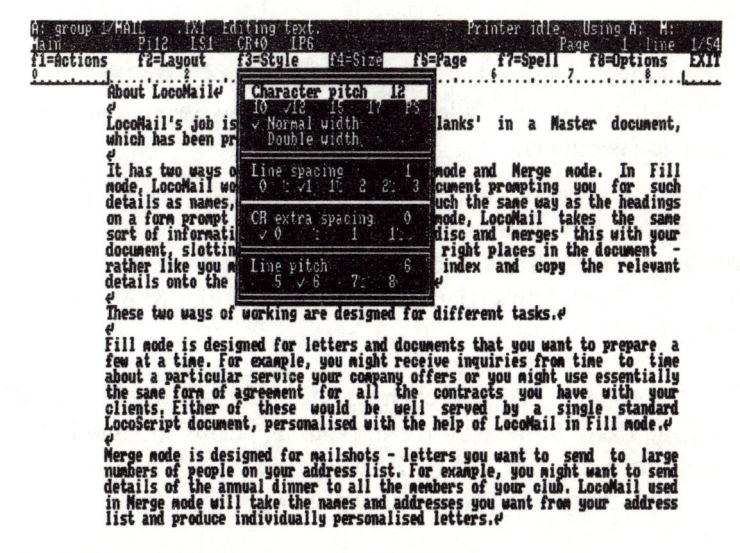

Fig. 5: Line and Character Spacing Flag Menu.

81

■ SECTION 4-10
Changing The Character And Line Spacing

The flag menu illustrated on the previous page, enables you to change a number of things about the way your document will be printed. The first section is character pitch.

3 Move the highlighting bar down one line. You will see a tick against the current setting. Tap the **[SPACEBAR]** and you will see the menu cursor and the tick jump to the next setting on the right. Keep tapping **[SPACEBAR]** until the tick lands on the setting you want.

'Normal width' and **'Double width'** refer to how much space each character will use. On your daisy wheel printer a 'double width' character will have extra spacing - j u s t l i k e t h i s . On a dot matrix printer, each character will be literally twice as wide as normal.

4 Move the bar down to the 'line spacing' section - onto the row of numbers. Here also, tapping the **[SPACEBAR]** will move the tick to let you select the setting you want. Choose, say, double spacing (i.e. the number 2).

The *'CR extra spacing'* setting determines how much vertical space is entered into the text when you press the [RETURN] (Carriage Return) key. We shall leave that as it is for now and the same goes for the Line pitch setting (i.e. how many lines the printer will print per inch).

5 We have specified the changes we want, so tap **[ENTER]** to tell the PCW to execute them. Nothing seems to have happened on screen so tap **[DOC/PAGE]** and watch as your cursor moves through the text, resetting as it goes.

SECTION 4-11
Justifying Text To Both Margins

If you want a really professional looking finish to your text then one of the devices you can adopt is **Right Justification** - making the right hand ends of the text line up with the right margin. The text you are reading now is right justified.

This paragraph, on the other hand, is not right justified - it has a 'ragged' right edge. You need to make up your own mind about which looks best, but it is generally held that justified text looks better - probably because it is hard to do with a typewriter. Some experiments have shown that justified text is *marginally* (!Ho, Ho..!) more difficult to read.

Here is how you would justify your text. There are three methods.

1 Begin by switching your machine on and then start up with a *copy* of your LocoScript Start of Day disc. Wait for LocoScript to display the disc management screen.

2 Highlight the file *'LSINFO'* in the 'A: group 1' group of files. Tap **[E]** and **[ENTER]** to call that file onto your screen.

At the moment the text in this file is UNjustified. We shall justify it to see how it looks.

3 Hold down a **[SHIFT]** key and tap **[f2/f1]**. Move the black bar to the *'Change layout'* option and tap **[ENTER]**.

The LocoScript control area reminds you that you are editing a layout. Look at the bottom line of the control area, see the actions you can carry out now.

4 Hold down a **[SHIFT]** key and tap the **[f8/f7]** key.

The first option on this flag menu is concerned with justification. At the moment there is no tick against it which means that it has not been set on.

SECTION 4-11
Justifying Text To Both Margins

5 Tap the **[SPACEBAR]** once and the tick appears. Tap **[SPACEBAR]** again and it goes again. So the **[SPACEBAR]** acts like a '**toggle**' switch. Tap **[SPACEBAR]** once more to turn justification on. Then tap **[ENTER]** followed by **[EXIT]** to get back to text editing mode.

(You can use the **[SPACEBAR]** as a **toggle** on many of the PCW's flag menus.)

Nothing has happened to your text yet. It still has a ragged right edge.

6 Hold down a **[SHIFT]** key, tap the **[DOC/PAGE]** key and watch the change ripple through the text.

Now for the second way of altering the justification setting. Let us assume for the moment that you want all of the text justified except for the last but one paragraph. Here's how to do it. Remember that at the moment justification is ON for the whole document.

1 Hold down the **[ALT]** key and tap **[UNIT/PARA]** twice. (Remember that the **[ALT]** key reverses the action of most of the special cursor keys.)

Your cursor should be somewhere around line 44 on page 1 of the file - at the start of the paragraph which begins *'LocoScript also organises'*.

2 Tap the **[-]** (CLEAR) key followed by the letter **[J]** to turn justification OFF at this point in the text. Now tap the **[UNIT/PARA]** key and watch the paragraph reset to a ragged right edge.

SECTION 4-11
Justifying Text To Both Margins

3 With your cursor at the start of the last paragraph, turn justification back ON again. Tap the **[+]** (SET) key followed by the letter **[J]**.

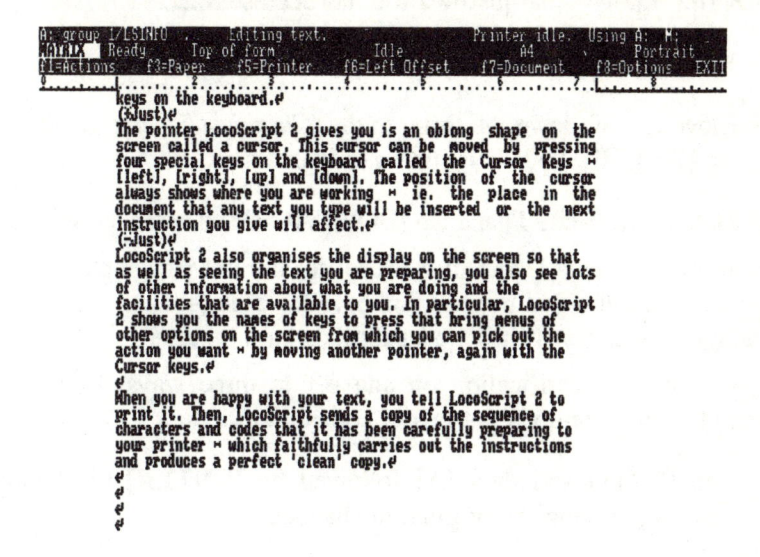

```
A: group 1/LSINFO     Editing text.              Printer idle. Using A: M:
          Ready       Top of form         Idle              A4        Portrait
f1=Actions    f3=Paper    f5=Printer    f6=Left Offset   f7=Document   f8=Options   EXIT

             keys on the keyboard.
             (xJust)
             The pointer LocoScript 2 gives you is an oblong shape on the
             screen called a cursor. This cursor can be moved by pressing
             four special keys on the keyboard called the Cursor Keys -
             [left], [right], [up] and [down]. The position of the cursor
             always shows where you are working - ie. the place in the
             document that any text you type will be inserted or the next
             instruction you give will affect.
             (-Just)
             LocoScript 2 also organises the display on the screen so that
             as well as seeing the text you are preparing, you also see lots
             of other information about what you are doing and the
             facilities that are available to you. In particular, LocoScript
             2 shows you the names of keys to press that bring menus of
             other options on the screen from which you can pick out the
             action you want - by moving another pointer, again with the
             Cursor keys.

             When you are happy with your text, you tell LocoScript 2 to
             print it. Then, LocoScript sends a copy of the sequence of
             characters and codes that it has been carefully preparing to
             your printer - which faithfully carries out the instructions
             and produces a perfect 'clean' copy.
```

Fig. 6: Justified and Unjustified text.

The third way of switching justification on and off is also very easy, but you need to see the justification codes you have put into the text, so:

1 Hold down a **[SHIFT]** key and tap the **[f8/f7]** key. Tap the **[SPACEBAR]** to toggle the codes display on and then tap **[ENTER]** and you will be able to see the codes you have just put in.

2 Move the cursor to the start of the text with **[ALT]+[SHIFT] and [DOC/PAGE]**.

3 Hold down a **[SHIFT]** key and tap the **[f2/f1]** key.

SECTION 4-11
Justifying Text To Both Margins

Notice that this is also the first step in the first procedure I described above. The bottom line of this menu says *'Clear justification'*. So LocoScript 'knows' that justification has been set on.

4   Hold down a [SHIFT] key and tap [f2/f1] again.

5   Move the bar down the menu to the *'Clear justification'* option and tap [ENTER]. LocoScript puts a code into your text.

6   Hold down [SHIFT] and tap [DOC/PAGE] and watch the screen.

Now all of the text is UNjustified except for the last paragraph. The last paragraph is still justified because you have the code (+Just) at the start of the paragraph which switched the justification back on again.

So you can turn justification on and off in three ways. Remember that the last two methods put layout codes into the text.

7   Tap [EXIT] and then [A] followed by [ENTER] to abandon this file, leaving the original unchanged.

SECTION 4-12
Centring And Right Aligning Lines

In this section we are going to look at how you can position single lines of text across the page. The natural position of a line of text is with its first character level with the left margin. In typographic jargon, normal text is: '**ranged left**'. But you can also **range** the text about the **centre** of the page and you can **range** it to the **right**. As usual with LocoScript, there are various ways of positioning the text.

1   Begin by switching your machine on and then start up with a *copy* of your LocoScript Start of Day disc. Wait until LocoScript displays the disc management screen.

2   Highlight the file *'POEM.EG'* in the 'A: group 1' group of files. Tap **[E]** and **[ENTER]** to call that file onto your screen. Hold down a **[SHIFT]** key and then tap **[f2/f1]**.

At the bottom of this 'layout flag menu' you will see three options. The last one - Set justification - allows you to control the text in the whole document. The other two control the position of single lines and these are the ones that concern us here.

3   Move the highlighting bar down the menu to the *'Centre'* option. Keep your eye on the first line of the poem and tap **[ENTER]**.

Everything **to the right of the cursor** is moved across to the centre of the page.

4   Now hold down a **[SHIFT]** key and tap the **[LINE/EOL]** key, to move the cursor to the start of the next line. We shall centre this line too, but by a different method.

5   In quick succession, tap these keys: **[+]** (SET) then **[C] [E]** to centre the second line of text. Keep repeating this same procedure and reset the whole of the first verse to the centre (**[SHIFT] [LINE/EOL]** then **[+] [C] [E]**).

SECTION 4-12
Centring And Right Aligning Lines

So you have seen two ways of centring the text between the margins. Use the one which suits you best. My own preference is the SET KEY method, because I find it quicker, but perhaps you are not in such a hurry as I am.

Next we will look at aligning a single line of text with the right margin - i.e. *ranging right*. The procedures are very similar.

1 Move your cursor to the start of the second verse. Hold down a [SHIFT] key and tap [f2/f1]. Move the highlighting bar down the menu to the *'Right align'* option and tap [ENTER].

This time everything to the right of the cursor moves right across the page so that the last character in the line is level with the right margin. Now, again, for our second method of right aligning the text.

2 Hold down a [SHIFT] key and tap [LINE/EOL] to get to the start of the next line. Now tap [+] (SET) followed by [R] [A]. Again keep repeating the procedure to reset the rest of this verse ([SHIFT] and [LINE/EOL] then [+] [R] [A]).

Here also, choose the method you prefer. I think you will agree that neither of them is difficult. Of course if you wish to make more specific indenting of text, keeping each section left aligned, you can use the indenting of paragraphs described in the section *'Indenting Text Temporarily'*.

SECTION 4-13
Creating A New Standard Template

You will know that LocoScript divides up the storage space on a disc into eight 'compartments' and it deals with those compartments as if they held eight different groupings of files. Start up LocoScript and you will see what I mean.

1 Switch your machine on and start up with a *copy* of your LocoScript Start of Day disc. Make sure that you use a copy because we will be saving our work. Wait until LocoScript displays the disc management screen.

If you scan through the list of files in each group on the disc you will see that most of the groups contain a file called *'TEMPLATE.STD'* (In fact, the majority contain nothing else). Although they all have the same name, they are different files - one for each group. So why are they there? To answer that question you will have to think about the procedures you go through when you create a new document. Before you start keying in text, you will have to have an idea of the tabs you may require, how wide the text should be on the page, whether you want headers or footers, what size paper you want the document to be printed on and potentially there are many more things you might wish to specify.

If you had to specify all the features of the document each time you started a new file, I'm sure that you would find that unacceptable. So LocoScript provides you with three options:

- In default of any instructions from you, LocoScript will set up certain basic features for the new document - based on the assumption that you will be using a certain size of paper and that you will be printing the document with a particular printer. (These are known as the *'Default Settings'*.)

89

■ SECTION 4-13
Creating A New Standard Template

- You *can* (if you want to) tailor these default settings for **an individual document** - for example, by putting in special tabs, or adding headers or footers. But then you will have to remember these settings for the next time you decide to create a similar document.

- You can set up a standard pattern or template for each *type of document* you may create, then store that template in a compartment on the disc (a group) which is set aside for that one type of document.

It is the third option which concerns us here, because that is the function of those files you can see called *TEMPLATE.STD*. So how do you set up a template of your own design?

The actual process of setting up a standard template file is very straightforward. You create it (under the name TEMPLATE.STD) just as you would create any other document - and we will see that in a moment. As for the template itself - in other words the *contents* of the template file - well you can make that as complicated or as simple as you like. Your LocoScript User Guide (in Session 21) takes you through a very detailed explanation of just what is possible, but in this section I want to concentrate on the sort of settings you are likely to use for the majority of work.

1 Move your groups cursor into the 'group 1' group on the disc in A: and then tap **[C]** to create a new document. Key in the file name: **TEMPLATE.STD** and tap **[ENTER]** to open the file and get the blank page display on screen.

Had there already been a file called TEMPLATE.STD in this group LocoScript would have displayed an **error flag** giving you the chance to choose another name for the file, replace the existing file with the one you are about to create, or abandon the activity.

SECTION 4-13
Creating A New Standard Template

Because group 1 does not contain a 'template' file, the page display you have now is the one which embodies the LocoScript *default* settings. We shall set up a template which is going to be of practical use in the future - a template for your letters.

What are the design criteria for letters?

- We shall use the most popular paper size (e.g. A4 in Europe)
- We may need to use tabs
- The standard template should include your address
- We want the text to be easy to read, so it should be not wider than 5.5 inches and it should be UNjustified
- We do not want the pages numbered
- We shall use a printer setting of 10 characters per inch (cpi)

So let's set up the template to meet these criteria.

1 First, to set up the basic 'layout' of tabs and margins, hold down a **[SHIFT]** key and tap the **[f2/f1]** key. Select 'Change layout' and tap **[ENTER]**.

2 The left margin is set at 10, which is fine, so move the ruler line cursor to character position 65 (so the text will be 55 characters wide - or 5.5 inches at 10cpi). Tap the **[f2/f1]** key. Select 'set right margin' with the **[DOWN ARROW]** and tap **[ENTER]**.

3 Now tabs. Three will usually be enough. Move the ruler line cursor to character position 15 (half an inch in from the left margin) and then tap **[f4/f3]**. A simple tab will do, so just tap **[ENTER]**. Do the same at character positions 20 and 25 and then tap **[EXIT]** to get back to editing mode.

SECTION 4-13
Creating A New Standard Template

Now let us just check that the other criteria are set as we want them. Hold down a [SHIFT] key and tap [f1/f2].

The bottom line on that flag menu tells us that (right) justification is NOT set on at the moment, so that is okay.

4 Tap the [CAN] key and then hold down a [SHIFT] key and tap [f4/f3].

Here we can see that the printer settings are also as we want them. (Notice, the character pitch is 10.)

5 Tap the [CAN] key, and let's key in your address.

Note: You will want to select your own style for the address, but for this exercise I'm assuming that you want your name in double width with the address in normal width text. I'm also assuming that the whole thing will be printed in a bold typeface.

1 As we shall be putting in some print control codes, it will be helpful if we can see them, so hold down a [SHIFT] key and tap [f8/f7] now tap the [+] (SET) key and the [ENTER] key.

2 Tap the [+] key followed by the letter [B] (for bold print) and now [+] [P] for Pitch, the number [10] and then the letter [D] for double width (NOT double *strike*). Finally, tap the [ENTER] key. Remember that when you print with a daisywheel printer, double width actually means double spacing between the characters, l i k e   t h i s.

3 Now key in your own name, but *don't* press [RETURN] when you have finished, because we want the rest of the text to be in normal width characters. Instead, tap [-] (CLEAR) followed by [P] to switch the pitch change off, *then* tap [RETURN].

■ SECTION 4-13
Creating A New Standard Template

4   Now key in your address, one line at a time. Do *not* press [RETURN] on the last line.

5   Remember that we set bold printing on at the start of this text, so now let us switch it off again. Tap [-] (CLEAR) and then [B]. And now tap **[RETURN]**.

So there is your name and address lined up with the left margin, but it is likely that you would prefer it either in the centre of the page, or aligned to the right.

1   Move the cursor up to the first line of the address ([ALT + DOC/PAGE]) and then tap the [+] key followed by [C][E] to centre it or [R][A] to right align it. Repeat the process for the complete name and address block, moving down a line each time with **[SHIFT + LINE/EOL]**.

2   You can see the text *and* the control codes you have inserted. Clear the control codes setting **[SHIFT] [f8/f7] [-] [ENTER]**.

3   And remember that your name is set in double width characters, which explains the odd looking layout. With the cursor on the first line, tap the **[DOC/PAGE]** key to tidy up.

Unless you want to make any further changes of your own, that's all there is to creating our new template.

4   Tap **[EXIT]** and then **[ENTER]** to save a copy of the file in group 1 on the disc in drive A:

You probably will not want this template in group 1 so let us MOVE it into the letters group.

■ SECTION 4-13
Creating A New Standard Template

1 Make sure that the files cursor is on **TEMPLATE.STD** in group 1 and then tap the **[f4/f3]** key.

2 Highlight the *'Move file'* option and tap **[ENTER]**. Now move the files cursor one column to the right and tap **[ENTER]**.

3 Tap **[ENTER]** again to confirm your actions and after a short pause you will see an error flag.

The problem is that you cannot have two files with the same name in the same group, so you can either 'cancel the operation', **or** you can choose another name for your file (but if you do that it won't work as a template file - It MUST be called TEMPLATE.STD), **or** you can replace the existing file with this one. That is what we must do, and that option is highlighted, so:

4 Tap **[ENTER]** and wait for the display to update itself. With your cursor still in the LETTERS group, tap **[C]** and **[ENTER]** to create a new file. And there you are with a working template.

5 Tap **[DOC/PAGE]** and then key in some experimental text. When you have finished, save and print your 'letter'.

6 Don't forget to erase the test document when you have read the print out.

So now you have seen that the actual procedure for creating a new template file is not difficult or complicated. It is really just like creating any other kind of document.

But remember, that if you want the file to work as a standard template for documents within a certain group, then the file must be called *TEMPLATE.STD* and it must be stored in the group in question.

Chapter Five
Enhancing The Printed Page

SECTION 5-1
Introduction

There are occasions when, in addition to controlling the layout of the actual text on the page, you need to highlight certain parts of the text for emphasis. With LocoScript, you can do this in a number of ways, underline, embolden, italicise or reverse the printed words. In this section we shall look at some of these only, but the same principles will apply to the others, so you may like to experiment with them later on your own.

SECTION 5-2
Printing Words Underlined

1 Switch your machine on and start up with a *copy* of your LocoScript Start of Day disc. Wait until LocoScript displays the disc management screen.

2 Move your files cursor onto the file called *LSINFO* in the group 1 column. Tap **[E]** and then **[ENTER]** to edit this document.

3 Tap the **[UNIT/PARA]** key to move to the start of the second paragraph. Now tap **[+]** (SET) followed by the letters **[U]** and **[L]**.

Nothing seems to happen, but:

4 Move the cursor to the right until it is in the space after LocoScript. Now tap the **[-]** (CLEAR) key followed by **[U][L]** and watch what happens.

5 Tap **[UNIT/PARA]** again, followed by **[+][U][L]** followed by **[DOC/PAGE]**. Again, watch your screen.

6 Turn the underline function off again with the combination of keys you used before: **[-][U][L]**.

So, while you are editing existing text you can add underlining with the method you have seen. But you can also key in text which will be underlined automatically.

1 Tap **[DOC/PAGE]**. Tap **[RETURN]** a couple of times so you are clear of the end of the text.

2 Now tap **[+][U][L]** and then key in: *'Now is the winter of our discontent'*

SECTION 5-2
Printing Words Underlined

Notice that all the letters *and* all the spaces *and* all the punctuation marks are underlined.

3 Now, tap **[-][U][L]** to switch this form of underlining off again. We can now try something slightly different. Tap **[+]** and the letter **[W]** and then complete the sentence by keying in *'made glorious summer by this..'*.

This time all the letters and all the punctuation marks are underlined, *but* the spaces are not. This form of underlining is called *'Word Underline'* - hence **[+] [W]** instead of **[+] [U][L]**. As with many of LocoScript's features, you can set them and clear them in two ways - either via the **SET** and **CLEAR** key menus, or by using one of the **function keys**.

1 Tap the **[f4/f3]** key and watch the screen.

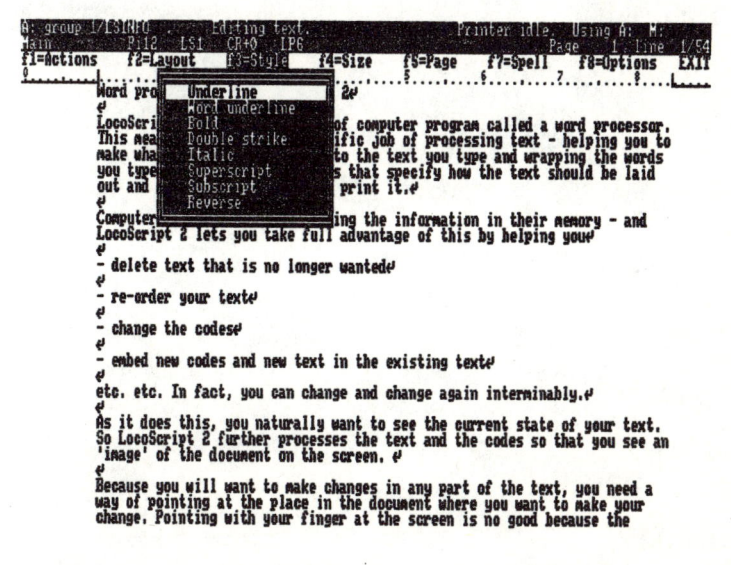

Fig. 1:   *Print Attributes* Flag Menu.

SECTION 5-2
Printing Words Underlined

You will see the flag menu, illustrated on the previous page, which allows you to set or clear 8 different **print attributes** (as they are sometimes known). But you should find that using the [+] key is quicker in most instances - except perhaps if you want to set, say a heading, to be underlined and bold, in which case, using this menu may be quicker.

2 Tap the [CAN] key to get rid of the menu and then abandon the file in memory by tapping [EXIT] then the letter [A] then tapping [ENTER]. The disc copy of the file will be unchanged.

■ SECTION 5-3
Printing Words In Bolder Type

1 Switch your machine on and start up with a *copy* of your LocoScript Start of Day disc. Wait until LocoScript displays the disc management screen.

2 Move your files cursor onto the file called *'LSINFO'* in the group 1 column. Tap **[f4/f3]** followed by **[ENTER]** to copy this file. Move your groups cursor to the 'group 1' group on drive M: and tap **[ENTER]** twice to make the copy.

3 Tap **[E]** then **[ENTER]** to edit this document.

You can **'embolden'** parts of your text to make them stand out from the rest. You have a choice between **bold** type - where each character is printed several times in the same place or **double strike** - which, as the name suggests is the same as bold except the character is struck only twice and it, therefore, does not create such a dark image.

As with other 'print attributes' you can set bold and double strike printing on/off in two ways: Either through the **f3** *'style'* menu or with the **SET** and **CLEAR** keys. For example:

1 Tap the **[f4/f3]** key.

The third and fourth items on the flag menu are *'Bold'* and *'Double strike'* respectively, which tells you that you can set them on or off from here. A quicker way to set bold or double strike on and off is with the **[+]** and **[-]** keys.

2 Tap the **[CAN]** key to get rid of the *'style'* menu. Before we start, we'll set LocoScript so it shows the print control codes. Hold down a **[SHIFT]** key and tap the **[f8/f7]** key. Tap the **[+]** (SET) key to put a tick against the 'Codes' option and then tap **[ENTER]**.

SECTION 5-3
Printing Words In Bolder Type

You won't see any changes on screen because we have not yet put any control codes in.

3 Tap [+] followed by the letter [B] (for bold). Now tap [LINE/EOL] to move your cursor to the end of the line, tap [-] [B] to clear the bold setting and you will see the codes added to the text.

So now the heading will be printed in a bold typeface. What about double strike? Well it's the same procedure, except you use [+] [D] (instead of [+] [B]).

What I want you to do now is to work through the complete file and put in the control codes to set the name 'LocoScript' to be printed in double strike. We can use another LocoScript tool to make the job easier.

1 First, hold down the [ALT] key and tap [DOC/PAGE] to get back to the start of the text.

2 Tap the [EXCH/FIND] key. When you see the flag menu, key in **LocoScript** exactly as it appears here. When you have done that tap [ENTER] and watch the screen. The cursor jumps immediately to the first occurrence - in the title (which is already set in bold).

Note: You **can** use 'double strike' and 'bold' in combination to get an even darker image on the page. So:

3 Tap [+] and [D] to set double strike on. Now move the cursor onto the opening bracket immediately AFTER the number 2 and key in [-] (CLEAR) [D].

SECTION 5-3
Printing Words In Bolder Type

4 Tap **[EXCH/FIND]** and tap **[ENTER]** to find the next occurrence and again set double strike on and then off again. Remember, the OFF command goes **after** the 2!

5 Repeat the 'FIND' and then the 'double strike on/off' sequence for the rest of the file.

You may have found that a pretty tiresome process, but think how much longer it would have taken without the FIND facility and how easy it would be to miss an occurrence of the word you wanted to enhance. So now you have seen a good example of how you can use a combination of tools to make your work easier, yet more thorough.

1 Let's look at the text without the control codes. Hold down a **[SHIFT]** key and tap **[f8/f7]**. Tap the **[-]** (CLEAR) key and tap **[ENTER]**.

2 If you want to see how this looks when it is printed out, tap **[EXIT]**, select the Save and Print option and then tap **[ENTER]**. If you do not need to see a printed copy, tap **[EXIT] [A]** and **[ENTER]**.

SECTION 5-4
Paper Sizes And Types

When you create a document with LocoScript it has to make certain assumptions about the paper you will be printing on. If it didn't know the width of the paper, how would it 'know' where to set the margins? If it didn't know the length of the paper, how would it know when to start a new page?

LocoScript has been set up to work with a standard size of paper which it will use in default of any instructions from you to do otherwise. How then do you instruct it to use a different size of paper for a particular document?

1 Switch your machine on and start up with a *copy* of your LocoScript Start of Day disc. Wait until LocoScript displays the disc management screen.

2 Move your files cursor to highlight the file name *'LSINFO'* in the group 1 column on disc A: and tap **[E]** and **[ENTER]** to edit this file.

3 Look at the top of your screen and make a note of the number of lines per page - 54 in Europe with A4 paper and margin settings of 10 and 72. On A4 paper this document ends at line 5 of 54 on page 2.

Paper size is one of the items specified in the set-up details for this (and every other) LocoScript file. So let us change it to see the effect.

1 Tap the **[f2/f1]** key. Make sure that *'Document setup'* is highlighted and tap **[ENTER]**.

LocoScript is now in 'Document setup mode'. As you can see on screen this is where you can set headers and footers as well as various other features - look in the bottom row of the LocoScript control area.

SECTION 5-4
Paper Sizes And Types

2 Tap the **[f6/f5]** key to gain access to the 'page' options. Make sure that *'Paper type'* is highlighted on the flag menu and then tap **[ENTER]**.

This flag menu shows you the paper types which LocoScript 'knows' about. The one which has been selected for this document has a tick mark against it. (In Europe this will be A4.)

3 Move the highlighting bar to another - smaller - paper setting (in Europe, select A5) and tap the **[+]** (SET) key. The tick mark moves to the new selection, then tap **[ENTER]**.

4 We don't need to alter anything else now, so tap **[EXIT]** and then **[ENTER]**. You are still in Document setup mode, so tap **[EXIT]** and **[ENTER]** again to get back to where we were.

Notice that the margins are the same, but the page length has changed. In Europe, the cursor is now on line 1 of 34.

5 Hold down a **[SHIFT]** key and tap the **[DOC/PAGE]** key, to move the cursor to the end of the document. The cursor, you will see, is on line 24 of 34 on page 2.

So changing the paper type has automatically caused LocoScript to compensate by changing the page length. Let us set the paper type back to what it was.

6 Tap **[f2/f1]** and tap **[ENTER]**. When the display settles down, tap **[f6/f5]** and tap **[ENTER]**. Make sure the highlighting bar is on the PREVIOUS paper selection, then tap **[+]** (SET) and **[ENTER]**.

While we are at this flag menu let us have a look at one of the other items.

105

SECTION 5-4
Paper Sizes And Types

1 Move the highlighting bar onto the Page layout option and tap **[ENTER]**.

This flag gives you a detailed description of the various 'zones' which have been set up for this page. The numbers on the right refer to the number of lines set aside for each zone. Remember that the standard line setting is 6 lines to the vertical inch of paper.

2 Tap **[ENTER]**, then **[EXIT]**, then **[ENTER]** followed by **[EXIT] [ENTER]** again to get back to the document.

Notice that once again LocoScript processes two pages but the cursor is now on line 5 of 54.

3 Tap **[EXIT] [A]** and **[ENTER]** to abandon this document.

LocoScript recognises a reasonable selection of paper types and sizes. If you have the need to use a special size of paper - one which LocoScript does not recognise - you can add the details of the paper to LocoScript's list. See session 19 in your LocoScript User Guide.

SECTION 5-5
Using Other Printers (with LocoScript)

Although LocoScript's ability to use virtually any type of printer is a valuable feature, I suspect that the 'typical' user will be quite happy to work with the printer which comes with their machine. We shall not be covering any of the technicalities associated with using other printers in this section but, we do want to discuss some of the things you will have to bear in mind.

Why would you want to use another printer?

There would seem to be two main possibilities: Firstly you might want a faster printer, or secondly you might want access to a wider range of type faces and 'print enhancement' options.

What types of printer are available?

For typical word processing work there are two main types: The **'Daisy Wheel Printer'** and the **'Dot Matrix Printer'**. There are other types of printers, such as Ink Jet, Thimble, Line, Laser, but at the time of writing these are less widely used than the two main ones I have mentioned, though laser printers are becoming more and more popular.

What are the differences between the two main types of printer?

The **daisy wheel** printer has at its 'business end' a print wheel which has letters at the end of thin flat 'spokes' which radiate from the centre of the wheel like daisy petals (hence the name 'daisy wheel').

The printer prints a letter on the paper by moving the appropriate petal into the right position and then striking the back of the petal with a print 'hammer'. The letter moves forward against the ribbon and then against the paper, so producing a letter on the page, in essence the printing method is the same as an ordinary typewriter.

You get different styles of print by changing the print wheel - each type of print wheel having a different type face and that's something you can't do with an ordinary typewriter.

SECTION 5-5
Using Other Printers (with LocoScript)

The **dot matrix** printer prints in a different way. Instead of having a fixed selection of characters ranged around a wheel which are then struck by a single hammer, the **print head** itself is formed of a bundle of thin rods which can all be moved independently.

In effect, each rod works like a print hammer which strikes the ribbon, creating a printed dot on the paper. When several rods move forward at the same time they create a pattern of dots on the paper - and if you move the right pattern of rods forward at the same time, they create the shape of a letter.

Why would you use one type of printer rather than another?

A **daisy wheel** printer generally produces much better quality print, the image is crisp and clean because the shapes of the characters are formed by lines and curves. In fact daisy wheel output is often referred to as **letter quality** printing.

But the printing mechanism has to work very hard to achieve high printing speeds. A rating of 50 characters per second (50 cps) is a good one for a daisy wheel printer. But speed ratings can be misleading. Often the speed rating given for a printer is actually its maximum speed. A printer with a maximum speed of 50 cps is likely to have an average printing speed of somewhere between 30 and 40 cps.

So, if *quality* of output is paramount, then you would probably want to use some kind of daisy wheel printer with a single strike ribbon (that is a ribbon which can be used just once).

If, however, speed is more important than quality, (for producing drafts, for example) then you would do better to opt for a **dot matrix** printer. In fact, some of the modern printers can produce a pretty acceptable finish - **Near Letter Quality** or **NLQ** as it is known.

SECTION 5-5
Using Other Printers (with LocoScript)

Generally speaking, because the dot matrix printer forms the outline of a character with dots rather than lines and curves, the quality of output cannot be as crisp and clean as the daisy wheel (that's why the best output is called *near* letter quality rather than letter quality).

Where speed is concerned, the picture is reversed: A dot matrix printer in drafting mode might well print at 350 cps plus. And even in NLQ mode, speeds of 80 cps are quite common.

If and when you do decide to use another printer with LocoScript, you need to remember some key points. You will realise that LocoScript has to be instructed to stop using one printer and to use another one instead. But there is more to it than that - as you will see on the next couple of pages.

Before LocoScript can carry out your instruction to use another printer it has to 'know' certain things:

- **Which printer** - and how it works
  There is no all embracing standard which governs how printers interpret instructions from a computer. Also, different printers have different features - for example, some dot matrix printers have an NLQ mode, others don't. So LocoScript has to have a record of the printer's name and the list of instructions it can understand and implement - these details about the printer are held in a **printer driver** file. Your computer together with LocoScript probably comes with a range of printer drivers as standard. You can - and may have to - add others.

- **Which print wheel** - for a daisy wheel printer
  Earlier on in this section I said that a daisy wheel printer prints by 'moving the appropriate petal into the right position and then striking the back of the petal with a print hammer'.

SECTION 5-5
Using Other Printers (with LocoScript)

If you think about it you will see that it can only do that if it 'knows' *how many* petals there are on the print wheel. It also needs to know *which* characters are on the print wheel and *where they are* located. (Don't forget, it also needs to know how many characters should be printed per inch.)

We have seen that LocoScript needs to know certain things about the printer so it can issue the appropriate instructions. But before it can issue those instructions it also needs to know:

- **How the instructions are to be communicated**
  LocoScript 'talks' to the printer by transmitting characters and control codes along a printer cable. But it can send that information 'down the line' in two ways: Either as a steady stream of characters, **one after the other**, like a ribbon of electrical signals, or it can chop up the stream of signals into regular lengths of, say, 8 units and then transmit them **8 at a time**. The first method is known as **serial transmission**, the second, as **parallel transmission**.

Both the printer and LocoScript must be set up to work in one or other of these modes - in other words they must **both** be set up to work either via a **serial interface** or via a **parallel interface**. The key point here is that the two methods of transmission are quite different - they require different types of cabling and they require different kinds of plugs, so LocoScript and your computer must know which plug socket to use when they talk to the printer.

Your computer probably has two printer sockets (or **printer ports**): One for the serial interface and a parallel port which conforms to the *'Centronics'* standard. If your computer does not have both of these and you want to add a port, you can buy one from your dealer and attach it to the computer at the **expansion** port at the rear of the monitor unit.

SECTION 5-6
Changing A Print Wheel

In this section we shall simply be looking at how you swap the print wheel on a daisy wheel printer. The procedures will not be exactly the same for all daisy wheel printers, though they might be similar. I am assuming that your system is switched on and that you have started up with LocoScript.

Don't forget that when you change a print wheel and when you want to use a different printer you *must* make the relevant adjustments to LocoScript's printer settings (the f6 menu from the disc management screen). For detailed instructions, see your LocoScript User Guide, session 20.

1 Look at the top of your printer. Toward the front edge you will see a translucent grey plastic lid or dust cover. The dust cover is hinged. Hinge this cover up and then down again - to reset the position of the print mechanism.

2 Now hinge the dust cover up to the vertical position and lift it clear of the printer so you have clear access to the innards of the printer.

3 You need to get at the mechanism below the ribbon cartridge, so the next step is to remove the cartridge. Note where the ribbon itself runs, then grip the cartridge by the two prongs which point away from you.

4 Gently tilt the cartridge upward - you will feel it click clear of a retaining clip - then lift the cartridge clear of the printer and put it to one side.

5 The print wheel is locked in position, so the first thing to do is to unlock it. Looking down on the mechanism you will see, on the left hand side, a black plastic coated lever. Pull that lever toward you to unlock the print wheel.

SECTION 5-6
Changing A Print Wheel

6 You will see the print wheel loosen as you unlock it. Now simply lift the printwheel upward - holding it gently by the 'petals'.

7 Take your replacement print wheel and, holding it between the finger and thumb of one hand by the petals - with the characters facing toward the printer roller, lower it gently into position, just in front of the two ribbon guide lugs.

8 Release the print wheel and it should slip down into the correct position. You do not have to line it up in any special way.

9 Now lock the new wheel into position by pushing the black plastic coated lever toward the printer roller - you will feel and see the lever taking up the slack and then you will feel it lock into position.

10 Take the ribbon cartridge, with the ribbon end away from you and with the ribbon tensioner to the top. If you look at the end nearest you, you will see two small lugs. Those lugs fit into two slots in the ribbon cartridge carrier on the printer.

11 Slip the cartridge into position, making sure the lugs are located properly, and then apply gentle but firm pressure to the top of the cartridge until you feel it click into place firmly. Check that the ribbon itself runs between the print wheel and the printer roller.

12 Take the dust cover lid and, holding it vertically, slip the right hand end over the hinge and then the left. Finally, close the dust cover.

SECTION 5-7
Changing A Ribbon Cartridge

1 Look at the top of your printer. Toward the front edge you will see a translucent grey plastic lid or dust cover. The dust cover is hinged.

2 Hinge this cover up to the vertical position and lift it clear of the printer so you have clear access to the innards of the printer.

3 The next step is to remove the old cartridge. Note where the ribbon itself runs, then grip the cartridge by the two prongs which point away from you.

4 Gently tilt the cartridge upward - you will feel it click clear of a retaining clip - then lift the cartridge clear of the printer and put it to one side.

5 Take your replacement cartridge with the ribbon end away from you and with the ribbon tensioner to the top.

If you look at the end nearest you, you will see two small lugs. Those lugs fit into two slots in the ribbon cartridge carrier on the printer.

6 Slip the cartridge into position, making sure that the lugs are located properly.

7 Then apply gentle but firm pressure to the top of the cartridge until you feel it click into place firmly.

8 Check that the ribbon itself runs between the print wheel and the printer roller.

9 Take the dust cover lid and, holding it vertically, slip the right hand end over the hinge. Then click the left hand end downward into position. Finally, close the dust cover.

Chapter Six
Mailmerge With LocoMail

SECTION 6-1
Some Background

If you ever need to produce several copies of the same document, each one only slightly different from the others, then this chapter, along with Chapter 9, are for you.

Whether you are:

- The treasurer of a club or society who has to send letters to all the members, reminding them that their subscriptions are due
- The chairman of a fund raising project who has a long list of people to contact
- The person responsible for sending out a firm's invoices and statements
- The person responsible for sending out a firm's marketing mailshots
- A sales manager who wants to keep existing customers in touch with new services or products

somehow you have to make contact with a lot of people, and you have to do that in the most efficient way you can. Your PCW can help you, but what are the alternatives?

A letter seems to be the best vehicle for making contact. Now all those letters are going to be very similar, so one device might be to have several copies of a standard letter printed. To make it worthwhile, you would need to have at least 100 copies, but, often, you don't need 100 copies - and, in any case, how would you personalise them? There are bound to be small but noticeable details which will give the game away - e.g. the absence of a date.

The ideal solution is to print each letter individually on the PCW's printer - The quality of print is certainly good enough. But you won't want to print the same, or very nearly the same, letter over and over again.

SECTION 6-1
Some Background

Now, one simple solution might be to create a standard letter and then edit and print each letter individually, using the original as a master. But that is a fairly time consuming process. What we need is some device which will enable you to slot the 'personalising' information into a standard letter (either by hand, or automatically) *during* the printing process.

Well you have such a device. The PCW9512 with LocoScript and LocoMail!

LocoMail does the job for you. In your User Instructions Book the job it does is referred to as **mail merging** (see session 21 on page 249). This is actually quite a good descriptive title, because the way it works is by 'merging' information from two sources into a single finished document. Some other word processors call it **merge printing**.

You can use LocoMail in either of two ways: If you have only a few letters to process, then you can **fill** in the details manually from the keyboard. But, if you have a lot of letters to process, then you can instruct the PCW to **merge** the details automatically from a separate list of personal details. So LocoMail has two 'modes': **FILL** mode and **MERGE** mode.

Both modes have a common starting point - a standard or **'master'** document, so let us prepare one which you can use if you want to.

SECTION 6-2
Creating A Master Letter

1 Switch your machine on and start up with a *copy* of your LocoScript Start of Day disc. Wait until the PCW displays the disc management screen. Move your groups cursor onto 'Group 1' on Drive M: Tap the letter **[C]** to create a new document. Key in the name **MASTER** and then tap the **[-]** (CLEAR) key to get rid of the rest of the file name. Tap **[ENTER]** to open the file.

Our MASTER letter is going to be just like any other letter, except that it will have specially marked pigeon-holes set aside for the personal details we want to include later.

2 The first thing to do **for this exercise** is to instruct the PCW to display the text control codes, so hold down a **[SHIFT]** key and tap the **[f8/f7]** key, then tap the **[+]** (SET) key followed by the **[ENTER]** key.

3 Now, key in your own address (unless you intend to use a pre-printed letterhead). Tap **[RETURN]** a couple of times to separate your address from the rest of the text.

We shall put our first pigeon-hole in here; for the date. Now, when the PCW comes to process this letter it will print your address, then it will move the paper up a couple of lines and then it will reach the pigeon-hole which we shall create in a few moments. We shall make this one for the date, which might be one of the things which will vary from letter to letter. But how will the PCW know what to put in here? Well it can either ask you to supply the details, or it can look in another file on the disc. But first, let us see how to get the PCW to prompt *you* to enter the right details for this part of the letter.

SECTION 6-2
Creating A Master Letter

1 Tap the **[+]** key followed by the letter **[M]** (for 'mail') and watch the screen. You can see that you have marked the start of the pigeon-hole.

2 Tell the PCW to prompt you for the details by keying in a question mark, followed by a semi-colon **[?] [;]**, followed by the words you want it to use, for example **[today's date]**. Now tap **[-]** (CLEAR) followed by **[M]** to mark the end of our first pigeon-hole and tap **[RETURN]** three times to separate the date from the next part of the text.

3 The next thing we want here is the name of the person we are writing to. Again this will vary from letter to letter (in other words, it is one of the **variables** as the jargon has it). So key in **[+] [M] [?] [;]** followed by **[name]** which in turn is followed by **[-] [M] [RETURN]**.

Now for the address. This is variable in more ways than one. Not only will it change from letter to letter, but there is no standard form of address - it may be just a couple of lines long (a local one for example), or several lines long (e.g. an international one). LocoMail can adapt to that. All you have to do is to put in a single pigeon-hole and the PCW will sort things out automatically.

When LocoMail comes to process this letter it will prompt you to key in details (as we have seen), but it will NOT process the details until you press the **[ENTER]** key. If you key in an address in response to a LocoMail prompt, the carriage returns are processed as carriage returns and nothing else. This is a very neat solution, because with other word processors you often have to have a separate prompt for each line of the address. With LocoMail nothing is processed until you press **[ENTER]**, so it doesn't matter how many lines there are in your addresses.

SECTION 6-2
Creating A Master Letter

4 Create the address pigeon-hole by keying in: **[+] [M] [?] [;] [address] [-] [M]** then press **[RETURN]** four times, to separate the end of the address from the rest of the text. (Not to leave room for the address!)

Our next variable will be the salutation. You could use a **constant** like 'Dear Sir' or 'Sirs', but that is not very personal. On the other hand, there will be some people whom you would address by name or nickname (Dear Fred,). Being slightly more formal, you may want to address someone as Mr, or Miss, or Mrs, or even Ms. You might even want to address someone as 'Your Highness'. The point is that it is best to treat the salutation as a variable.

5 Key in: **[+] [M] [?] [;] [salutation] [-] [M]** then tap **[RETURN]** twice and we are ready to key in the body of the letter. Key this in:

Our records show that payments from you for invoice/s number/s **[+] [M] [?] [;] [number] [-] [M]** are overdue. The total amount outstanding is **[+] [M] [?] [;] [amount] [-] [M]**. I should be grateful if you would clear this within the next seven days.**[RETURN]**

[RETURN]

If I do not receive your cheque within seven days, I shall be forced to **[+] [M] [?] [;] [action to be taken] [-] [M]**.**[RETURN]**

[RETURN]

[+] [M] [?] [;] [close] [-] [M] [RETURN]

6 Now save the file. Tap **[EXIT]** and then move the highlighting bar down to *'Save and Continue'*.

SECTION 6-2
Creating A Master Letter

Before tapping [ENTER], notice some things about this text. Firstly, you can 'drop-in' a pigeon-hole wherever you want to include information that is likely to vary from letter to letter (the variable does not have to be on a line of its own).

Secondly, we started the letter with a variable for the salutation so we have to finish with a variable for the close (*Yours sincerely, Yours faithfully, Bye for now,* and so on). Thirdly, you have allowed yourself the flexibility to treat different customers in different ways.

```
A: group 1/MASTER          Editing text.              Printer idle. Using    M:
MAILIX  Ready     Top of form            Idle            A4          Portrait
F1=Actions   f3=Paper   f5=Printer   f6=Left Offset   f7=Document   f8=Options   EXIT
........|.......|.......|.......|.......|.......?.......|........
    John Smith
    21, Old Street
    MEXTOWN
    NN1 6OD

    (:Mail) today's date (:Mail)

    (:Mail) name (:Mail)
    (:Mail) address (:Mail)

    (:Mail) salutation (:Mail)

    Our records show that payments from you for invoice/s number/s
    (:Mail) number (:Mail) are overdue. The total amount outstanding is
    (:Mail) amount (:Mail), I should be grateful if you would clear this
    within the next seven days.

    If I do not receive your cheque within seven days, I shall be
    forced to (:Mail) action to be taken (:Mail)

    (:Mail) close (:Mail)
```

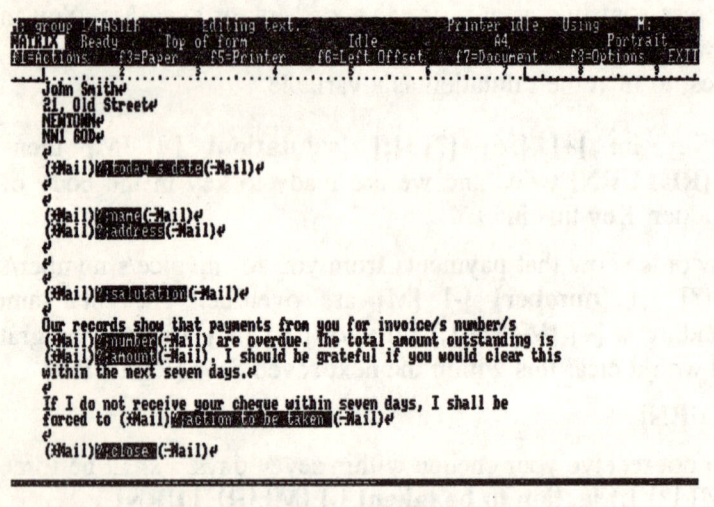

Fig. 1: Master Mail Merge letter.

Now you have your Master letter, let's move on to print it.

7 Tap [ENTER], then tap [EXIT] [A] and [ENTER] to abandon this letter. If you intend to take a break now, **before switching your machine off**, make a permanent copy of the *master* letter on one of your discs. (See, *'Making A Copy Of A File'* .)

SECTION 6-3
Printing A Master Letter (FILL)

1   With the Disc Management display on screen, make sure that the files cursor is on the file called 'MASTER' **not** *MASTER.EG* (If you do not have a copy of this file, please work through the previous section.)

Remember that LocoMail has two modes - FILL, in which you key in details as they are required, and MERGE, in which LocoMail reads the details in from another file and merges them with the master. Whichever mode you use, you must start by selecting the master document - the one you want to print. We shall use FILL mode for our master.

2   Tap the letter **[F]** and then tap **[ENTER]**.

You will see the letter appear on screen with the cursor flashing just after the first (date) pigeon-hole.

3   Key in today's date and then tap **[ENTER]**. (!..**[ENTER]** **not** **[RETURN]** ..!)

You will see your input accepted and then the cursor moves down to the next pigeon-hole.

4   Make up some details and fill in all the pigeon-holes. **Remember** press **[ENTER]** to complete an entry.

5   When you get a flag menu on screen, put some paper in the printer. Then, move the highlighting bar onto the *'Print result'* option and tap **[ENTER]**. Because you have adjusted the printer you will see PCW9512 flashing at the top left of your screen. Tap **[EXIT]** to clear the printer message, then after a short pause, tell the PCW to proceed by tapping **[ENTER]**.

SECTION 6-3
Printing A Master Letter (FILL)

The printer prints your 'FILLED' letter and you are offered the opportunity to 'Fill again' or 'Finish'. If you want to print another copy of this letter with some different details, by all means do so.

6 When you have finished, move the highlighting bar down to the 'Finish' option and tap **[ENTER]** to get back to the disc management screen.

SECTION 6-4
The Master (MERGE) Document

1 Switch your machine on and start up with a *copy* of your LocoScript Start of Day disc. Wait until the PCW displays the disc management screen. Move your files cursor onto the file called *'LETTER.2'* in the 'Group 1' on the disc in A: and then tap **[E] [ENTER]** to 'edit' this file.

The text in this section assumes that you have read the previous sections in this chapter. That being so, you will recognise where the pigeon-holes are in this letter. But you will also recognise that they are different from the ones you have seen so far.

The first two (name and address) do not contain the prompt codes (? ;) because this letter has been set up to be used as a MERGE document which gets the details for the pigeon-holes from another file (a **data file**), so it does not need to prompt anyone to key in anything for these slots. But should you use this document while you are in FILL mode, LocoMail *will* prompt you to key-in details, by highlighting the name of the pigeon-hole (in capital letters, followed by a question mark).

The third pigeon-hole is different again. The 'date' is the date on which the letter is being sent and that sort of information will not be in the data file, so here we have a special kind of FILL command.

For the first letter you MERGE print, the command works just like the fill commands you have seen; you will be prompted to key in today's date. When you do so, LocoMail fills in the pigeon-hole, but it also makes a note of what you keyed in and stores it under the name 'Date' as a **temporary variable**. For subsequent copies of the letter, LocoMail will **not** prompt you to fill in the date. Instead, the exclamation mark (!) and the word **'Date'** tell it to use whatever details it has stored under the name 'Date' - which is, of course, what you keyed in for the first copy (or *'pass'*) of the letter.

SECTION 6-4
The Master (MERGE) Document

The interesting thing to note about this feature is that once LocoMail has made a note of the variable information held under the name 'Date' (or any other name) you can use that same information elsewhere in the letter. For example, if you wanted today's date repeated in the first sentence of the letter, you could insert something like this: (Please note that) **as from [+] [M] [Date] [-] [M]** (we shall be trading as..).

When LocoMail reaches the mail command in the first line, it will automatically fill in the 'Date' information. This is a significant feature which we will expand upon when we look at data files.

1 Let us try MERGE printing this file. First of all, get back to the disc management display by keying in **[EXIT] [A]** and **[ENTER]**.

Notice that there is a file called *ADDRESS2.LST* near the top of the 'Group 1' column. That is the data file I want you to use in a few moments.

2 With your files cursor still on the file *LETTER.2* tap the letter **[M]** to Merge print this MASTER DOCUMENT.

A flag menu appears, asking you to select a 'merge data document' (that is the data file I referred to).

3 Move your files cursor onto the file *ADDRESS2.LST* and tap **[ENTER]**.

The next flag menu asks you to confirm that it has the details correct for the job you want to do, *and* it offers you the choice of either **Manual** or **Automatic processing**. (With Manual processing you get the chance to by-pass (or discard) a set of details if you do not want to use it (just like when you completed a FILL process). With Automatic, LocoMail uses all the sets of data in the data file.

SECTION 6-4
The Master (MERGE) Document

4   For this exercise, simply tap **[ENTER]** to go ahead with a Manual merge print. You will see LocoMail fill in the name and address pigeon-holes with data it got from the data file and then it will prompt you to key in today's date. Key in the date now and then press **[ENTER]**.

LocoMail looks for more pigeon-holes, but it does not find any, so it displays a list of options. If you would like to see a printed version of this letter, go ahead and select the 'Print result' option, then put paper in the printer and follow the screen prompts. Otherwise:

5   Simply tap the letter **[D]** followed by **[ENTER]** to discard these details and start another pass. Watch the screen and you will see LocoMail pick up the next set of details from the data file and merge them into the letter.

Notice that this time LocoMail does not prompt you for the date - it uses the details you keyed in for the first pass.

6   Tap **[D]** and **[ENTER]** at the end of each pass until you reach the end of the data file, at which point LocoMail will return you to the disc management screen.

SECTION 6-5
Creating A Merge Data File

The data file which LocoMail uses is a bit like a stack of cards - each card holding a complete set of information. But how does LocoMail know *where* on the card to find the bit of information it wants?

In data file jargon, the information on a single card is known as a **record**. (So each card holds a single record). Every record is comprised of the same *types* of information *in the same sequence*. Each of those types of information is known as a **field**. So each record contains the same fields in the same order. Therefore, Locomail does not have to know what is in a field, or precisely where it appears on the card; it merely needs to know whether it is the first, or second, or third, or fourth, etc. field in the record.

This being so, it means that you have to set up the records in your data file in a precise and consistent way.

1 Switch your machine on and start up with a *copy* of your LocoScript Start of Day disc. Wait until the PCW displays the disc management screen. First, let us have a look at an example data file. Move your files cursor onto the file called *ADDRESS2.LST* in the 'Group 1' column on Drive A: Tap **[E]** and **[ENTER]** to have a look at this file.

The screen display you have now illustrates the idea of each record being on a separate 'card'. In fact each one is on a separate page in the file. Let us look a little closer.

The first page (or record) in the file is the one which tells LocoMail how the records in the rest of the file are made up. Notice three things about the first page:

- It defines how many fields there are in a record
- It defines the names of each of the fields
- It defines where one field ends and the next one begins

SECTION 6-5
Creating A Merge Data File

In this file there are four fields in each record. They are called: 'Name', 'Address', 'Country' and 'Language'.

The first field in every record is the **Name** field. The second field is **Address**. That is easy enough for us to see because the screen layout gives us lots of clues about where the name ends and the address begins. But remember that the computer will not be reading the screen layout. All it has to work with is a stream of letters and spaces, so how does it tell them apart? For example, if you were to read this:

Mr Samuel Black Hill Lane End Tillington

How would you know where the name ends and the address begins? Is it,

Mr Samuel, Black Hill, Lane End, Tillington

Mr Samuel Black, Hill Lane End, Tillington

Mr Samuel Black Hill, Lane End, Tillington

In these examples the commas helped you interpret the same sequence of letters in different ways - they separated out the various components of the name and address. In principle, LocoMail does the same thing, but it is not limited to using commas as **separators**.

Notice that in the first record in the file, 'Name' ends in a carriage return and 'Address' ends in a semi-colon. Put another way, if you had been told to look at a record and find the details for an address, you would scan the record to find the first carriage return, then you would look for the first semi-colon. Once you had found them you would know that everything between those two points constituted the *'Address'* part of the record in question. Essentially, that is also how LocoMail selects the right information from each record. That being so, it is clear that you have to remember certain things when you are using a data file.

SECTION 6-5
Creating A Merge Data File

You have a wide choice of possible separators for any field, but you must be careful to choose one that does **not** appear in the field details. (For example, it would be silly to use a carriage return to mark the end of the address, because the address itself will contain carriage returns and LocoMail will not be able to tell which is the right one.)

The name of a field is very specific. Remember that you select information for a variable by quoting its name in the **Mail** command. The field name you use must be exactly the same in both the data file and the Mail command.

You do not *have* to use every field in the data file in your master document. If your records contain 10 fields and you need only 1 for the job in hand, then that is fine. Remember LocoMail **selects** just the details you ask for in the Mail commands.

If, for some reason, you do not have any data for a particular field in one of your records (which frequently happens) you must still mark the field's place in the record - **even though the field is empty!** You will see an example of this in the records on screen. If you look at the third record, for Dr H Quentin, you will see that there are no details for the Address field, but the semi-colon is still there. So LocoMail can still find the right Country details and the right Language details.

Earlier, we saw that when you use a special version of the FILL mail command (the 'Date' example), LocoMail creates **'temporary variables'** which work just like the field names in the data file. They will remain in LocoMail's memory for the duration of a print run, but then they have to be created again, because they do not actually appear in any data file.

SECTION 6-5
Creating A Merge Data File

1   Tap **[EXIT]** then **[A]** and **[ENTER]** to abandon this file. Then move your groups cursor onto 'Group 1' on drive M: We shall create our own data file. Tap **[C]** and then key in the filename **TESTDATA** and tap the **[-]** CLEAR key to delete the spare numbers and tap **[ENTER]** to open the file.

Before we start, we must have a clear idea of what we want to achieve and that depends on how we shall be using the data in this file. So let us imagine that we are going to create a data file which we can use for mailshots to businesses. The records in our file will therefore have to hold at least the following details:

> **The name of the recipient**
>
> **His/Her job title**
>
> **The name of the company**
>
> **The address of the company**
>
> **The salutation**
>
> **The close**

Once we know this, we can go ahead and create the first record in the file - which, if you remember, defines the names and the sequence of the fields in the rest of the records in the file.

1   Key in, **[name]** and tap **[RETURN]**.

Notice two things here: firstly I have adopted the rule of using only lower case letters for field names to avoid confusion, secondly I have used a carriage return to mark the end of this field, because a name field should never have to contain a carriage return. The same applies to the next two fields.

SECTION 6-5
Creating A Merge Data File

2 Key in **[job] [RETURN]** then **[company] [RETURN]**. Next, key in **[address]** BUT this time we cannot use a carriage return to mark the end, so tap **[;]** then without tapping the **[SPACEBAR]**, key in **[salutation]** and tap **[RETURN]** (because the salutation should never have a carriage return in it either). Now key in **[close]**, but nothing else for the time being.

The close will be the last field in the record, so we need to mark the end of the record AND the end of the page (or card). The easiest way to do that is to put in a **forced** page break.

3 Hold down the **[ALT]** key and tap the **[RETURN]** key and you will see page 2 open up. You are now set up to start keying in personalised details.

Special Note For U.K. Users.

If you do decide to keep information of this sort on your computer - you may have to record that fact on the **Data Protection Register**. Information held for certain uses is exempt (e.g. personal, or household, or recreational uses) but it is safer to check. Contact:

The Office Of The Data Protection Registrar
Springfield House
Water Lane
WILMSLOW
Cheshire SK5 5AX

Let us create our first record, with imaginary details!

1 Key in the entry you will see on the next page. Make sure you use exactly the same keystrokes.

SECTION 6-5
Creating A Merge Data File

2 Key in:

>Philip Wells**[RETURN]**
>Sales Manager**[RETURN]**
>Aqua Ltd**[RETURN]**
>The Old Pump House**[RETURN]**
>BATH BD4[;]Dear Phil,**[RETURN]**
>Best wishes**[RETURN]**
>**[RETURN]**
>**[RETURN]**
>**[RETURN]**
>**[RETURN]**
>**[RETURN]**
>Sam**[RETURN]**
>**[ALT][RETURN]**

Notice that this does conform with the definition on the first page of the file. In particular, the 'close' begins after the carriage return which marks the end of the salutation and ends with a forced page break, so all the **[RETURN]**s in the close will not confuse LocoMail.

Subject to the 'Data Protection' warning above, you are now ready to create your own data file. Remember to save a permanent copy of the file though, because at the moment you are working with the memory drive.

SECTION 6-6
Implementing A Mailshot Run

In this final section of the chapter, I want to round things off by drawing together a summary of the main points. This will take the form of a checklist for undertaking a mailshot run. You will decide how you want to set about it, but what I can do is to describe how I do it, in the hope that you might pick up some ideas.

1 Start by thinking through what you want to *achieve* by doing a mailshot. Ask yourself if there is a better way of achieving the same objective. **Define the problem.** In other words, check that you really do want to do a mailshot, rather than something else (like telephone people, for example).

2 You will have a mental note of the people you will be writing to. Choose one of the people from the list and write the master letter to **that person**. Forget about the others for the time being.

There are two reasons for writing to a specific person: Firstly, it is much easier to write the actual words if you have a clear idea of who you are 'talking' to. Secondly, you will arrive at a more natural layout for the letter.

3 Once you have saved a copy of the letter, get a print out of it and then go through the text marking up those items which will vary from copy to copy. Also check that the letter is appropriate for everyone you will be writing to. Edit the letter, replacing the variable items with 'Mail' commands.

If you intend to FILL this letter and you think you will need prompts, use the form of the Mail command which includes the '**?** **;**' prompt definitions.

4 Save the edited version of the master letter.

SECTION 6-6
Implementing A Mailshot Run

If you are going to FILL the letter you are now ready to test if it works as you intended. If you are going to MERGE print the letter, you will next need to create your data file.

If you already have a data file, you will need to check that the records in the file contain the information you will need for your letter and you must check that the letter and the data file both use the same names for the variables (e.g. if you have marked a pigeon-hole in your letter as being the slot for the 'salutation', check that you have not called it something else, such as the 'start', in the data file).

5 Define how you are going to use the data file (not just for the job in hand, think also about any follow-up there may be to this mailshot).

6 Create the data file as we discussed earlier in this chapter. **Remember**, that if you do not have data for one of the fields, you must still mark its position. In other words, even if a field is empty it **must** still appear in the record once you have defined that it will.

7 Carry out a test MERGE print run. If all is OK, go ahead with the real print run.

Chapter Seven
Checking Your Spelling With LocoSpell

SECTION 7-1
Introduction

There are times when you are creating or editing a document, when you are unsure of the correct spelling of a word or words. We all have word blind-spots! The most efficient way to deal with these is to key in the spelling you think is correct and then, when the document is complete, use LocoSpell to run a check on your whole document.

If, however, you do wish to check a particular word as you go along, this is also possible as we shall see.

Before we look at how LocoSpell works, we need to know how it sees words and what it will be looking for.

LocoScript ignores single character words like 'I' and 'a' and words of more than thirty two characters, as it assumes if you are using such a monster you will have checked the spelling yourself!

LocoScript also ignores words which you have added to the dictionaries. More about this in a moment.

LocoScript works by checking the words in your document against those in its dictionaries. A word is a set of characters between 'terminator' characters or codes: spaces, carriage returns, tabs or codes such as CentrE, RAlign and end-of-page. Words divided by 'separator' characters, and these are , ; : . ' - ( ) ! / (but not including soft hyphens), are checked in parts. The exceptions are the common abbreviations like we're and can't which are included in the dictionaries.

Words including special 'killer' characters like " $ £ @ * and Greek and Cyrillic characters, numbers, fractions and the less common accented characters are assumed to be correct and you should check these carefully for yourself.

139

SECTION 7-1
Introduction

Accented characters which are included are:

a e i o u (acute, circumflex, grave, umlaut) y (umlaut) c (cedilla) a (ring) o (slash) n a o (tilde) and their upper case equivalents. Your use of these accents must match those in the dictionaries, however, or the word will be shown up as incorrect.

To see how this works out and what options are available when running a spelling check, we shall work through a short sample document which has been specifically created to demonstrate LocoSpell.

SECTION 7-2
Checking Your Spelling

1 Switch your machine on and start up with a *copy* of your LocoScript Start of Day disc. Wait until LocoScript displays the disc management screen.

Make sure that LocoSpell has loaded (if you have an early version of the Locomotive software, see notes about installation in your User Guide).

We shall start by copying a file to the M: Drive so that the original is not changed. (If LOCOSPEL.DCT is not on drive M: you will need to copy that across also.)

2 Highlight the file *'MISTAKE.EG'* and tap the **[f3/f4]** key. Select 'Copy File', move the cursor to the required group on drive M: and tap **[ENTER]** twice. Now tap **[E]** and **[ENTER]** to call the file onto your screen.

You will notice that this short document contains a number of mistakes and we are going to use these to examine the various ways in which LocoScript lets you handle these.

3 Tap **[f7/f8]** and the flag menu appears offering the options to check *'All of document'*, *'Just forwards from here'*, *'Single word'* or *'User dictionary upkeep'*.

We shall look at these options shortly, for the moment,

4 just tap **[ENTER]** to select *'All of document'* and the spelling check starts.

The first word LocoScript finds is 'fedding'. This is highlighted and a flag menu tells you this is the word stopped at and suggests 'feeding' as a possible replacement.

SECTION 7-2
Checking Your Spelling

5   Since this is the word we want, tap **[ENTER]** to select *'Use suggested replacement'* and LocoScript moves on to the next word.

The next word LocoScript stops at is *'discusin'*. This time the suggested replacement is not the one we want, but it would make it easier to key in the correct version if we simply edit its suggestion.

6   Select *'Replace and then edit'* and then key in the letters **[sion]** to complete the word correctly, followed by **[ENTER]** to proceed.

The next word *'tye'* has produced *type* as the suggested replacement. This is because LocoScript uses the first two letters as its main prompt in finding an alternative. This time it will be easier to edit the word as it stands, so:

7   Select *'Edit this word'*, use the delete left key and then key in the correct letters **[he]**, then tap **[ENTER]**.

Really that is all there is to using LocoSpell.

Of course you may well want to update LocoSpell's dictionary(ies) with words that are special to the work you do, or even consult the dictionaries to check a spelling before you key a word in. You can see how to do that by looking in your User Guide.

At the end of your spelling check, a flag message appears, telling you how many words LocoSpell has checked and how many words it has added to the dictionary. You then have the option to update the *user dictionary* or leave it unaltered.

If you have not already created a *user dictionary*, LocoSpell will create one called *USERSPEL.DCT* which will be stored in the same group as the document you have been editing. So if you have been working on the memory drive, make sure you copy the new user dictionary to a floppy disk before you close down.

Part Two
General Applications

INTRODUCTION
What The Rest Of This Book Covers

Part two of this book is concerned with more general applications of computers. We mustn't forget that the PCW is indeed a full blown general purpose computer. This means that you can use it to do any of the day to day jobs you might expect an office computer to do - (which includes enabling you to play games to while away the time waiting for the next customer to phone you).

The list of things your PCW can do is virtually endless. All you need is the right software and you're in business. But there isn't room in this book to cover every possible application, so we have had to concentrate on the most popular ones:

- Word processing
- Databases
- Spreadsheets.

And even with this restricted list there are many alternatives open to you - i.e. there are lots of word processing programs, lots of database programs and lots of spreadsheets. So, even here we have had to be selective. We have concentrated on describing the three *'types'* of application, to try and show what's possible.

Because this is a *Step By Step* book, we demonstrate the points by working through examples with specific software.

Our reasons for arriving at the final selection of software to be covered were various. For example, we chose *LocoFile* as an example of a particular class of database program, principally because it provides a familiar working environment for the LocoScript user. We chose *dBase ll* and *SuperCalc^2* because they are already very popular with PCW buffs. And we chose *mini Office Professional* because it is a low cost example of a single package which *integrates* the major types of application (plus a couple of others) into a single working environment.

INTRODUCTION
What The Rest Of This Book Covers

We make no value judgments about the software we describe, nor does the fact that we have selected one rather than another imply that we are recommending that software. Of course if we believed a piece of software was poorly done, then we would not have selected it, but that does not mean that we have necessarily selected the *'best'* software in each class.

There is one simple reason why we would not be so rash as to set ourselves up as arbiters of quality: the word *'best'* is so indefinable! After all, one person may believe that a grotty 'card index' program that costs 30p per dozen is the best database system for their needs. Another might believe that an all singing and dancing database program which allows the users to create their own software programs is best - and they would probably ignore the fact that the price ticket has three numbers before the decimal place. *'You pays yer money and you takes yer choice..!'*

All we can hope to do is to give you some idea of what to start looking for. But we don't want to influence your buying decisions. Naturally we have our favourites, but that's because we work in a particular way, doing particular kinds of work, with our computers. Your needs will be different from ours.

So let's get on with looking at the general purpose software.

Chapter Eight
General 'Housekeeping' With CP/M

SECTION 8-1
Introduction

If you have been using your PCW9512 exclusively as a word processor or have been working only with the LocoMotive software packages, you may not have met CP/M, so what is it?

CP/M stands for Command Program for Microcomputers. It is the Operating System for your PCW9512 (and a range of other '8 bit' computers) a computer program which controls or manages the way the computer and all the other items of hardware linked to it operate together as a single system.

When you start up LocoScript, you go straight to the Disc Management screen of the relevant programs. But your system will have used CP/M to get there. In this section we shall look at how CP/M sets your system up ready to use programs and how you can use CP/M to do all the 'housekeeping' jobs you need to.

You can do many housekeeping jobs while LocoScript is running, but from time to time you may want to work on a number of discs and files and do several housekeeping jobs in one session. When this happens, you will find it much quicker to do the jobs without starting up LocoScript first. This section describes how to do those jobs with your CP/M Operating System. In essence, you work with CP/M when you want to use the PCW as a general purpose computer.

SECTION 8-2
Discs And Drives

Your computer has at least one floppy disc drive built into it. It is through this disc drive that you feed information to the computer, once you have switched on the power. The first information you must give the computer is its operating system, CP/M. In doing so, you also create another disc drive, a memory disc drive which you can use to work in while the PCW is switched on. You will be able to work at greater speed in the memory drive, which is called Drive M:, but if you want to keep your work you will have to save it to a floppy disk before you switch off. The PCW warns you of this when you start to work in Drive M:.

You must beware of damaging your floppy discs, because if you do, it is almost certain that you will lose all the files on the disc.

You should ALWAYS have at least two copies of every disc - The 'MASTER' and the 'BACK-UP' (which is simply a duplicate copy of the master). This may sound a bit over-cautious, but what costs more: a disc, or the time you would have to spend re-creating it?

SECTION 8-3
Some Tips On Looking After Your Files

- Make a back-up of a *Program Disc* as soon as you get it. **If you have not made copies of the PCW's master discs, do so now!** (See the section on *'Copying Discs'*.)
- Work with your back-up discs not your master discs
- Once you start working with your PCW you will start to create data files. You should back-up those files, at the end of each working session at the very least
- If, during a working session, you create or edit several files, then you should back-up each file as soon as you finish working with it
- *Always* store master discs and back-ups in separate boxes. and preferably in separate rooms. *Always* store discs in a dust proof container of some kind and at room temperatures
- *Never* touch the magnetic surfaces of the disc
- *Never* switch the computer *On* or *Off* with a disc in a drive
- As a general rule, try to keep data files (the work you've done) on separate discs from programs (program files)
- Unless you *need* to save information on your program disc, it is a good idea to write protect it before you start work. Push the *'write protect tab'* (in the top left hand corner of the disc) down towards the letter A or B
- Make sure that you establish a routine procedure for identifying discs (and what's on them) - an index of some kind

Perhaps these tips seem a bit obsessive, but that's because you've never been in the position of damaging a disc which holds several weeks, perhaps months, of work. When it happens, and you experience that sick feeling, then you'll see what we mean. But then it will be too late.

SECTION 8-3
Some Tips On Looking After Your Files

Now the comments on the previous page do not apply *only* to LocoScript files.

Certainly, at first you will probably be using the PCW mostly for word processing with LocoScript, but the whole purpose of this book is to suggest that you might consider using it to do other kinds of work. For a start, there are several other word processor packages available for the PCW. And when you start to use other software you will inevitably have to carry out a whole range of *'housekeeping'* tasks - e.g. copying files, renaming files, getting rid of redundant files, moving files about, and so on.

It is true that with LocoScript you can do many of the housekeeping tasks via the system itself, but what happens with the other software? Is there perhaps a quicker way to do more general housekeeping? And how do you control the computer when you are *not* working in LocoScript?

Let's have a look at some procedures.

SECTION 8-4
Resetting (Rebooting) The PCW

Let's assume that your machine is already switched on.

1 Start by getting your *working copy* of the disc labelled 'CP/M Plus' and put it in the disc drive (the left hand one if you have two disc drive slots).

2 With your left hand, hold down the keys labelled [SHIFT] and [EXTRA] then with your right hand, tap the key labelled [EXIT]. You will see the PCW go through its CP/M start up sequence.

Holding down [SHIFT] + [EXTRA], then tapping the [EXIT] key is the procedure you use to *'Reset'*, or *'Reboot'* (yes honestly) your computer.

3 The Reset procedure overrides anything the computer is doing at the time, *but* be careful with it, because resetting the PCW involves flushing out the memory and the memory drive (drive M:). So if you had been working on something in drive M: and you had not saved it on disc, you would lose it forever. Also, with certain software packages, you might scramble the data files if you do not close down properly *before* resetting!

4 If you reset the computer with the LocoScript disc in the drive, then you will simply re-start LocoScript. But if you reset with the CP/M Plus disc in the drive, you will get access to the CP/M Plus Operating System.

An *'Operating System'* is a computer program which manages the way the computer system works. It enables the various bits of the hardware system - the disc drive(s), the monitor, the central processor unit, the keyboard and the printer to work as a single unit. Associated with the operating system there is a set of *'utility programs'* or *'commands'* which enable you to carry out your housekeeping tasks. It is those commands that this chapter is about.

SECTION 8-4
Resetting (Rebooting) The PCW

You will know when the operating system has loaded, because several lines of text will appear on screen and then the disc light will go out. On the last of the lines of text to appear you will see: **'A>'** (This is known as the *'A Prompt'* or CP/M's *'System Prompt'*. It lets you know that CP/M is ready to carry out your instructions.) In other words, that the computer system is waiting for you to give it a command.

So let's see the sort of tasks you can get it to perform and let's look at the sort of commands you can give it.

154

SECTION 8-5
Finding Out What Is On A Disc

When you start up your word processing system in the normal way, the screen displays a complete list of the files on your disc - separated into groups. If you change the disc in the drive and then tap the **[f7]** key, that display will change to tell you which files and groups are on the new disc. So when you are word processing it is very easy, but perhaps a bit cumbersome to find what you are looking for.

But what happens when you decide to use the PCW for something other than word processing and you want to keep your filing system up to date? Or if you have simply lost track of a file you need? Is there a quicker way to get a listing of the files on a disc? Well, yes there is. Let's assume that your machine is already switched on.

1 Start by getting your working *copy* of the disc labelled 'CP/M Plus' and put it in the disc drive (the left hand one if you have two disc drive slots).

2 With your left hand, hold own the keys labelled **[SHIFT]** and **[EXTRA]**. Then with your right hand, tap the key labelled **[EXIT]**. You will see the PCW go through its CP/M start up sequence.

3 When you reset with the CP/M Plus disc in the drive, and when you get the 'A' prompt on screen, CP/M is ready to accept your commands .

4 We want to get a list or *'directory'* of the files on a disc, but if you enter the directory command now, you will get a list of the files on the CP/M disc - not the one you want to check out. So replace the CP/M disc with the one you want to check. and *then* key in: **DIR** and press the **[RETURN]** or **[ENTER]** key. You will see a list of the file names appear on screen.

SECTION 8-5
Finding Out What Is On A Disc

Note: That you are given a directory of the disc in drive A: (you can tell that because each line of filenames is preceded by 'A:'). There are three things to notice here:

- When you start up under CP/M, the computer assumes (in default of any contrary instruction from you) that any command you key in applies to the disc in drive A: (in other words, drive A: is its 'default drive') and that's why you got a **DIR**ectory of the disc in drive A:

- You can elect to work on another drive, by simply keying in the identifying letter of the drive you want and then pressing **[RETURN]**

  e.g. **M: [RETURN]** or **m: [RETURN]**

This process is known as *'logging-on'* to a drive.

- You can get a directory for another disc drive without having to log-on to that drive. For example - If you now want to find out which files are in the memory drive (drive M:), but you don't want to log to that drive, key-in:

  DIR M:[RETURN]

5 (!! If you have a twin drive machine, put a disc in the right hand drive now !!) Try keying in: **DIR B:** and now press **[RETURN]**. If you have a twin drive machine you will get a list of the files on the disc in drive B:. If you have the single drive machine, see the next page.

SECTION 8-5
Finding Out What Is On A Disc

6 On a single drive machine, when you ask for a directory of drive B: you hit a slight logical problem, you have only one drive - and that's called drive A: ! But the PCW can cope. The screen prompts you to provide a disc for B:.

What it means is: *'For the time being, let's pretend that your drive A: is called drive B:, so put another disc in the drive then tap the* **[SPACEBAR]** *to let me know when you've done it.'* (Clever isn't it!?)

7 Now, normally, you would do as you are told. But let us cheat a bit, don't change the disc. Just tap the **[SPACEBAR]**. And away goes the PCW, giving you a directory of what it thinks is drive B:. Again, you can tell because each row of filenames is now preceded by 'B:'. (So it's really quite dumb!)

8 The **DIR** command has other variants which you might find useful, so it is worth looking in the PCW User Instruction Manual.

157

SECTION 8-6
Checking The Space Left On A Disc

You can get a lot of information on a disc, but there is a limit. Before you start what looks like being a lengthy job, it is a good idea to check that there will be enough room on the disc for the document you are going to create. The precise amount you need will vary with the page layout, but for word processing, if you work on a maximum of 65 characters per line, with 55 lines per page (for 11 inch continuous paper) you can see that you will have to allow for roughly 65 times 55, or 3575 characters for each page. (In fact, an average of 2.5 to 3 thousand characters per page is usually close enough). So now you know how much space you need, how do you find out how much you've got?

Well you need the CP/M program called SHOW.COM which is on your CP/M disc. So make sure you have your working copy of the disc to hand.

1 Put your working *copy* of the CP/M disc in drive A:. (If you have two drive slots the left hand one is drive A:.) Also put any other disc in the right hand drive.

2 RESET your system - Hold down **[SHIFT]** and **[EXTRA]**. Then tap the **[EXIT]** key. The PCW will carry out a series of jobs (e.g. reading certain files on the disc in A: and putting copies of them onto the memory drive (drive M:).

3 When the PCW screen settles down and you get the system prompt (**A>**) key in: **SHOW B: [RETURN]**.

With a twin drive system, the PCW goes ahead, but with the single drive system you'll be prompted to provide a disc for B: first. For now, just tap the **[SPACEBAR]** as if you had swapped discs.

■ SECTION 8-6
Checking The Space Left On A Disc

4 The SHOW command tells the PCW to look at the disc in the drive you have specified (B: in this case) and report on how much free space remains. You should see a display something like this:

B: RW, Space 100k

The *'RW'* signifies that you can 'read' from this disc and 'write' to it - i.e. use it normally.

'Space 100k' tells you that you have enough room to fit another 100 thousand ('100k') 'bytes' on the disc. (Think of a 'byte' as one character of information.)

SECTION 8-7
Making A Duplicate Copy Of A Disc

We have already explained that you should make a back-up of any disc that you are using and that, at least with program discs, you should use that back-up disc to work from. Provided the disc you are using was created for the PCW9512, you can follow the procedure described in this section. If you are wanting to use a program written for the PCW8256 or PCW8512 then you will need the special facility '8000COPY' which is described in the next section.

1 Start by getting your working *copy* of the disc labelled 'CP/M Plus' and put it in the disc drive (the left hand one if you have two disc drive slots). Make sure side 1 is uppermost. Have a new or blank disc to hand.

2 With your left hand, hold down the keys labelled [SHIFT] and [EXTRA], then with your right hand, tap the key labelled [EXIT]. You will see the PCW go through its CP/M start up sequence.

When you reset with the CP/M Plus disc in the drive, and when you get the 'A' prompt on screen, CP/M is ready to accept your commands.

We want to copy a disc and to do that you need to use a program called DISCKIT which is on your CP/M Plus disc (which should still be in drive A:).

3 Key in: **DISCKIT [RETURN]**.

The PCW responds by running the DISCKIT program. You'll see a message on screen telling you how many disc drives DISCKIT has found and asking you to remove the disc(s) and then press a key.

4 Push the button on the front of the disc drive to release the disc and then tap the **[SPACEBAR]**.

SECTION 8-7
Making A Duplicate Copy Of A Disc

DISCKIT displays a 'menu' which offers you four options: **COPY** (tap the key labelled '**f6/f5**' in the pad of keys at the left of the keyboard), **FORMAT** (tap **f4/f3**), **VERIFY** (**f2/f1**), or tap the **[EXIT]** key to leave DISCKIT.

5   We want to copy a disc, so tap the **[f5/f6]** key.

Single Drive Machine: DISCKIT asks you to put the disc you want to read - copy **from** - in the drive and then tap the letter **[Y]**.

Double Drive: DISCKIT asks you which drive you want to read - copy **from** - (tap f4/f3 for drive A: or f2/f1 for drive B:). Next you will be asked to specify which drive you want to 'write' to - copy **to** (tap f4/f3 for drive A: - f2/f1 for drive B:).

6   *Single Drive:* Put the disc you want to copy **from** into the drive, then tap the letter **[Y]**. Have your new or blank disc ready.

Double Drive: (Recommended procedure) Put the disc you want to copy **from** in drive A: and then tap **[f4/f3]**. Put the disc you want to copy **to** in drive B: and tap **[f2/f1]**, then tap the letter **[Y]**.

DISCKIT will now copy your disc for you. If you have a single drive machine (or if you had elected to read from one drive and write to the same one) DISCKIT will prompt you to swap discs at the appropriate times.

Note: If the disc you are writing **to** is brand new you will see a message telling you that DISCKIT will *'format'* while it is copying (see *'Creating A (data) Disc'*).

SECTION 8-7
Making A Duplicate Copy Of A Disc

If you are working with a single disc drive DISCKIT will format and copy a disc in three parts, each part has 53 tracks. In the top left hand corner of the screen DISCKIT keeps a count of where it has got to during the copy process. You will see it read from and write to 'tracks' 0 to 159. When it has finished, the screen will ask you to remove the disc(s) and tap a key.

Note: (a) Get into the habit of always putting the discs in a drive with side 1 uppermost.

Note: (b) If, during the copy process, you are asked to swap discs and you put the wrong disc in the drive, or put the right disc in upside down, DISCKIT will spot your mistake and ask you to rectify it.

Note: (c) If, during the copy process, you do not push the disc home securely in the drive, DISCKIT will think that the disc is missing altogether and it will prompt you to provide the right disc and then tap **[R]** to retry the activity (or tap **[C]** to cancel).

6 When prompted by DISCKIT, remove the disc(s) and tap the **[SPACEBAR]**.

DISCKIT asks if you want to make another copy.

7 If yes, tap the **[Y]** key and repeat the process. If no, tap the **[SPACEBAR]**.

DISCKIT displays its main menu again (the one with 4 options).

8 Tap **[EXIT]** to leave DISCKIT. Don't forget to put a label on your new disc.

SECTION 8-8
Copying A Disc From 8000 Format

The floppy discs that you use with your PCW9512 look the same as those used with the PCW8256 and PCW8512. They are, however, formatted differently, i.e. the number of tracks laid down on the surface of the disc electronically is greater, 720 as opposed to 180.

This means that you can store a great deal more information on the disc and therefore work more efficiently. But it also means that if you want to use a program which has been created in the 8000 format or if you want to use work that you originally set up on an 8000 series machine you need to copy this to a disc which you can use on your PCW9512.

On your CP/M disc you will find a file called '8000COPY' which is the one you use instead of DISCKIT to copy a disc.

1 Start by getting your working *copy* of the disc labelled 'CP/M Plus' and put it in the disc drive (the left hand one if you have two disc drive slots).

2 With your left hand, hold down the keys labelled **[SHIFT]** and **[EXTRA]** and with your right hand, tap the key labelled **[EXIT]**. You will see the PCW go through its CP/M start up sequence.

Before you can start the copy procedure you will need a disc which is formatted for the PCW9512, ready to receive the information you are going to copy. If your disc is not already formatted for the 9512, follow the steps described in the section titled, *'Formatting A New Disc'*.

3 With your CP/M Plus disc in the floppy drive, at the 'A' prompt, key in: **8000COPY [RETURN]**.

SECTION 8-8
Copying A Disc From 8000 Format

You will see some text appear on screen, explaining the 8000COPY procedure. You have the option to create a disc which will start CP/M Plus automatically when you switch your machine on and insert the new copy disc. Since this is the most straightforward option, we shall follow it through here. The text then reminds you that you must have a formatted disc ready to copy to, and it displays the warning, for single disc drive machines 'This will erase all files on drive M:'.

Note: If you do have a single drive machine and if you have any information on drive M: which you have not yet saved to disc, copy that information to disc now **before** you start the 8000COPY procedure! I.e. tap [N] in response to *'Do you want to continue'* and this will take you back to the 'A' prompt.

4 To proceed with 8000COPY, tap [Y] in response to *'Do you want to continue (Y/N)?'*.

5 You are then asked if you want to make the destination disc - the disc you are copying to - 'bootable', i.e. it will start up CP/M automatically. Tap [Y].

6 Make sure your CP/M disc is still in drive A: and tap the [SPACE BAR]. If you have a single drive machine, the system reads the CP/M system file and erases all files from drive M:. If you have a twin drive machine you should insert your destination disc in drive B:, the right hand drive slot, and the copy procedure will proceed without using Drive M:.

7 If you have a single drive machine, remove the CP/M Plus disc and insert the disc you are copying from, the one which is in normal, i.e. 180K or 8000 format, into Drive A:.

SECTION 8-8
Copying A Disc From 8000 Format

8 If the disc contains LocoScript files, tap **[Y]**, if not, tap **[N]** and the copying will begin. You can follow the progress on screen.

10 When prompted, remove the source disc and insert your destination disc and tap the **[SPACEBAR]**.

When copying is complete, you will be asked 'Do you have another normal capacity disc to copy?'. If the answer is Yes, tap **[Y]** and continue until all copying is complete, then tap **[N]**. All files on drive M: are erased and you return to the A prompt.

Note: You should be able to copy the contents of four normal capacity discs to the higher capacity discs. In each case you will be asked if the disc contains LocoScript files. Tap **[Y]** or **[N]** as appropriate. If you attempt to copy a file which already exists on the destination disc, a warning message appears on screen and you have the option to overwrite the original version or not as you wish.

To use your new disc:

1 Reboot the system by holding down **[SHIFT]** and **[EXTRA]** and tapping **[EXIT]**. To start the program you want, key in the appropriate instruction as shown in your program documentation.

■ SECTION 8-9
Booting Automatically Into A Program

One additional refinement to the process of creating working discs is to make the new disc automatically boot into a program when you start up (either by switching on or by resetting/rebooting the system). To do this you have to put a copy of the file SUBMIT.COM and an amended version of the file PROFILE.SUB on your new disc as follows.

1 Start by getting your working *copy* of the disc labelled 'CP/M Plus' and put it in the disc drive (the left hand one if you have two disc drive slots).

2 With your left hand, hold down the keys labelled **[SHIFT]** and **[EXTRA]**, and with your right hand, tap the key labelled **[EXIT]**. You will see the PCW go through its CP/M start up sequence.

3 At the A prompt, key in:

PIP [RETURN]
m:=submit.com [RETURN]

4 Remove your CP/M disc, insert the new disc and key in:

a:=m:submit.com [RETURN]
[RETURN]

You are now ready to copy the file PROFILE.SUB in the same way.

5 Insert your working copy of CP/M PLUS and at the A prompt key in:

PIP [RETURN]
m:=profile.sub [RETURN]
[RETURN]

SECTION 8-9
Booting Automatically Into A Program

This returns you to the 'A' prompt once more and you can now alter the PROFILE.SUB file to work with your new program.

1   Key in **RPED [RETURN]**. This loads a small program (written in the *BASIC* programming language) which you can use to alter text files. (If a message appears on screen, *RPED?* followed by the 'A' prompt, key in **SUBMIT RPED [RETURN]**.)

2   At the Menu Screen, tap **[f1]**, insert your new disc and key in **PROFILE.SUB [RETURN]**. The destination disc is the same as the source disc in this case, so tap **[RETURN]** if you want the new version to replace the existing one or key in a new name (e.g. THISPROG.SUB) and tap **[RETURN]**.

What you will see on screen are the instructions that CP/M follows when you start up, or boot up, your system. It includes copying certain files to memory, drive M: and directions on the sequence in which instructions are to be carried out. What you need to add now are the start up instructions for your new program.

This may simply be a single word as for example with mini Office Plus, or it may include other instructions such as SETKEYS as with SuperCalc.

3   Use the cursor arrows to move the cursor down to the bottom of the file and key in the new instructions.

Note: When working with RPED, the DELete, ALT+Delete and CUT keys can be used to remove text. To insert text, you move the cursor to the line where you want the text to appear, hold down ALT and tap the DOWN ARROW key if you need to insert a line and key in the text. Use the arrow keys to move to the next line if need be. The [RETURN] key simply moves the cursor to the start of the next line.

SECTION 8-9
Booting Automatically Into A Program

Note: For full details of how to create and edit text files using RPED, refer to the CP/M section of the PCW9512 User Instructions.

4 Once you have completed the changes, tap the **[EXIT]** key to return to the Menu Screen and **[EXIT]** again to go back to the system prompt.

5 With your new working disc still in drive A:, hold down **[SHIFT]** and **[EXTRA]** and tap **[EXIT]** and the system should load up your program automatically.

Note: If this does not happen, check that the new PROFILE.SUB contains the correct instructions by keying in TYPE PROFILE.SUB. This command will give you a display of the contents of the PROFILE.SUB file. Repeat the above procedure if necessary.

■ SECTION 8-10
Creating A (data) Disc

It is a good idea to keep programs and data on separate discs - if nothing else, you will be able to get more data on a disc if it is dedicated to one job!

> **BEWARE.!** You will be 'formattting' a disc, and formatting a disc entails destroying any information already on that disc.
> You can use the FORMATTING process on any disc - Make sure before you start that the disc you intend to FORMAT is really one that you can wipe clean without losing some vital information!!

Before you can use a new disc to hold data files (or program files for that matter) you will have to go through a procedure to prepare the disc for its job. When you get a brand new disc it is simply a thin sheet of plastic material which is coated with a magnetic medium. Before you can use it to store information of any kind, you will have to 'mark out' a pattern of tracks on the surface. These tracks hold the magnetic 'pigeon-holes' for the data and they have to be laid out in a very precise format. That is why the preparation procedure is known as FORMATTING the disc.

FORMATTING is very easy to do - dangerously easy! **See the 'Health Warning' above.**

Have your CP/M disc to hand as well as your brand new disc.

SECTION 8-10
Creating A (data) Disc

1 Start by getting your working *copy* of the disc labelled 'CP/M Plus' and put it in the disc drive (the left hand one if you have two disc drive slots). Make sure side 1 is uppermost.

2 With your left hand, hold down the keys labelled **[SHIFT]** and **[EXTRA]**, then with your right hand, tap the key labelled **[EXIT]**. You will see the PCW go through its CP/M start up sequence. This procedure is known as RESETTING or BOOTING your system.

When you reset with the CP/M Plus disc in the drive, and when you get the 'A' prompt on screen, CP/M is ready to accept your commands.

We want to FORMAT a disc and to do that you need to use a program called DISCKIT which is on your CP/M Plus disc (which should still be in drive A:).

3 Key in: **DISCKIT [RETURN]**.

The PCW responds by running the DISCKIT program. You'll see a message on screen telling you how many disc drives DISCKIT has found and asking you to remove the disc(s) and then press a key.

4 Push the button on the front of the disc drive to release the disc and then tap the **[SPACEBAR]**.

DISCKIT displays a 'menu' which offers you four options: COPY (tap the key labelled [f6/f5] in the pad of keys at the left of the keyboard), FORMAT (tap [f4/f3]), VERIFY (tap [f2/f1]), or tap the [EXIT] key to leave DISCKIT.

5 We want to FORMAT a disc, so tap the **[f4/f3]** key.

SECTION 8-10
Creating A (data) Disc

Single drive machine: You will be asked to provide the disc which is to be formatted.

Twin drive machine: You will be asked to tell DISCKIT which drive will hold the disc to be formatted (I recommend that you get into the habit of putting the disc in drive B: - with side 1 uppermost - and then nominating that drive).

> And remember! You can use the FORMATTING process on any disc. Make sure before you start that the disc you intend to FORMAT is really one that you can wipe clean without losing some vital information!

6 When you are sure that you are ready, tap the letter **[Y]** to start the formatting process.

You will see disckit keep a count as it lays down 160 tracks (numbered 0 to 159) on the surface of the disc.

Once the disc is formatted, it will be ready for use as a data (or program) disc.

SECTION 8-11
Naming And Storing Your Document FILES

When you create a document file (or any other kind of file) which you intend to store on a disc, you will have to give it a name. That name will have to conform with the following simple rules:

- **Two parts**: The file names you use can have two parts: a TITLE and a code to identify what *type* of file it is (e.g. whether it is a letter, a report, a quotation and so on)
- You don't **have** to use both parts, but if you do, you must separate them with a full-stop (or 'dot'), e.g. *'thispage.txt'*
- The TITLE can be anything between 1 and 8 characters in length
- The TYPE code can be anything between 1 and 3 characters in length
- You must **not** have a space anywhere in your file name and you must **not** use a full stop *other than* to separate the title and the type code. If you need to split the file title into more than one part (e.g. chapters of a book), use the underscore symbol, e.g. *'pcw_6.txt'*

You can use most of the keys on the keyboard in your file names, but for day to day purposes I would advise you to stick to letters and numbers. You won't make any mistakes that way, but perhaps more importantly, you're more likely to be able to interpret your file names in six months time. After all, you store a file so you can refer to it at some time in the future. and that means you must be able to find the file again. So keep your file names simple! Use a system that comes naturally to you, or one that fits in with the way you do things normally. (You will find a list of the characters to avoid on page 364 of your PCW 9512 'User Instructions'.)

SECTION 8-11
Naming And Storing Your Document FILES

It doesn't matter whether you key in the file name in capitals or in lower case. The computer will convert all letters into capitals.

Caution: Certain file type codes have specific meanings to your computer, and some have specific meanings to particular software packages, so be careful with them. In particular do not use: 'COM' 'EXE' 'HEX' 'ASM' 'BAS' 'PRN' 'INT' 'SUB' '$$$' unless you are told to in the instructions for the software you are using at the time.

SECTION 8-12
Matching Up File Names ('masks')

There will be times when you want to carry out the same command for several files with very similar names (for example, make a copy of a set of files called 'chap1, chap2, chap3, etc.'). There will also be times when you are looking for a file whose name you cannot remember exactly. CP/M has a feature which you will find useful under these and many other circumstances. CP/M allows you to use *'ambiguous file names'* in many of your commands.

You create an ambiguous file name by replacing parts of the name with special symbols. You can use the question mark symbol (?) to represent a single character or you can use the asterisk (*) symbol to represent a group of characters. e.g.

1 To make a copy on drive M: of several files, all called 'chap followed by a number, (which are on the disc in drive A:) you would key in:

PIP M:=A:CHAP? [RETURN].

In response to this **single** command, CP/M will copy **all** the files which match the ambiguous name.

(See also *'Making A Duplicate Copy Of A Document File'*)

2 To find a file called 'LETTER.(something-or-other)', key in:

DIR LETTER.* [RETURN].

In the first example you could have used **CHAP*** as your ambiguous filename. In the second example you could have used **LETTER???**

Just remember that a question mark takes the place of a single character and the asterisk represents several characters. So **???????????** and ***.*** means all files called 'something dot something'. In other words, **all** files!

SECTION 8-12
Matching Up File Names ('masks')

- So the command: DIR followed by either of these two and then **[RETURN]** will give you a normal directory:

    e.g. DIR *.* [RETURN]

- ???????? or * on its own means all files which do not have a file TYPE extension.

    e.g. DIR ???????? [RETURN]

- ????.* means any file which has only four characters in the first name and has any file type extension.

- *? means a file which has any name, but which has only one character in its file type extension. There are lots more possible combinations for you to try.

■ SECTION 8-13
Making A Duplicate Copy Of A File

When you want to tidy-up or reorganise your disc filing system, one of the jobs you will want to do is to make copies of one or more files. Don't forget that you will also need to make safety (back-up) copies of all your files - see the section titled *'Discs And Drives'*.

So how do you make copies of a *file* rather than a disc? Well you need the CP/M program called PIP.COM which is on your CP/M disc. So make sure you have your working copy of the disc to hand.

1 Put your working copy of the CP/M disc in drive A:. **(If you have two drive slots** the left hand one is drive A:.)

2 RESET your system - Hold down **[SHIFT]** and **[EXTRA]**, then tap the **[EXIT]** key. The PCW will carry out a series of jobs. One of those jobs is to read certain files on the disc in A: (including **PIP.COM**) and put copies of them onto the memory drive (drive M:). This is PIP.COM in action, under the control of the PCW. As you can see, it can even copy itself!

3 When the PCW screen settles down and you get the system prompt (A>), key in: **M: [RETURN]** You will see the 'system prompt' change to (M>) which tells you that M: is now your default drive. (If you key in: **DIR [RETURN]** you will see which files are on the M: drive.)

4 Leave your CP/M disc in drive A: for the time being, but let's pretend for the moment that it is one of your 'data' discs which holds files you want to copy. (Remember, that we are 'logged' to the M: drive and there is a copy of PIP.COM on this drive.)

SECTION 8-13
Making A Duplicate Copy Of A File

Let us further suppose that you want to make a duplicate copy of a file you have which is called 'SHOW.COM' and you want that copy on M:. (In reality of course you would not use the 'COM' extension in your own file names - see *'Naming And Storing Your Document Files'*.)

5 Key in: **PIP M:SHOW.COM=A:SHOW.COM** (don't press **[RETURN]** yet).

Let us examine this command in more detail to find out what it all means.

1. Remember, you want to use PIP.COM (the copying program) so that is the first thing you key in, but, because it is a **COM**mand program you don't need to key in the full name to **run** the program.

2. Notice also that the PIP command is separated from the rest of the instruction by a space AND that there are no other spaces in the instruction. PIP is the command, the other details are known as the *'parameters'* of the command. (Don't ask us why - perhaps it's just to make things seem more difficult than they really are.)

3. Notice how the parameters are expressed. They are in the form of a mathematical equation which describes *how you want things to be -* rather than what you want PIP to do! I.e. You want to end up with a file on M: called SHOW.COM (M:SHOW.COM to be precise) which is going to be the same as (or equal to) a file on A: called SHOW.COM.

6 If that's clear, press **[RETURN]** now to implement the PIP command. If it's not clear, turn to the section headed, *'Some General Points About CP/M Commands'*.

177

■ SECTION 8-14
Getting Rid Of Unwanted 'Files'

From time to time you will want to clear old files from your discs - to make more room, or simply to minimise the clutter. Here's how you do it.

1 Start by double checking that you really do not need to keep the file. If you *do* need the file, but you don't want it on the disc you are using, you can COPY the file onto another disc - see the previous section, *'Making A Duplicate Copy Of A File'*.

The structure of the command to use is:

ERA file-name [RETURN]

- So to **ERA**se a file called LETTER.TXT which is on the drive you are 'logged' to, you would key in:

ERA LETTER.TXT [RETURN]

- To **ERA**se a file which is on a drive *other than* the one you are logged to, you must precede the file-name with the appropriate drive identifier. e.g.

ERA B:LETTER.TXT [RETURN]

- To **ERA**se a group of files with similar names you can use file name masks - see the section, *'Matching Up File Names ('masks')'*.

ERA B:LETTER.* [RETURN]

Note: The PCW will check that you really do want to erase a number of files. You will have to confirm by tapping the letter **[Y]**. You can erase several, or even *all*, the files on a disc in one go by using file name masks. As an added safety measure you can get the PCW to check with you before it erases each file (provided you have a copy of ERASE.COM available preferably on the disc you are logged to).

■ SECTION 8-14
Getting Rid Of Unwanted 'Files'

1 So, assuming you were logged to drive M: with ERASE.COM on that drive (i.e. copied across from the CP/M disc), you can selectively erase all the files on the disc in drive A: with this command:

      ERA A:*.* [C] then press the **[RETURN]** key.

The PCW will present you with the name of a file on the disc and then ask you to *confirm* that you do want it erased, before removing the file from the disc.

Note: The ERAse command does *not* put the file into 'limbo' as LocoScript's erase/delete procedure does. Once you have ERAsed a file you cannot get it back - unless you have special software.

■ SECTION 8-15
Renaming A Document File

From time to time you will want to give your files different names (e.g. because you have changed your filing system, or more often because you want to denote that a file is a 'back-up' copy of another file). This is how you do it:

1   To rename a file which is called LETTER.TXT and to give it the new name LETTER.BAK you would key in:

   REN LETTER.BAK=LETTER.TXT [RETURN].

Note: the formula, *newname = oldname* !!!

If you want to change the name of a file which is on a disc *other than* the one you are working on (i.e. other than the one you are 'logged to') you will have to precede the file names with the appropriate drive identifying letter. For example, if you are logged to drive M: and you want to change the name of a file which is on drive A: you would key in:

   REN A:LETTER.BAK=A:LETTER.TXT [RETURN].

Note: the REName command changes only the name of the file - it does not affect the file in any other way.

If you try to rename a file to a filename which already exists, just as if you try to rename a file in LocoScript to one which already exists in the same group, a message will appear warning you that there is already a file of that name. You then have the option **Y/N** to cancel or proceed with the operation.

If for some reason you do wish to replace an existing file which already has the name you want to use, as for instance when you are setting up a new keyboard configuration for a foreign language, make sure you copy or rename the original file first as it will be deleted if you proceed. See this section and, *'Making A Duplicate Copy Of A File'*, above.

SECTION 8-16
Some General Points About CP/M Commands

A 'typical' CP/M command takes the following form:

PIP M:SHOW.COM=A:SHOW.COM [RETURN].

We are using PIP in this example, but the points we are going to make here apply generally to CP/M commands.

1 It is less complicated if you have a copy of the program on the disc in the drive which you have logged to. E.g. If you are logged to drive A: and PIP.COM is on drive M: then you would have to precede the command with the drive 'identifier', i.e. you would have to key in **M:PIP** etc.

2 You write the command line in the form of an equation. Here, it reads: 'make a copy so we end up with a file on M: called SHOW.COM which is the same as the file on A: called SHOW.COM'. Think of CP/M commands as having the form **'destination = source'**.

3 If you want the copy to have the same name as the original file, there is no need to specify the name for the 'destination' file, e.g. **PIP M:=A:SHOW.COM [RETURN]** would be Okay.

4 If you want the copy to have a different name from the original, then you have to specify that name (for the destination file) in the command, e.g.

PIP M:LETTER.BAK=A:LETTER.TXT [RETURN]

would create a file called LETTER.BAK on M: which is a copy of the file LETTER.TXT on the disc in your drive A:.

SECTION 8-16
Some General Points About CP/M Commands

5 You can use file name masks in many CP/M commands. For example, let's imagine we want to copy *all* the 'COM' files on a disc into memory. You would key in:

PIP M:=A:*.COM [RETURN]

To copy all files called 'SHOW' something, you would key in:

PIP M:=A:SHOW.* [RETURN]

To copy ALL the files onto M: key in:

PIP M:=A:*.* [RETURN]

For more information, see the section headed, *'Matching Up File Names ('masks')'*.

6 Remember that to work with a file which is on a disc other than the one you are logged to, you must identify the drive which holds the program, e.g.

A:PIP M:=A:SHOW.COM [RETURN].

SECTION 8-17
Personalising Your System

What CP/M does when you start up, is controlled by a file called PROFILE.SUB. The contents of this file are displayed on screen when you start up CP/M. As we indicated earlier in the section *'Making A Disc 'boot' Into A Program'* you can edit this file to extend these operations.

We have already seen, in that you can alter your system to meet your needs more closely, e.g. by changing a printwheel to use a different set of characters. You can also set up a dot matrix printer on your system.

Broadly speaking, you can add a Parallel printer which you plug into the Parallel Port at the back of your PCW9512 and then tell CP/M to direct any printer information to the Parallel Printer Port by keying in the command, DEVICE LST:=CEN.

You can also set up a Modem link so that your system can communicate with electronic mail services such as Telecom Gold. To do this you will need to buy and attach a Serial Interface. Details of this are in Part 1, Chapter 3 of your PCW9512 User Instructions.

Once you have a modem attached, you need to set it up as described below, but you can tell the system to talk to it in much the same way as when you change to a different printer, DEVICE LST:=SIO.

To return to the built in printer at any time while you are still working, you key in DEVICE LST:=LPT.

Note: To set up your modem once it is attached, you need to identify how it is to handle the transfer of information. You use the utility SETSIO (set the Serial Interface Output) which is described in Part Three, Chapters 2 and 5 of your PCW9512 User Instructions.

These are quite dramatic changes to the standard system, yet you can build them in as an option rather than a permanent change. There are also a number of smaller changes you can make to create a more efficient system for you.

SECTION 8-18
Setting Up Special Function Keys

There may be functions or operations you perform regularly that do not appear on the standard keyboard set up, or require lengthy instructions. You can set up function keys or combinations of shift and other keys to do these at a stroke.

The shift keys, [SHIFT], [ALT] and [EXTRA] already have functions in combination with specific keys. For example [EXTRA] + [U] produce an up pointing arrow, [ALT] and the number keys produce fractions, [EXTRA] and [C] produces the Copyright symbol. Some combinations are not defined, however and you can use these to set up special features for yourself.

If you regularly use the text editor to set up new files, you might like to set up a function key to open up RPED.

To do either of these you need to create a text file and save it with a name that gives an indication what it contains. For example where you want to include a few foreign characters but do not want to change the whole keyboard configuration you could create a file called EUROKEYS or simply MYKEYS. There are already three files on your CP/M disc which set up different keyboard configurations, KEYS.WP, KEYS.DRL and CPMKEYS. These call up the Word processing, DRLogo and PCW's normal keyboard settings.

1 Start by getting your working *copy* of the disc labelled 'CP/M Plus' and put it in the disc drive (the left hand one if you have two disc drive slots).

2 When CP/M has finished loading, at the 'A' prompt, key in **RPED** (in capitals or lower case) and tap **[RETURN]**. (If you see the cryptic message, *'RPED?'*, key in, **SUBMIT RPED[RETURN]**.)

SECTION 8-18
Setting Up Special Function Keys

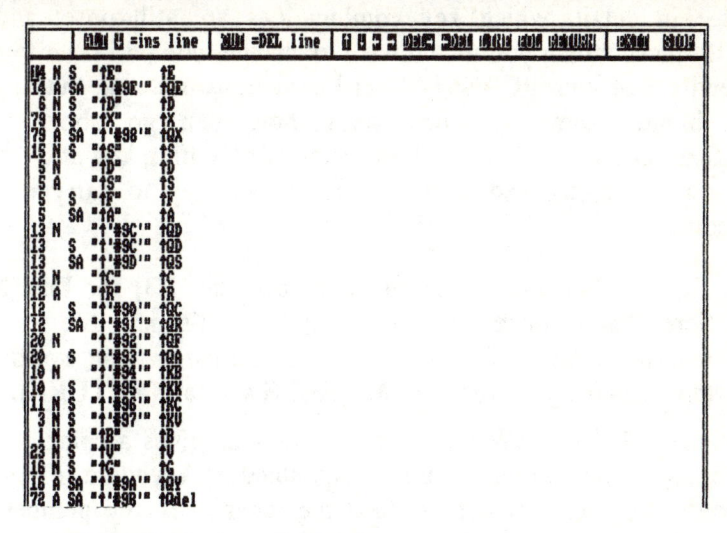

Fig. 1: KEYS.WP displayed in RPED.

3 We shall start by having a look at how an existing file looks, so tap **F1** and key in **keys.wp [RETURN]**, then tap **[RETURN]** again to call up the first part of this file.

It all looks a little confusing at first, but it is quite simply designed to tell the PCW9512 what should appear on screen when each key is struck.

The first column gives the number of the key. A full plan of the numbers appears on page 544 of the PCW User Instructions. The second and third columns give a code for the shift key to be used, e.g S=Shift, E=Extra, A=Alt and N=Normal. What appears in inverted commas is the instruction for the key setting and the last column gives a brief description of what this setting does.

185

■ SECTION 8-18
Setting Up Special Function Keys

To see in detail, which key combinations are still unset and to identify those which you would wish to change, you will need to read Appendix 1 of your PCW9512 User Instructions in detail, but to give two simple examples which show how you go about these modifications, we shall look at an example of setting key strokes for a foreign character and setting one function key to carry out an instruction.

1 Tap **[EXIT]** and at the Menu Screen, tap **[f3]** for Edit New Screen and, since you will be adding this new file to your working copy of CP/M, this is the destination disc, so key in the filename you want e.g. **MYKEYS** and tap **[RETURN]**.

Appendix 1 in the PCW9512 User Instructions gives a complete list of the key combinations set up for the standard keyboard. From the keyboard diagram you will see that the letter N is key number 46. We are going to set the combination of Extra + N to create a lower case n tilde. List 1.4 *'The Complete Character Set'* on page 547, shows that lower case n tilde has a Decimal value of 249.

2 At the RPED text editing screen, key in:

46 E "⇑'#249'" Lower case n tilde

Note: 46 is the N key, E = Extra, next is the up arrow - which you get by keying in [EXTRA] and [U] or [EXTRA] + ; and 249 is the decimal value for the character. The decimal number should be in single inverted commas and the whole *value* expression should be in double quotation marks (shifted '2' key on the main keyboard).

SECTION 8-18
Setting Up Special Function Keys

To set a Function key to perform a command you need a similar line of text but with the expression given as a string of characters and codes rather than a number. For example:

3 Key in **E #81 "rped ⇑ M"**

Note: *E + #81*, or *129*, is the token for (i.e. it represents) the function key F1/F2 in its hexadecimal and decimal values, *RPED* is the command to start the text editor and ⇑ *M* puts a carriage return at the end of the command. (Remember, [EXTRA]+[U] gives the ⇑ symbol.)

4 To exit from RPED and save the new file, tap **[EXIT]** to leave the screen and save the information, then tap **[EXIT]** again to leave the program and return to the A prompt.

5 To set the keys to the new configuration, key in **setkeys mykeys [RETURN]** and try them out. To return to the standard PCW keyboard, key in **setkeys cpmkeys [RETURN]**.

SECTION 8-19
Protecting Your Files

Perhaps the person we most need to protect our files from is ourself. Although the PCW goes out of its way to stop us erasing or overwriting our documents, it can happen in a moment of lost concentration. So the system lets us protect our files from accidental damage.

We have already seen that we should make working copies of our software to protect master discs from damage, and we should make back-up copies of our work wherever possible.

Some files are vital to the computer, system files, and we can separate these from our document files. Two additional features available to us are, creating read only files and adding password access to discs and files.

1 Start by getting your working *copy* of the disc labelled 'CP/M Plus' and put it in the disc drive (the left hand one if you have two disc drive slots).

2 When CP/M has finished loading, at the 'A' prompt, key in **set filename [RO]** (in capitals or lower case) and tap **[RETURN]**. (RO stands for *Read Only*, i.e. anyone can examine the file but not edit or erase it.) To return it to normal, key in: **set filename [RW][RETURN]**.

You can use wild cards to protect groups of files, as for example if you wanted to make all your 'system' files read only.

1 To separate system files from other files you will first need to identify them. Key in **set filename [SYS][RETURN]**. Repeat this for any other files you wish to designate. These files are hidden when you list the files on a disc. They are not copied, erased or renamed with 'non-system' files.

188

SECTION 8-19
Protecting Your Files

2 To make a file a 'non-system' file again, key in **set filename [DIR][RETURN]**.

Program files with User Number 0 can be made available to other User Numbers by making them System Files. See Section 2.13 in Part Three of your PCW9512 User Instructions for setting up User Numbers if you are likely to need this facility.

SECTION 8-20
Setting Passwords

If more than one person is using your system and you want to restrict access to certain discs or files, you can set up password access - not only to prevent access, but to control the operations that can be performed when access is given. There are three modes of protection, read, write and delete as we shall see. The initial thing you need to do when setting up a password is to switch on the password protection for the drive. When you are setting up or using passwords they appear on the screen so you need to be sure unauthorised users are not able to observe the screen while you are using passwords.

1 Start by getting your working *copy* of the disc labelled 'CP/M Plus' and put it in the disc drive (the left hand one if you have two disc drive slots). When CP/M has finished loading, at the A prompt, key in **set a: [PROTECT = on, PASSWORD = password][RETURN]**. (You use a password for this to prevent other users turning the protection off.)

You now have three 'modes' of protection which you specify as follows. To control access for:

- Reading, copying, changing, deleting or renaming - READ
- Changing, deleting and renaming - WRITE
- Deleting - DELETE

If you copy a password protected file to a different disc using the same name, the same password and protection mode will be maintained. If you give the copy a new password, by adding it after the new filename, the protection will be set to READ.

3 To set the password, key in **set filename [PASSWORD = password, PROTECT = mode]**. Groups of files can only be copied if they share the same password and you set the Default password to this password first: **set [DEFAULT = password]**.

SECTION 8-21
Installing & Using Commercial Software

Commercial software written for CP/M will run on the PCW9512 but it needs to be modified or installed to give the correct on-screen and printer results. The software that you want to use must be written for CP/M version 2.2 or CP/M Plus (CP/M3), the same operating system as your machine. It must also be available on 3" Compact floppy discs in Amstrad CPC or PCW format.

If you have any problems with any of these requirements you should consult your dealer.

Before starting to use your system and master discs you should 'write protect' them to prevent accidental damage. To do this, open the write protect holes at the top left corner of each side of the disc by pushing the cover back in the opposite direction to the arrows A and B.

Start by creating a working copy of the discs using DISCKIT or 8000COPY as described in earlier sections. Then proceed as follows:

1 Start by getting your working *copy* of the disc labelled 'CP/M Plus' and put it in the disc drive (the left hand one if you have two disc drive slots). When CP/M has finished loading, at the 'A' prompt, remove the CP/M disc and insert your new working disc and key in the appropriate command to run the program.

If you want to keep your data separate from the program disc, you will need to create a data disc as described in an earlier section. If you wish to make the program self-booting, you will need to replace the file J10CPM3.EMS with J30CPM3.EMS from your PCW9512 start up disc. You must also ensure that you can get this file, along with the software program(s), any CP/M utilities you need *and* the PROFILE.SUB and SUBMIT.COM files on the same disc.

■ SECTION 8-21
Installing & Using Commercial Software

To install the software, provided it was written for a range of computers which includes the PCW9512, you should follow the instructions in the software pack. These usually take the form of a sequence of questions and answers. You can find a full list of the PCW9512 parameters on page 425 of your User Instructions. If the program lists a Zenith Z19/Z29 or similar monitor and a Diablo 630 or similar printer, select these.

If the software was not written for the PCW9512, you should consult your dealer before installation.

You may want or need to change some of the key settings to run your new program. If you do, follow the procedure described above in the section *'Setting Up Special Function Keys'*.

Chapter Nine
Storing Information With A Database Program, LocoFile & dBase II

SECTION 9-1
A Word About Databases In General

If, up to now, you have used your PCW9512 simply as a word processor, you may still be using a card index to store details of your customers and suppliers. You could say that you are using a database, but is it the *best* type of database for you, or would a computer database be better? Let's be clear, a card index might well be the database best for you.

So what *is* a database? Essentially, it is simply a store of information which is organised in a particular way; a telephone directory is another database we all know. A database *program* (such as LocoFile or dBase enables us to create and maintain (keep up to date) our own store(s) of information on a computer - the PCW in this case.

A database program, to be worthy of the name, must enable us to carry out certain basic tasks:

- organise information
- store that information
- retrieve any bits of information we want quickly

and, ideally, it should also enable us to

- sort the information
- analyse the information
- present the same information in different forms

A Reminder For U.K. Users.
If you do decide to keep information about other people on your computer - you may have to record that fact on the **Data Protection Register**. Information held for certain uses is exempt (e.g. personal, or household, or recreational uses) but it is safer to check. (See section 6-5 for the address of the registrar.)

SECTION 9-1
A Word About Databases In General

Setting up an address file for mailmerging letters is part of what you can do with a database, but the flexibility of indexing should allow you to call up a whole range of information, such as all clients in a particular county when planning visits, historical records of outstanding accounts, suppliers of particular goods, club members whose fees are due, patients whose check-ups need booking and many more.

In this chapter we shall be looking at a couple of database programs, used by large numbers of PCW9512 owners. The aim is to introduce you to databases in general - their basic ways of working and those tasks they are particularly effective at performing.

We shall be looking in some detail at how you use LocoFile (as an example of a particular class of database programs), and we shall then look briefly at dBase II - a quite different kind of database program. We'll leave it up to you to decide whether you need a database program at all, and if so, which class of program would suit you best.

SECTION 9-2
An Introduction To LocoFile

LocoFile is a database program produced by LocoMotive Software, who also produced LocoScript, LocoSpell and LocoMail with which you may already be familiar. To set up LocoFile, you will need to prepare a working disc as we shall see shortly, but in doing so it will give you an updated version of the other LocoMotive software. You should therefore take note of any update information which comes with the package to show how it affects other work that you do.

Before you can use LocoFile, as with any other software, you should prepare a working copy of the master disc. With LocoFile you may also like to prepare a *'Samples'* disc which will contain the sample files supplied with LocoFile and which you will be able to use as a data disc once you start working on your own.

SECTION 9-3
Installing LocoFile

1 To create a working or Start of Day disc you will need a blank disc and the Locofile Master disc. Write-protect the Master disc by opening the write-protect holes. (See page 8 of your PCW9512 User Guide.) If your version of LocoScript is the same as the one on the LocoFile disc then you can add LocoFile to that and there is no need to create a new Start of Day disc.

Note: The version number is written on the front of the master disc. If you do not know which version is on your LocoScript Start of Day disc, start up or reset your machine with your Start of Day disc, tap F1 for the Actions Menu and the version number is displayed at the top of this menu. If your version of LocoScript is the same as the new disc then follow the steps to copy the relevant data from the LocoFile Master disc to your Start of Day disc. To create a new Start of Day disc, proceed as follows:

2 Switch on or reboot your machine with your current LocoScript Start of Day disc.

3 Show the hidden files by tapping **[f8]**, highlighting **Show Hidden Files** and tapping the **[+]** key followed by **[ENTER]**.

4 Move the cursor to Group 0 or System Group on Drive M: and erase any of the following files which appear, by highlighting the file name, tapping **[f3]** for the File Menu, selecting **Erase File** then tapping **[ENTER]** twice:

D630 .#CP
D630 .PRI
DMP .PRI
INSTALL .DRV
PCW9512 .#SF
PCW9512 .PRI

SECTION 9-3
Installing LocoFile

5 Label your new Start of Day disc '2.xx Start of Day disc'. Remove the LocoScript Start of Day disc from Drive A: and tap **[f2]** for the disc menu. Select **Copy Disc** and copy the LocoFile Master disc (Source Disc) to your new Start of Day disc (Destination Disc). Leave the new Start of Day disc in Drive A:.

If you are going to use only the built in printer, then continue with the steps below. If you will be using additional printers, refer to the section *'Using Different Printers'*.

1 To remove other printer files, tap **[f6]** for the Setting Menu. Select **For Printer** and tap **[ENTER]**. Use the **[CUT]** key to delete all printer names followed by a question mark (?) and return to the Settings Menu by tapping **[ENTER]**.

2 Move the cursor down and select *Write SETTINGS.STD* then tap **[ENTER]**. With the new Start of Day disc in drive A:, select *Write to the disc now in drive A* and tap **[ENTER]**.

All that remains is to copy any files which you wish to include in your new Start of Day disc to the appropriate group e.g. LOCOSPEL.DCT and USERSPEL.DCT from Drive M: to Drive A: Group 7. You can also copy any files you have created which you wish to continue using, e.g. phrases and data files, TEMPLATE.STD, KEYBOARD.JOY. See *'Making A Duplicate Copy Of A File'*.

1 To prepare a Samples disc, which can become a data disc if you wish to use the sample database file for your own records, insert your write protected LocoFile Master disc into drive A: and tap **[f2]**. Check that **Copy Disc** is highlighted and tap **[ENTER]**.

Note: If your start of day disc is not the same version as LocoFile master disc, follow the installation instructions given in the *'Update Information'* supplied with LocoFile.

SECTION 9-3
Installing LocoFile

2   Select *Copy 720k disc using Drive A* and tap **[ENTER]**. When copying has finished, select *Return to Disc Manager* and tap **[ENTER]**.

3   Insert the new disc in Drive A:, tap **[f8]** and select *Show Hidden Files*. Tap the **[+]** key followed by **[ENTER]**. Move the file cursor in turn to each file in Group 0, tap **[f3]**, select *Erase File* and then tap **[ENTER]**.

You should now have 0 files in Group 0.

You are now ready to start looking at LocoFile. We shall use an example file to see how you can use LocoFile and then modify sample files to create the structure you need for your records.

1   Start by switching on your PCW9512 and inserting the LocoFile Start of Day disc or inserting the disc and resetting with **[SHIFT]**, **[EXTRA]** and **[EXIT]**. See *'Resetting Or Rebooting Your PCW9512'* if you are unsure what to do.

2   To check that LocoFile is installed on your disc, tap **[f1]** for Actions (see the illustration on the next page) and you should see three new options, *Run LocoFile, Create LocoFile data* and *Squash LocoFile data*.

Note: If these do not appear you need to repeat the installation procedure described above.

SECTION 9-3
Installing LocoFile

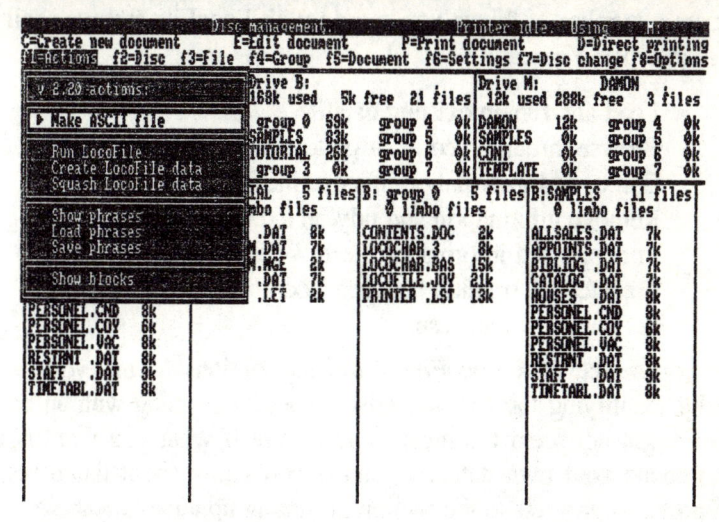

Fig. 1: LocoFile Actions menu.

3 Tap **[CAN]** to clear the Actions Menu when you have finished checking it.

■ SECTION 9-4
Running LocoFile

There are a number of things you can do with LocoFile and we shall look at these in order. You can:

- Load and run an existing datafile
  Browse through records or go to a particular record
  Edit or add information in a datafile
  Remove information and tidy up a datafile
  Print selected information from, a datafile
  Transfer information between LocoFile and LocoScript
  Set up a new database.

When you select *'Run LocoFile'* from the Actions Menu, you have to begin by identifying the file you wish to access. Starting with an existing datafile might not seem the most logical point if what you want is to be able to create your own database, and if you know about databases, you might prefer to progress to the section on setting up a new database.

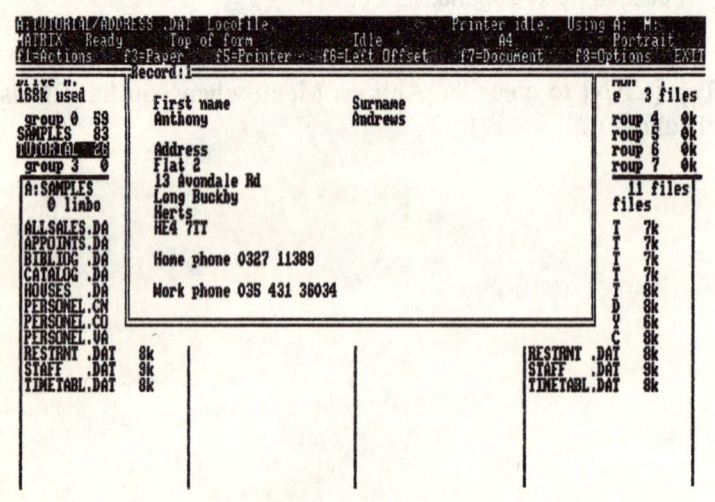

Fig. 2: A LocoFile Record Card.

SECTION 9-4
Running LocoFile

However, LocoFile comes with a number of sample files built in which you could quite easily modify to the structure you need, so there is a logic to starting with the existing before going on to the new.

1 At the Disc Manager Screen, move the cursor to Drive M: Group Tutorial using the Shift and Arrow keys, then check that ADDRESS.DAT is highlighted and tap **[f1]**, select **Run LocoFile** and tap **[ENTER]**, then **[ENTER]** again.

The first 'record card' appears and we shall use this to find out something about how LocoFile creates a record.

So far we have loaded and run LocoFile and have gained access to a file that was already saved. The record overlays the Disc Management Screen, but a new menu has appeared at the top of the screen. We can see the name of the group and the file, the state of the printer, the index currently in use, the item currently selected, the position of the cursor in the record and along the bottom line a series of menus accessed through the function keys.

2 Move the cursor around the record using the arrow keys to move a single space or line in each direction. When the cursor lands on an item it is outlined and the spaces allocated to it are shown by dots. The item name then appears in the top menu. To move from one item to the next, use the **[ENTER]** key and to move back to the previous item tap **[RELAY]**.

3 Move the cursor to the Address Item and add the letter **'a'** after Flat 2. Notice that the word Changed appears on the top right border of the record to show that a change has been made to the contents of an item.

SECTION 9-4
Running LocoFile

4 To move to the next record, tap **[Page]** and you see that the items of information (what's known as the *fields* in most databases) are the same, but the contents of each item (each field) is different.

5 Tap **[Page]** again and you will see the word 'Unique' appear in the second menu line. This tells you that the index item, in this case the surname, appears only once in the file.

6 Tap **[Page]** again and you will see that in Record 4 one item has no information recorded in it. So you do not need information for each item for every record; you can leave some items blank.

The [Page] key moves forward one record at a time. To move back one record you hold down the [ALT] key and tap [Page] once for each page. Clearly, if you have a large number of records you need to be able to move more quickly around the datafile. To move back to the First Record you hold down [ALT] and tap the [DOC] key (Shift + Page). To go to the last record, you just tap [DOC].

Notice as you move around the datafile that the records do not appear in number order. This is because, the record number, shown at the top left of each 'record card' refers to the order in which the information (data) was added. The current file is ordered (or '*indexed*') alphabetically by surname. That order would change if you change the index item, as we shall see shortly.

SECTION 9-5
Finding A Particular Record.

But what if you want to find a particular record, to edit it or check some detail? To 'Go To' a particular record, you use one of the options shown at the top of the screen. You tap [f5] to call up the 'Goto' menu.

1 Tap **[f5]** and the menu appears.

This menu provides an alternative means of moving through the records to using the Page and Doc keys. Provided you are not currently on the first or last record, you will have the options to go to the next record, the previous record, the first record of the current index or the last record of the current index.

The one option which you can use only through this menu is to go to a record that you identify, so how does this work?

2 With the Goto menu on screen, key in the word **'Smith'**. (Capitals or lower case letters will do.) Check that *'Record with this key'* is selected, i.e. it has a small triangle beside it, and tap **[ENTER]**.

The record for Nicola Smith appears.

Note: If a message appears saying *'No match found'* you may have mistyped the name. LocoFile will take you to the next nearest record to the name you typed, warn you and then the warning message disappears. You may need to use the Doc/Page key to get precisely where you want.

3 You can see that this is not a unique record, so tap **[Page]** and you will find another Smith. Tap **[Page]** once more and there is yet another, John Smith. Notice that they are listed in Record Number order, not alphabetically by first name.

SECTION 9-6
Changing The Index Key

There are a number of occasions when you might want to include more than one key for your index and LocoFile allows for this. You can make changes through the f2 Index Menu.

1 Tap **[f2]** (Shift + f1). The index menu appears giving a list of the record items, with a tick against *'Surname'*; the current index key. To change the index key, highlight the one you want, in this case *'Full Name'*, check that *'Use this index'* is selected and tap the **[+]** followed by **[ENTER]**.

2 Nothing appears to have happened, but now tap the **[Page]** key and Nicola Smith appears after John Smith. If you look at the top of the screen, you will see that Index has changed to *Full Name*.

3 To show that you now have two keys to the index, tap **[f5]** to display the Goto menu.

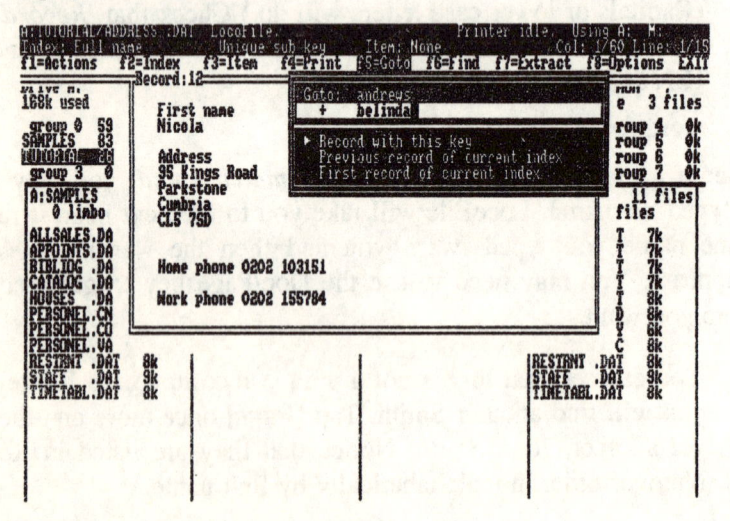

Fig. 3: The LocoFile 'Goto' flag menu.

SECTION 9-6
Changing The Index Key

The word 'Smith' which you keyed in before, is still there but you now have a second line for the first name. When you use Full Name for the index you have a Main Key, the *surname*, which Locofile sorts first, then a Sub Key, *first name*, which further sorts identical surnames.

4 Delete the word Smith using the **[DEL]** key and key in **'Andrews'**, tap the down arrow and key in **'Belinda'**. Check that 'Record with this key' is selected and tap **[ENTER]**.

5 To check the details of this full name index, tap **[f2]**, use the down arrow to highlight **'Inspect index'** and tap **[ENTER]**. The index specification appears.

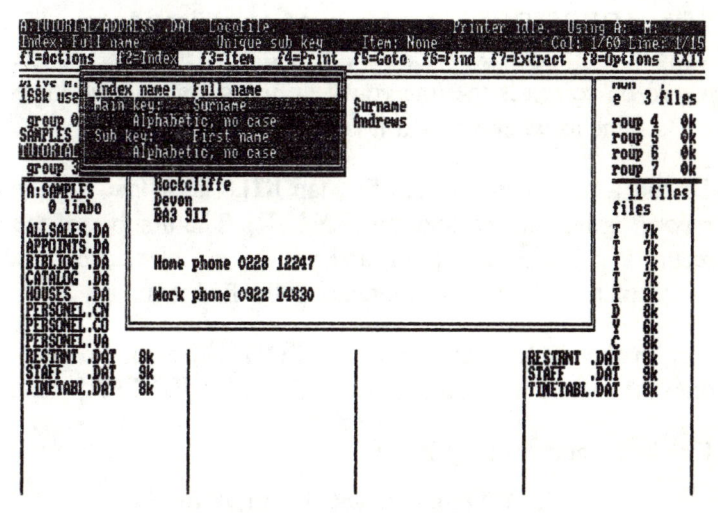

Fig. 4: The Full Name index.

6 Tap **[CAN]** then **[EXIT]** to return to the Disc Management Screen.

SECTION 9-7
Making Changes To A Datafile

We have already seen how you move through an existing datafile and how you can find specific records and make minor changes to individual records. We shall move on now to show how to add records to a datafile, how to erase records you no longer need and how to change information in individual records.

We shall assume that you are going to perform these operations from the Disc Manager Screen, although you can make these changes at any time while you are using LocoFile.

1 If you are starting up anew, switch on your PCW9512 and insert your LocoFile Start of Day disc. Move the cursor to ADDRESS.DAT on Drive M: as you did before.

2 With *ADDRESS.DAT* on Drive M: highlighted, tap **[f1]** for Actions, highlight *'Run LocoFile'* and tap **[ENTER]** twice. The record on screen is the one you were using last and the index key is the same as when you left it last.

3 To add a new record to the file, tap **[f1]**, check that *'Create new record'* is highlighted and tap **[ENTER]**. The number of the new record appears at the top left and you have a blank 'record card' to complete with the cursor already at the first item.

4 Key in the name **'Mary'** and tap **[ENTER]** to move the cursor onto the second item. Key in **'Smith'** and tap **[ENTER]** again.

5 Key in the address as follows:

> 23 Whiteley Street [RETURN]
> Blacktown [RETURN]
> Anyshire [RETURN]
> AN1 SH4 [ENTER]

SECTION 9-7
Making Changes To A Datafile

6 Add the home phone **'091-234-5678' [ENTER]** and the work phone **091-345-6789 ext 123**.

7 To check that the new record appears in the right place in your datafile, tap the **[Page]** key and you should find Nicola Smith.

Now that we have a record for Mary Smith, we shall use it to illustrate how to make changes to a record.

1 Hold down the **[ALT]** key and tap **[Page]**, to return to Mary Smith's record.

We'll assume that she has married and changed her name and address. In order to demonstrate another feature of working with Locofile, we'll assume that she has married Anthony Andrews and changed her address to his.

2 Move the cursor onto the Surname item and use the **[DEL]** key to delete **'Smith'**, then key in **'Andrews'**.

(You can also use the [CUT] key to delete text from a record.)

3 Tap **[ENTER]** to select the address item, then tap **[CUT]**. Use the arrow keys to highlight the whole address, then tap **[CUT]** again.

4 Tap **[f5]** to call up the Goto menu. Delete any name which appears here using **[DEL]** and key in **'Andrews'** on the first line, tap the **[Down Arrow]** and key in **'Anthony'** on the second line. Check that *'Record with this key'* is selected and tap **[ENTER]**.

SECTION 9-7
Making Changes To A Datafile

5 Check that the address item is selected, then tap **[COPY]**, highlight the address and tap **[COPY]** again. Tap **[0]** to identify the block.

6 Tap **[Page]** twice to get back to Mary Andrews and with the address item selected, tap **[PASTE] [0]**. The new address appears in the item slot. Notice, the word *'changed'* has appeared in the top right corner of the record card.

7 Try using the same procedure to change the Home phone number.

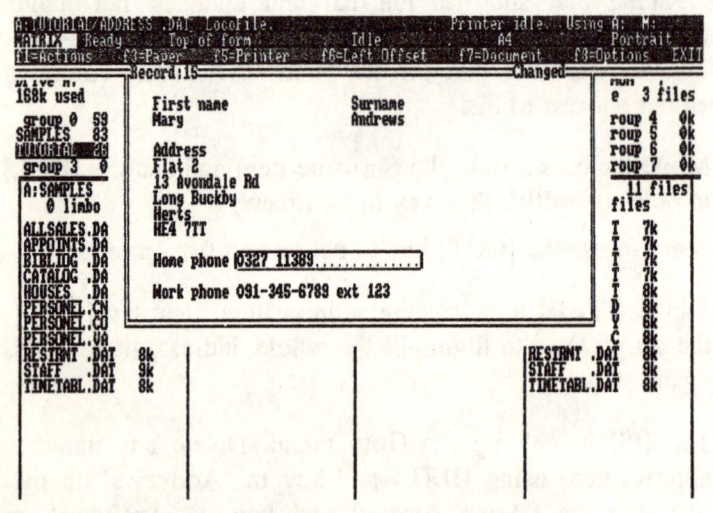

Fig. 5: A *Changed* record card.

Using Cut, Copy and Paste might seem somewhat complicated at first, but it will save writing details down then keying them in again and avoid the silly mistakes that can often creep in when you're trying to copy information.

SECTION 9-7
Making Changes To A Datafile

Just remember that the same principles you use when dealing with blocks of information in LocoScript apply here and you can't go far wrong.

Note: When you move on from a record that you have changed, using the DOC/PAGE key, a message appears on screen offering you the option to move on from the old value or the new value. Once you have made changes to a record, any effect that a change in an index item might have on the position of a record is implemented, hence this option.

Note: If you do make a mess of a record, you have one other option, which only appears when you have made a change to a record, 'Undo alterations' on the F1 Actions menu. This can only be applied to the record while you are displaying it. Once you move on to a new record the changes are fixed.

■ SECTION 9-8
Getting Rid Of Unwanted Records

Once a record becomes out of date, it will save space and time if you clear it from your datafile. To do this you need to have the record on screen.

1 We shall erase the record we added, which should still be on screen, Mary Andrews. Tap **[f1]**, move the cursor down to *'Erase this record'* and tap **[ENTER]**. The record is removed from the datafile and the next record is displayed on screen. If the record you erased was the last in the datafile, the new last record will appear on the screen.

Note: Once you have erased a record, you can call it back using 'Recover from limbo' in the F1 Actions menu, provided you have not changed or erased another record in the meantime.

Once you have erased a record, the space it occupied still forms part of the datafile. This is not a problem when just a few records are involved, but if you clear out large numbers of records then you need to get rid of the wasted space using the Squash LocoFile data option from the Disc Management F1 Actions menu.

1 Tap **[EXIT]** to return to the Disc Management screen. Move the cursor onto ADDRESS.DAT if it is not still there. Tap **[f1]**, move the cursor to Squash LocoFile data and tap **[ENTER]** twice. A message appears on screen showing LocoFile processing the records.

The new squashed file is normally created as a separate file with the old version kept as a limbo file as a back up, provided there is enough space available. If there isn't enough room, a warning 'Disc Full' message appears. If you don't have a backup copy of your datafile i.e. you have not saved a copy to disc, cancel the operation.

SECTION 9-8
Getting Rid Of Unwanted Records

2 If you do have a back up, select *'Run Disc Manager'*, create some space and tap **[EXIT]** and the squashing continues. The squashed file will now appear in the list of files.

Note: In some circumstances it is possible to recover a corrupted datafile using the *Squash* option. Details of this are given in Appendix III of the LocoFile User Guide.

■ SECTION 9-9
Using LocoFile

So far we have looked at how to make modifications to an existing datafile, how to add, edit and erase records. We shall move on now to look at how to adapt the sample datafiles which LocoFile offers you and how you use these to set up your own datafile.

1 Switch on and insert your LocoFile Start of Day disc. Once the Disc Management screen appears, if your sample files are on a separate disc, remove the start of day disc, insert your Samples disc and tap [f7] to Change the disc.

We'll use the same datafile we have used before, ADDRESS.DAT. As working on Drive M: is much quicker, if you don't already have a copy of this file on Drive M:, use the F3 Copy File option.

2 Move the cursor onto **ADDRESS.DAT** in Drive M: and tap [f1] for Actions. Select **'Run LocoFile'** and tap [ENTER] twice. The last record you used appears, but to proceed it doesn't matter which record you have on screen.

Before you set up your own datafile, you need to think about what information you are going to include, how you want to set that information out and what size of 'card' you want. It may be that if the style and content of card you want is substantially different from any of the samples, it will be easier to start from scratch as we shall see later, but for the moment let's assume that this file forms a useful basis for your own address datafile.

3 The facility you want is Datafile set-up in the Actions menu, so tap [f1], select **'Datafile set-up'** and tap [ENTER]. The display on screen changes to a 'blank' version of the record card. Each item title is shown, but lines of dots represent the spaces allocated for the information.

SECTION 9-9
Using LocoFile

This blank card acts as a template for all the records in the datafile, so it should include all the items you need, even if you don't have information on all items for every person. You can change the range of items from the current set-up or change the space allocated for items and you can change the card size, as we shall see now.

1 You will notice at the top of your screen that you are within Datafile set-up still and this has its own series of menus. Tap **[f5]** for the 'Card Menu'.

To change the card settings, you highlight the option you want and key in the new value, check that 'Use this format' is selected and tap [ENTER]. To change the character and line pitch you use the arrow keys to highlight the size you want and tap the [+] key to select it, followed by [ENTER] to confirm the setting.

Section 6.1 *'Changing the size of the card'* and Appendix II in your LocoFile User Guide give details of maximum card sizes related to paper types, but as a general rule of thumb, the overall maximum width you can use is 80 characters and maximum length 99 lines. If you try to make a change which creates a card size too small for the current items or too large for the paper type, an Alert message appears and you then have to make appropriate alterations.

2 Tap **[CAN]** to clear the Card Menu and we'll start to make some changes to the items on the card.

You can change the details of the existing items, their size, position, name etc., you can set up new items or remove items altogether. If you do remove an item, however, you lose all the data related to that item in the file you are using. You cannot recover this information, except if you have a back-up copy of your datafile.

■ SECTION 9-9
Using LocoFile

3 You should still be within Document set-up and have a blank card on screen. To change an item, you have to move the cursor to it using the [ENTER] or [RELAY] key, so outline the First name item, then tap **[f3]** to call up the Item Menu.

4 From here you can make a series of alterations, as you can see. For now, check that **'Change item'** is selected and tap **[ENTER]**.

5 We're going to change this item to Company name and increase the item width to 53 characters, the same as the Address item. So, with 'First name' highlighted, key in **Company name** and tap **[DEL>]** four times.

You'll notice half way down the menu box 'Place at ? o'clock'. That refers to the position of the name relative to the item. Think of the card divided into the twelve clock positions starting at the middle top and moving around, so that 11, 12 and 1 are along the top, 2, 3, and 4 down the right side and so on. We'll leave this item where it is, but we shall have to move the second item in a moment.

6 To alter the Item width, move the highlighting down to **'Item width'** and key in **[53]**. Tap **[ENTER]** to confirm the new settings.

An alert message appears warning you that items now overlap. You have the option to 'Try again' and correct the overlap or 'Continue' and sort the problem out later. You will not be able to leave Document set-up until you have corrected any overlap, however.

216

SECTION 9-9
Using LocoFile

7 Move the cursor down to **'Continue'** and tap **[ENTER]**. Now tap **[ENTER]** to select 'Surname'. Next, hold down **[ALT]+[SHIFT]** and use the cursor arrow keys to move the 'Surname' item down two lines and across to the left just below 'Company name'. Tap **[f3]** and change the item name to **'Contact'**. Tap **[ENTER]** twice to confirm the change.

8 We no longer need 'Home phone' so, select 'Home phone' and tap **[f3]**, select **'Remove item'** and tap **[ENTER]** twice. A warning message appears telling you that all home phone records will be destroyed, but since this is no problem for us, select **'Remove item'** and tap **[ENTER]** and Home phone disappears from the card.

9 Tidy up the card by moving the Address item down two lines as follows. Tap **[RELAY]** to highlight the Address item, hold down **[ALT] + [SHIFT]** and tap the down arrow twice.

10 Tap **[ENTER]** to position the cursor on **'Work phone'**, tap **[f3] [ENTER]** and change the name to **'Phone'** by deleting the word 'Work' and the space. Tap **[ENTER]** to confirm the change and move the item left to line up with the other items.

11 To add a new item, move the cursor, using the right arrow key, five spaces to the right of the 'Phone' item and tap the **[+]** key. The cursor becomes a box. Use the right arrow key to extend the box until it is level with the right hand edge of the Address item.

Note: In effect you are pulling out the box from the top left corner and could stretch it down as well as across if you had more room and needed it.

SECTION 9-9
Using LocoFile

12 We'll use this item to identify the type of company, so tap **[ENTER]** to show that you are ready to add the details of the new item, and a menu appears. The item width, height and position are shown, all you need to do is key in the name, so key in **'Type'**, change the position to **9 o'clock** and tap **[ENTER]**.

An alternative way of setting up new items is discussed in your LocoFile User Guide, Section 6.2.2.

13 Tap **[EXIT]** now to leave *'Datafile set-up'* and return to the record you were on previously. (Notice that where you have changed item names, First name, Surname, the information has transferred to the new item. Where you have removed an item, Home phone, the data has disappeared, and where you have created a new item, *'Type'*, the entry is blank because there was no data for this in the original file.)

Two problems remain from the changes before you can set up and use this datafile for your own records. Firstly you still have records which you do not want in your own version. This you can remedy by leaving Document set-up, Erasing records and, if necessary, Squashing data, as described earlier in this section. Do this now if you wish, then we'll copy this new datafile under a new name onto your Samples disc as follows.

1 Tap **[EXIT]** to leave LocoFile and return to the Disc Management screen. With ADDRESS.DAT in Drive M: still highlighted, tap **[f3] [ENTER]** to select 'Copy File'. Your Samples disc should still be in drive A:, so move the menu cursor to Drive A: Group 0 and tap **[ENTER]**, key in **'MYADDRES.DAT'** for the New Name and tap **[ENTER]**.

218

SECTION 9-9
Using LocoFile

Note: When you were working on ADDRESS.DAT in Drive M:, the changes you made were incorporated in that file. Once you leave LocoFile by switching off or rebooting, the ADDRESS.DAT on Drive M: will be a copy of ADDRESS.DAT on your LocoFile Start of Day disc. The copy of your new file will only be on your Samples disc.

The other problem is that you have now removed or altered some of the Index items. So we'll move on now to look at making changes to the Index.

SECTION 9-10
Changing The Index

1 Switch on your PCW9512 and insert your LocoFile Start of Day disc in Drive A:. When the Disc Management screen has loaded, if your sample files are on a separate disc, either remove the Start of Day disc and insert your Samples disc into Drive A: or if you have a twin drive machine, put your Samples disc in Drive B: and tap **[f7]** for change of disc.

2 Move the cursor to **'MYADDRES.DAT'** and tap **[f3] [ENTER]** and copy the file to Drive M:. (The reason for making the copy is that your PCW9512 can work more quickly in Drive M: and if you do make a mess of things you can always abandon what you're doing without having damaged your original file. LocoScript will warn you to save your work to floppy disc before you switch off or reboot.)

3 With MYADDRES.DAT still highlighted, tap **[f1]** move the cursor down to **'Run LocoFile'** and tap **[ENTER]** twice. The last record card you were using appears on screen, although if you erased records it may be blank and if you squashed the datafile it will be the only record.

4 Tap **[f1]** for the LocoFile Actions menu and select **'Datafile set-up'**, tap **[ENTER]**. The new blank card you set up earlier appears.

5 You can set up new indexes from here, inspect indexes and remove existing indexes. First, use the **[ENTER]** or **[RELAY]** key to select the item you want as the main key to your index (in this case select 'Type') and then tap **[f2]** (SHIFT + F1) for the Index menu.

■ SECTION 9-10
Changing The Index

6 Check **'Create new index'** is highlighted and tap **[ENTER]**. The Main key menu appears with the new item names you created and the word 'Type' should have a tick against it and should be highlighted, so tap **[ENTER]**.

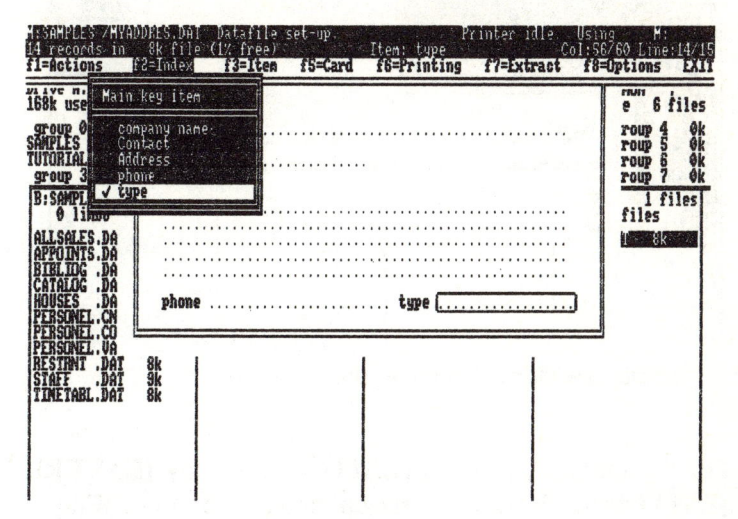

Fig. 6: *'Create new index'* flag menu (1).

7 This calls up the Main key type menu. We shall leave the sort as alphabetic, but notice the other options available to you. We are using the standard keyboard and we can ignore the case, so tap **[ENTER]** again.

The next menu that appears tells you what you have selected so far. It also offers you a number of alternative ways to proceed from here. You can Add a sub-key, Change the main key, set Alternative main keys and sub-keys, so LocoFile gives you a great deal of flexibility in your indexing.

SECTION 9-10
Changing The Index

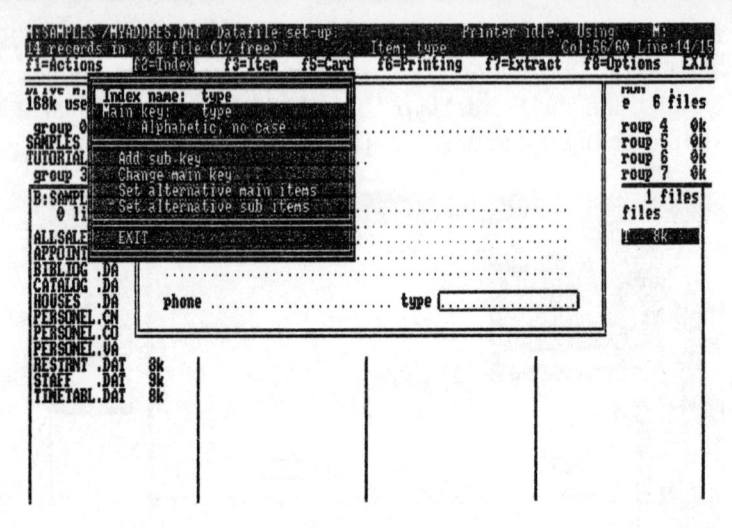

Fig. 7: *'Create new index'* flag menu (2).

8 For the moment, just tap **[EXIT]** followed by **[ENTER]**. Tap **[EXIT]** to finish 'Datafile set-up' and return to LocoFile.

9 You still have to set the current index to your new item, so tap **[f2]** (SHIFT + F1) and the Set current index menu appears. Move the highlighting down to **'Type'** and tap the **[+]** key to select it. Check that **'Use this index'** is selected and tap **[ENTER]**. Now when you enter some data in the type item, LocoFile will sort your records alphabetically by type.

You will notice in the *Set current index* menu, the list of items, apart from 'Type' is the original one from ADDRESS.DAT. This is because to create a new index you have to erase the old one first.

SECTION 9-10
Changing The Index

Note: Any new item in your datafile that you identify as a key item, as we did with 'type', will be added to the list and you must be careful that this does not bring the list up to more than eight which is the maximum.

You have to erase any items you no longer want, i.e. that you have altered or deleted from the record card and it is probably better to do this before you start identifying new key items.

1 Tap **[f1]**, select **'Datafile set-up'** and tap **[ENTER]**. Now tap **[f2]** (SHIFT + F1) for the Index menu, select **'Remove index'** and tap **[ENTER]**. The current list of index items will appear.

2 Move the cursor onto First name and tap **[ENTER]**. A warning message appears which you can ignore for now, move the cursor down onto **'Remove index'** and tap **[ENTER]**. Delete Surname and Full name in the same way.

3 Now, if you wish, you can add other items to your index list by moving your cursor to the item you wish to add, say, Company name, then tap **[f2] [ENTER]**. A tick appears against the selected item which is also highlighted. Tap **[ENTER]** twice to confirm your selection, followed by **[EXIT] [ENTER]** to return to Datafile set-up. Repeat for any other items you may wish to include in your index.

Note: You can check which items you have selected by leaving Datafile set-up (tap [EXIT]) and calling up the index menu ([f2]). You are now ready to identify Main keys and Sub-keys as described earlier and in your LocoFile User Guide.

Indexes are invaluable in giving flexibility to data access. There are occasions, however, when you might need to abstract selected information from records, to print out address labels or personalise correspondence. Using LocoFile, you can extract one or more whole items from a record card or copy part of the information contained in an individual item.

SECTION 9-11
Extracting Items

1   To set up Extract details for whole items, with MYADDRES.DAT open, tap **[f5]** (for Goto) and select **'First record in the current index'**, then tap **[ENTER]**. The extract details will only apply to a record which is shown on screen, although you can then use the same details subsequently for another record by calling that up on screen.

Note: LocoFile takes the items in their standard order, left to right and top to bottom, and sets them out according to their position on the record card with carriage returns where records are on different lines and tabs/spaces where they are side by side. For this reason it is important to think about how you set out the data on the record card *before* you start to set it up as we shall see shortly.

2   With the correct record on screen, tap **[f7]** for the Extract menu. The items that LocoFile expects you to want to extract will have a tick beside them. The number of the Block to which you want the information saved is shown at the top and you can alter this by highlighting it and keying in a new number between zero and nine. (To delete an item you highlight it and tap [-], to add a new one, highlight it and tap [+].) For now, check that Extract items is selected and just tap **[ENTER]**.

Note: You also have the option from the Extract menu to Select all or Select none of the items i.e. set or clear all items at one go.

You now have a block of items which you can paste into a document wherever and as many times as you wish. You can examine these blocks using the F1 Show blocks option, if too many build up and you need to check before deleting any. You can do this either from LocoFile or while editing a document or from the Disc Management screen.

■ SECTION 9-11
Extracting Items

To copy or remove part of an item, you move the cursor to the start of the section and tap [COPY], then move the cursor to the end of the text you want and tap [COPY] or [CUT]. You can now paste this in the usual way.

As we said just now, you can use this information in a number of ways and we shall come back to these. Since you are very likely to be anxious to get on and set up your own datafile, we shall deal with that next.

3 For the time being, tap **[EXIT]** to leave LocoFile. If you are finishing remove the disc and switch off your machine. If you are continuing, read on.

SECTION 9-12
Setting Up Your Own Datafile

The first task in setting up a datafile, and one which you must spend plenty of time thinking about, is creating the design. You need to decide what items you are likely to need to include. Then you need to determine a logical order and positioning, according to available space and how you are going to use the information and you need to allocate the maximum amount of space that item will need.

Once you have designed the card, you create a new datafile and set up a 'Pattern' card before inserting your data. You can either key data in direct or load it in from a LocoMail or ASCII datafile. If you are loading data from either of these you will need to use the same item names as they do. This must be a very important consideration in setting up your datafile.

1 With these points in mind, draw up a list of the items you want to include. Things like names, addresses, positions/contacts, categories or types, comments. Then try to estimate how many spaces the largest entry is likely to need and which items you might want to extract together. (Your LocoFile User Guide gives some ideas for how to go about this in Chapter 7, section 7.1.1, 7.1.3 and 7.1.4.)

Before you proceed to set up the Pattern card, check how you want to use the information you are going to put into the file and from this decide which items you want to index. Finally calculate the size of card you want and check that this is compatible with LocoFile's maximum size of 80 characters wide and 99 lines long and with the paper size set up for your printer.

A useful point to remember is that a maximum of 27 lines shows on screen at any one time, so for the sake of ease of reading try to stick within this limit or mark the card to show where the end of screen line comes.

SECTION 9-12
Setting Up Your Own Datafile

Draw out your plan onto a piece of lined or squared paper, or card, and you are then ready to set up your own datafile.

1 If you are not already in LocoScript, switch on and insert your LocoFile Start of Day disc.

Note: If you do not want to add your datafile to this disc you will need to create a separate Start of Day disc as we described earlier, then you replace the existing disc with the new one and tap [f7] for Change of disc.

2 At the Disc management screen, move the cursor to the group where you want to place your new datafile and tap **[f1]** for the Actions menu. Select **'Create LocoFile data'** and tap **[ENTER]**.

3 You now have a Selection menu where you can key in the name you want to give your datafile. Choose a name of not more than eight characters which will give an indication what is in the file and add the letters DAT after the full stop. Once you have keyed in the new name, tap **[ENTER]** to confirm the details and a blank card appears.

Note: If you add DAT to the name, the file will load automatically into Drive M: when you start up and working with the file will be much quicker. It does not matter which group you choose to put your datafiles in, but for the sake of tidiness it may make sense to keep them together.

■ SECTION 9-13
Setting Up A Pattern Card

1 With your card plan in front of you, start to insert the items. Use the arrow keys to move the cursor to the top left corner of the item you want to insert and tap **[+]**. The cursor changes to a box. Use the arrow keys to stretch this box to the size you want across and down. (The column and line numbers are shown at the top right of your screen which may help you.)

2 When the box is the right size, tap **[ENTER]**. Fill in the details on the name box, including whether you want the name to show or not and where it should appear. The item width and height will reflect the size of box you have just created but you can change it from here if your wish. Tap **[ENTER]** to confirm the details.

3 Repeat the above sequence to add the other items taking care not to overlap them.

Note: If you wish the name to appear to the left or right (e.g. at 9/10 or 2/3 o'clock) of the item, you will have to leave space for it when you place the item box, or a message on screen will warn of overlapping items.

Note: Remember you can always move an item by holding down [ALT] + [SHIFT] and using the arrow keys if you have a problem. LocoFile will not let you leave Datafile set-up until all items are laid out without overlap.

You can now proceed to identify index and extract items as we have seen before. There is also a minor refinement you can make through the F8 Options menu i.e. whether the zero has a slash through it or not.

■ SECTION 9-13
Setting Up A Pattern Card

4 Once you have set everything up as you want it, tap **[EXIT]** and a blank record card appears, ready for you to start adding data.

5 Select each item in turn using the [ENTER] or [RELAY] key and insert your data. When all information is entered, tap the **[PAGE]** key to move on to the next record. When you have entered all the records, tap **[EXIT]** to leave LocoFile and return to the Disc Management screen.

Note: You can go back into Datafile set-up at any time to alter the settings of your Pattern card if it is not working as you want, but remember that if you delete an item or reduce its size you will lose some of the data you have keyed in.

If you have been working on Drive M: by any chance, do not switch off or reboot before copying the file onto your floppy disc.

■ SECTION 9-14
Exchanging Datafiles With LocoMail

LocoFile is one of a suite of programs which work under the LocoScript Disc Management screen. LocoMail is another and it is easy to understand why one of the most useful jobs you can do with LocoFile data is to transfer into documents prepared using LocoScript.

The flexibility which indexing and extracting information gives you makes it a simple task to organise the data you want to select and insert. You can also transfer data from LocoMail files; as you can ASCII files.

You can convert your LocoMail datafiles to LocoFile datafiles to make searching, updating and restructuring easier. You can use data from a series of LocoFile datafiles to insert information into documents to a sophisticated level.

Before you insert data from LocoMail into Locofile you need to have a datafile set up with exactly the same names as the items you want to transfer from the LocoMail file. If you want to add information to an existing datafile you may have to change the item names, even if you change them back after you have transferred the data.

1 Switch on your PCW9512 and insert your LocoFile Start of Day disc. (If there is not already a copy of ADDRESS.DAT on Drive M:, use [f3] Copy file to make a copy.) With this copy of ADDRESS.DAT highlighted, from the Disc Management screen, tap **[f1]**, select **'Run LocoFile'** and tap **[ENTER]**.

2 Tap **[f1]** again for the Actions menu, select **'Insert data'** and tap **[ENTER]**. A message appears telling you to select the merge document.

SECTION 9-14
Exchanging Datafiles With LocoMail

3   Use the cursor arrows to move to **DATAFILE.MGE** in the Tutorial Group on Drive A:. Tap **[ENTER]** twice and the files merge. (This is a LocoMail file which has the same set of items as ADDRESS.DAT. If you choose a file which does not match, you have to choose another or change the item names in the LocoFile datafile. If only some of the items match you can cancel the merge or ignore those which do not match.)

The point of working with a copy of your LocoFile datafile is that if anything goes wrong, for instance if there is some error in the datafile you are merging, you still have the original to work with. (Your LocoFile User Guide gives additional details of how to cope with any problems that might arise, in section 8.1.)

4   Tap **[EXIT]** to leave LocoFile and return to the Disc Management screen.

As when merging LocoMail files into LocoFile files, when exchanging the other way round, item names have to match. To see how to merge a simple document and datafile, we shall use two samples from the Tutorial group.

1   Use the arrow keys to move the cursor to **MAILSHOT.MGE** in the Tutorial group on Drive A: and tap **[f3] [ENTER]** and copy the file to the Tutorial group on Drive M:.

2   With MAILSHOT.MGE still highlighted tap **[M]** for Merge, move the cursor to **ADDRESSM.DAT** and tap **[ENTER]**. Tap **[ENTER]** once more to confirm your selections and follow the on screen instructions to key in the index items and the merge will proceed.

231

■ SECTION 9-14
Exchanging Datafiles With LocoMail

For more information about merging datafiles and documents you should consult the LocoMail User Guide, or 'Script' - the newsletter published by Locomotive Software which updates information about the software.

We have looked at how to use and change a datafile, how to set up and change indexes, which gives flexible access to records, how to extract items and how to set up your own datafile, in addition to merging data between datafiles and documents.

This section should have given you an idea of what LocoFile can do and how to get started to use it for your own data. The LocoFile User Guide gives a great deal more detail on all aspects but the order is not in our view so logical for the average user. Once you have completed this section and experimented with setting up your own datafiles, you can refer to the User Guide for more detailed information.

SECTION 9-15
An Introduction to dBase II

We've seen that LocoFile works like an electronic card index program. There are times when you will want to do a lot more with your information. For example, LocoFile does not deal with numerical functions. So if you need to abstract statistical information from your database, or if you want to produce more complex print-outs which include financial analyses (e.g. sales reports), then a program like *'Dbase II'*, may be more useful to you.

So how does dBase II differ from LocoFile? Put very simply, dBase fulfils the same basic functions as any other database program in that it enables us to:

- organise information
  store that information
  retrieve any bits of information we want quickly

and, it also enables us to

- sort the information
  analyse the information
  present the same information in different forms

but dBase gives you much more control over how these tasks are performed. There is a drawback though. As with any computer program, the more powerful or versatile it is, the more there is for you to learn and remember (e.g. dBase has more than 80 different commands which you can use to manipulate your data). dBase also has very powerful routines for storing, searching, sorting, retrieving and printing out all, or selected parts of the information. But what makes dBase really quite different from LocoFile and from most other database programs is that it has what amounts to its own programming language built in. In short, dBase may have far too many features for your current needs. On the other hand, you don't have to use them all, and you may prefer to have them in reserve for the future. So let's have a quick look at dBase.

■ SECTION 9-16
Using dBase II On The PCW

Here we have to assume that you have installed dBase correctly for your machine.

1 Switch on your machine and put your dBase starter disc in drive A:. Hold down **[SHIFT]** and **[EXTRA]** then tap the **[EXIT]** key to reset the system and load dBase.

dBase will start running after the PCW has carried out some housekeeping and copied the dBase files to the memory drive (drive M:). The first thing that happens is that it displays a message telling you to press a key to get a display of the command files in your default drive (we shall see what command files are shortly).

This screen is actually a bit misleading, because you actually have two options here. If you tap the [EXIT] key you will go straight into dBase without displaying the command files, but if you tap any of the other normal keyboard keys (say, the [SPACEBAR]) you will get the promised listing.

2 Tap the **[SPACEBAR]**.

Once dBase has listed the files - all called *'something*.CMD', an on-screen message tells you *"you may choose to 'DO' any of the above command files"*. (Hmm.) What it means is, that a command file is a sort of program, written in the dBase programming language I mentioned earlier. If you want to run one of the programmes, you key in the word DO followed by a space and then the name of the command file in question. Like this:

3 Key in **DO WELCOME** (in upper or lower case) and tap **[RETURN]**.

The 'Welcome' program is quite a useful way to get to know how dBase works, and I recommend you work through it. We have structured the rest of this section as a sort of quick overview of the topics covered by Welcome (not quite in the same order). Our aim is to get you to the point where you can work happily with Welcome and with the dBasc manual.

SECTION 9-17
Working With The dBase Welcome Program

After a very polite opening screen, *Welcome* displays a menu of eleven options. The program is really a series of computer based learning sessions which look quite good. By that I mean that they don't seem to be as patronising as usual (though it still has a habit of congratulating you for pressing the right key from a choice of one).

The eleven options appear in four groupings, the first three of which, correspond with three major functions of databases:

- File Handling
- Data Handling
- File Interrogation

The fourth grouping enables you to exit from the welcome program itself, in either of two ways.

File Handling has sessions on:

- how to create a (database) file
- how to open and close files
- how to delete a file

Data Handling has sessions on:

- How to add data (information) to a file
- How to edit data in a file
- How to delete data from a file

File Interrogation shows you:

- how to list or display records in a file
- how to locate information in a file
- how to get *'reports'* (usually printouts) of selected parts of the data in a file

■ SECTION 9-17
Working With The dBase Welcome Program

Finally you can exit from the welcome program:

- either by leaving dBase altogether (back to the CP/M prompt)
- by going back to dBase proper and starting work for real

Each option has a reference letter and you choose the one you want by tapping in the relevant letter key.

1 Choose the last option in the list, by tapping the letter **[X]**.

The screen changes to display a closing down message from *welcome*. Just below the message there is a dot (full stop), with the cursor beside it. This is dBase's *'dot prompt'* - it has the same function as CP/M's A prompt. In other words, the prompt tells you that the computer is ready to receive the next instruction from you.

2 Let's stay with the welcome program. Key in **DO WELCOME** and tap **[RETURN]**. Tap the **[RETURN]** key a couple of times to get back to Welcome's menu.

3 Then tap the letter **[A]** and we can have a look at how to create a new database file.

Note: Before we go any further, a quick reminder of a couple of key concepts. (Now who's being patronising!?)

Remember, your database will be stored in a **file** of its own. each database file will hold a series of **records** and each record will be comprised of the same **fields** (types of information), in the same sequence.

When you want to start a completely new database with dBase you have to begin by creating a database file to hold the information. You use dBase's CREATE command to do it.

SECTION 9-18
Creating A Brand New Database

As with any database program, when you start to create a new database the first thing you should do is to sit down and think about how you are going to use the information it will hold. After all, even though we define a database as a *store* of information, nobody wants simply to hoard facts. Information has a value only if you can use it for some definite purpose. So, if you begin by worrying about how you are going to get the information *out* of the file, then you are more likely to come up with the best way to put the information into the file in the first place.

Take the example of a simple personal telephone directory. With this we shall usually want to find a telephone number by looking up the surname, then the first name - to discriminate between Roger Powell and Roy Powell, for example - then we want the number. So we need a very simple structure.

Starting at dBase's dot prompt:

1 Key in the command word **CREATE** followed by the name you want to call the database and then tap **[RETURN]**. e.g.

>create phone [RETURN]

dBase will automatically add a full stop and then the letters *'DBF'* to the filename you give it. So our telephone directory will be in a database file called *'PHONE.DBF'*.

dBase responds by displaying a screen which starts with a field number, then it wants you to define a **name** for the field, the **type** of data it will hold, the maximum **width** (or length) of the field and, for numerical fields, how many **decimal places** it should have.

Let's look at how you might respond to this screen.

Firstly, I would get into the habit of tapping the **[SHIFT LOCK]** key, to ensure you always refer to the correct field name when you are searching the files (see the sections on *'Interrogating'* the files).

SECTION 9-18
Creating A Brand New Database

2 Key in **SURNAME** (of the person) then a comma and immediately key in the letter **[C]** for the type - again followed by a comma.

Note: You can set the fields to be either:

- C type, which means it will hold alphanumeric characters
- N type, holding numerical information - in cases where you want to carry out mathematical operations with the data (e.g. working out totals on an invoice)
- L type which can contain only *'logic'* data entries - i.e. it can only hold T for true, F for false, Y for yes, or N for no

We shall set all our fields to be C type; even the field for the telephone number, because we will not want to do sums with the telephone numbers.

3 Next, key in the number **[20]** for the width of the field (don't forget you have [SHIFT LOCK] on) and tap **[RETURN]** to finish your definition of the first field.

You don't have to add an entry for decimal places because you specified that the field should be C type. dBase files away your definition, then it displays a number for the next field, ready for you to define what it should be. We actually need two more fields. Define them as follows:

002 **FORENAME,C,10 [RETURN]**
003 **NUMBER,C,20 [RETURN]**

4 dBase now displays the number of the next field (the fourth one), but we need only three, so tap **[RETURN]** and dBase offers you the chance to start entering data into your new database. We *shall* do this next, but I want to take you through the more usual procedure, so, for the moment, tap the letter **[N]**.

SECTION 9-19
Adding Records To Your New Database File

When you decide to add new data to one of your database files, you would:

1   Start up dBase by putting the starter disc in drive A:, holding down the **[EXTRA]** key and one of the **[SHIFT]** keys and then tapping the **[EXIT]** key. dBase should load into memory and run automatically.

2   When you get to the dot prompt you are ready to start.

Now, you know what you want to do, but dBase doesn't, so you have to tell it. Before you can add records to a file, dBase needs to know which file you want to work with, so:

3   Key in **USE** followed by the name of the database file you want to add to. e.g.

USE PHONE[RETURN]

After a few moments, the dot prompt returns. Now you are ready to add information to the file, so:

4   Key in **APPEND[RETURN]**

dBase displays the number of the record you are about to complete (in this example, '00001') and each of the fields in this (and every other record in the file). The cursor is in the first field waiting for you to make your entry. So you simply fill in the details you have, tapping [RETURN] at the end of each field. If you have no data for a particular field, just tap [RETURN] to skip to the next one.

By the way, this won't work for the first field in the record, because if you just tap [RETURN] there, dBase assumes that you have finished entering data and it goes back to the dot prompt. (So that's how you finish a data input session!)

■ SECTION 9-19
Adding Records To Your New Database File

When you tap return in the last field of the record, dBase brings up the next record number and a set of empty fields and you repeat the process until you have appended all your new data.

Now's the time to tap [RETURN] in the empty first field to stop adding data.

dBase may not have saved all the data you have keyed in (because it writes the records to disc in batches, to save time), so, just in case, close down the file (in our example, 'PHONE') and immediately open it again.

5 Key in **USE PHONE[RETURN]**

The USE command word tells dBase to close the file it is working on, saving data in the process, and then open up the file specified in the second half of the command line. (It's too daft to spot that they are the same.)

6 Have a go at putting about ten records into the file, so you can try out the next few activities. Key in **APPEND[RETURN]**, add your details and when you have finished, *'secure your data'* by keying in **USE PHONE[RETURN]**.

■ SECTION 9-20
Examining The Records In A File - BROWSE

(Assuming that dBase is loaded and running, don't forget to key in, *'USE PHONE'* before trying out these commands.)

Once you have a file with some data in it, dBase enables you to examine the data in various ways. Perhaps the most simple way is to use the BROWSE command. It's very straightforward, but also very powerful.

1 Key in **BROWSE** and tap [RETURN]. You don't need to tell dBASE which file you want to browse through, because you have already told it to 'USE' the file called 'PHONE'.

If you have more than 19 records in your phone file, dBase will display the first 19 on the screen, but you can scroll through the whole file. Notice it displays each complete record on a separate line. This is fine when each record is quite short (less than the width of the screen), but in files where each record is longer than the width of the screen, it will display only the left hand end of each record. The rest of the record will be off the screen to the right. dBase has special commands for panning and scrolling the screen display, so, even with very long records you will be able to read the whole file if you want to.

Your keyboard is 'live' while you are browsing, which is fine if you want to make small adjustments to any of the records, but it does also mean that you can't key in a normal command word to pan or scroll. Instead you use control codes (or ALT codes on the PCW) - see page 3-50 in your dBase manual. (You'll notice that dBase uses virtually the same control codes as WordStar.) You also have to use a control (ALT) code to exit from browse. Try this.

2 Hold down the **[ALT]** key and tap the letter **[Q]**.

241

SECTION 9-20
Examining The Records In A File - BROWSE

dBase immediately returns you to the dot prompt and an otherwise empty screen. When dBase displays the dot prompt it means it wants you to key in a command word, but you don't have to key in the whole word - just the first four letters will do, so try this:

3   Key in **BROW** - (that's the command), and if you key nothing else in, dBase will repeat the display you got a few moments ago.

But you can be a bit more selective about what you want to browse through. Let's imagine for the moment that your file actually contains very long records, with the telephone number as the last field. If you simply browse through the file, the telephone number will be off the screen to the right - in other words you won't be able to see it quickly. How can we get dBase to present us with just the key information we need (the telephone number for each surname in the list)? It is actually quite easy. You simply specify the fields you want to browse through, like this:

4   (Remember you have already keyed in *'BROW'*.) Tap the **[SPACEBAR]** to leave a space and then key in **FIELDS [SPACEBAR]**, then the name of the fields you want to examine like this: **SURNAME,NUMBER**. So the whole command should read:

   BROW FIELDS SURNAME,NUMBER

5   Now tap **[RETURN]** to get the display you want.

Note: Had you keyed in, **'brow fiel surname,number'**, this would have worked as well. Notice you can shorten the command words to the first four characters, but you must use the full name of the field you want to look at (though it does not have to be in upper case as you can see in this example).

6   Tap **ALT-Q** to leave browse.

SECTION 9-20
Examining The Records In A File - DISPLAY

As you get more familiar with dBase you will find there is a wide range of options for displaying and printing the contents of a data file. We want to examine just one more in this quick overview of dBase - the command, DISPLAY (actually, another command, LIST, works in a very similar way).

1 Start up dBase and key in **USE PHONE[RETURN]**.

2 First, key in **DISP STRU** (short for *'display structure'* of the database file) and then tap **[RETURN]**.

dBase provides you with a description of the file:

- its name
- the number of records it holds
- the date it was last updated
- whether it is the primary database you are using or not
- then a description of the field numbers, names, types, widths and any decimal places which have been defined for numeric fields.
- finally it tells you the total size taken up by the records (one character space is used by dBase for control information about the record).

3 Now key in **DISP**(LAY) on its own and tap **[RETURN]**.

Dbase displays the first record in the file. Move dBase's *'pointer'* to the end of the file, by keying in:

4 **GOTO BOTTOM [RETURN]** (i.e. go to the bottom of the list of records). Then key in **DISP [RETURN]** again to look at the last entry you keyed into the file.

SECTION 9-20
Examining The Records In A File - DISPLAY

5 Now get back to the start of the file by keying in **GOTO TOP** and tapping **[RETURN]**.

As you can guess, if you were to key in the display command again, you would now get a display of the first record in the file. Well that's a bit boring, so we'll try something else. In fact you can be very specific about which record or records dBase displays.

6 First, key in, **DISP ALL [RETURN]** and make a note of a record somewhere in the middle of the file. Jot it down on a piece of paper if you have to.

7 Now key in **ERASE[RETURN]** to clear the screen.

Let's say you have found a telephone number written on a piece of paper, but you can't remember who the number belongs to. Well you can search the database to find out, like this:

8 Key in, **DISP FOR NUMBER** = *(the number you made a note of just now)* **[RETURN]**, e.g.

    disp for number = 081 234 5678[RETURN]

dBase displays the record you made a note of so now you have a better chance of working out why you have a strange telephone number hanging around on your desk. Well that's a fairly simple example, but you can see the principle of searching the database by specifying, what you might call, 'limiting' information. Try keying in,

    list for number = "*the number you noted down*"**[RETURN]**

and you'll see you get the same result. In fact it is worth experimenting with display and list to see the possibilities.

SECTION 9-21
Sorting The Records In A File

So far we have been working with the database which has not been sorted in any way; it is just a record of the entries you made, in the order you made them. That doesn't make a lot of difference to dBase's search routines, but if you want a printed version of you telephone numbers file, you would probably want the records listed so the surnames were in alphabetical order. Here's how you sort the file into such a form.

1   Start up dBase and key in **USE PHONE[RETURN]**.

2   Key in, **SORT ON SURNAME TO TELBOOK[RETURN]**.

Translated, this command reads, '*sort the file you are using* (phones), *on the surname* (key) *field* (or prime index) *and put the results of your sorting in a file called telbook*(.DBF)'. dBase tells you when it has finished sorting the data and writing the new file.

The original file remains unchanged (key in LIST[RETURN] if you don't believe me). Before we can examine our sorted database we have to tell dBase to stop using PHONE and to start using the new file.

3   Key in **USE TELBOOK[RETURN]** and now key in either **LIST** or **DISP ALL** followed by **[RETURN]**.

4   Try sorting on the forename field, e.g.

   sort on forename to friends[RETURN]

Now get dBase to use the *friends* file and then list the contents.

Here again the principle is very straightforward, but the end results can be spectacular, so the message is, experiment!

■ SECTION 9-22
Programming With dBase

When you bear in mind that a computer program is really nothing more than a long list of commands, and you remember that dBase itself responds to a varied list of commands (far more numerous and varied than we have had space to explore in this quick overview), then you can begin to see how it might be possible to program dBase to do some pretty complex things.

If you can put a long string of dBase commands into a file (a COMMAND FILE) and then, as it were, *feed* that file into dBase, dBase will interpret each command and carry it out as if you had keyed it in direct.

And, of course, that is the big advantage of having a computer program - or a command file; you *don't* have to key in each command painstakingly while you are doing a job with the computer. That's particularly useful if you are doing a repetitive task, like making out invoices, or printing out a catalogue. All you have to do is key the commands in once (into a file called something.CMD), then test the resulting program and when you are satisfied it works properly, you can hand it over to someone else and let them *DO* the job *(remember DO WELCOME?)*.

You can produce the command file either through dBase or with your own word processor, but it must be called *something.CMD*.

So, if you want to write your own dBase programs (dbase *applications* in the jargon) then it will be worth your while getting to know a full range of dBase commands. Given the comprehensiveness of dBase commands, there seems to be virtually no limit to what you can make the computer do - in terms of business computing, we mean.

You may even be able to sell one or more of your programs, so it will pay you to get in touch with Ashton Tate Publishing group for details of their applications register.

Chapter Ten
Working With Numbers – SuperCalc^2

SECTION 10-1
A Word About Spreadsheets In General

When you read the blurbs for spreadsheet programs, they generally say something along the lines of, *'SuperMegaCalc provides you with a computer based version of the paper spreadsheets we all use...'* Personally I don't think I've ever used one and I'm not sure I'd recognise one if it leapt up and bit me. I suppose they mean that if you take a big bit of paper and draw lines and columns on it, you can spread that out on the table and use it to organise financial information. I only say that because that's what computer spreadsheet programs do.

Now, if they had said, *'SuperMegaCalc provides you with the computer equivalent of the back of an envelope'*, I'd know what they mean. That's where I work out all my quotes and costings, my invoice totals, income and expenditure projections and the like. And that is the sort of task that spreadsheet programs enable you to do - i.e. key in raw numbers and then work out a whole range of things from the basic data. But more than that, the spreadsheet program will do all the working out for you in a flash, which means you can play around with the numbers to see how to get the best results. In short, spreadsheet programs take all the hard work out of processing numbers.

They also enable you to store the results of your calculations, so you can call them back at some later time to try and find out why things went wrong. And they enable you to print out nice neat versions of the figures (presumably so you can hide the truth behind an impressive presentation).

All in all spreadsheet programs are useful tools (some refer to themselves as *decision aids*) and SuperCalc^2 is a good example of what a spreadsheet can do for you.

■ SECTION 10-2
Starting up SuperCalc - The Screen Display

1 Put your CP/M disc in drive A:, then hold down one of the **[SHIFT]** keys and the **[EXTRA]** key, then tap the **[EXIT]** key to reset your computer.

2 Remove you CP/M disc and replace it with your SuperCalc disc. Key in **SC8256** *(sic)* and tap **[RETURN]** to start up SuperCalc.

Before SuperCalc gets running it displays a copyright screen with a message near the bottom telling that you can get help if you press the question mark key, or you can simply tap [RETURN] to start working.

3 Tap the **[RETURN]** key, as the help screens in SuperCalc are not really that helpful - they seem to have been written for some kind of American computer buff. We have found this to be true even for much later versions of SuperCalc.

Once you get SuperCalc going you are faced with a virtually empty screen. All you can see is a row of letters across the top of the screen (A through to I) and a column of numbers - 1 through to 27 - down the left hand side of the screen. At the place where the 'A' column and line 1 intersect there is an area of highlighting.

4 Tap the **[RETURN]** key twice and watch what happens to the highlighting. (If nothing happens, tap the **[RIGHT ARROW]** key twice.)

It moves across line 1 to column C. This highlighted area is in fact the spreadsheet cursor. It functions like the cursor in a word processor, insofar as it tells you where the next thing you enter onto the spreadsheet will appear. The cursor occupies a section of the spreadsheet at the intersection of a line and a column. In other words, it sits in a *'cell'* or a pigeonhole into which you can put data. The position of the spreadsheet cursor tells you which cell is the *live* one - i.e. the one you are working with.

SECTION 10-2
Starting up SuperCalc - The Screen Display

On many occasions you will need to refer to a particular cell - e.g. to include it in a calculation, or to copy its contents, or to move it. You tell SuperCalc which cell you mean by quoting its co-ordinates. So the live cell at the moment is cell C1.

5   Move the spreadsheet cursor down, three lines (by tapping the down arrow three times), the live cell is now C4.

6   Tap the **[LEFT ARROW]** twice.

Below the column of numbers there are three further lines of information:

- The first line has on it *'< A4'*, which tells you, firstly, that if you press [RETURN] the spreadsheet cursor will move left (or at least it would if it weren't at the left hand boundary of the spreadsheet, and secondly it tells you the current location of the spreadsheet cursor.

- The next line tells you the current 'status' of the spreadsheet - it is empty at the moment, so it doesn't tell you much.

- The third line says '1>' and then there's another cursor. This line is the 'entry line' and the cursor here is the *'entry cursor'*. The number at the left tells you the position across the screen of the entry cursor.

7   Tap the **[RIGHT ARROW]** key twice to move the spreadsheet cursor to cell C4, then, keeping an eye on the number at the left of the *entry line*, key in the number **52** and tap **[RETURN]**.

The number appears in cell C4, but note that the spreadsheet cursor has moved one cell to the right. That is because its motion was set to *'rightwards'* the last time you pressed an arrow key.

SECTION 10-3
Putting Information Onto The Spreadsheet

1   **Move** the spreadsheet cursor, leftwards to **column A**, and then downwards to **line 8**.

You can put three main types of information onto the spreadsheet:

- Numbers (which you have already done in cell C4)
- Formulae
- Text

Let us now have a look at how you might use the other two types, first, text.

Note: When you key in a text entry, you must start with a double quotation mark (", a shifted number 2). So:

2   Key in, **"weekly cost** and notice as you do that nothing appears in the cell yet. The characters you key in appear in the entry line and while they are there you can edit and amend them.

Note: If you make a mistake while you are keying in an entry (data or commands), backspace with the [LEFT ARROW] key and then overtype the mistake. Or tap [ALT][Z] to clear the whole entry and start again.

3   Tap **[RETURN]** and the text should appear in cell A8. At the same time the cursor should move down to the next line. Tap **[RETURN]** to skip a line and then key in **"annual cost.**

Note: You put the double quotation mark (") only at the *beginning* of the text entry (not at the end as well), and you need it only for text entries.

4   Tap the **[RIGHT ARROW]** key once to move the cursor to cell B11. Notice that the two text entries you have made overlap into column B. That is no problem when the next cell (the one in column B on the same line as the text entry) is empty, but now tap the [UP ARROW] key once, you will see that anything put into that cell will truncate the text entry in column A.

■ **SECTION 10-3**
Putting Information Onto The Spreadsheet

Note: The *default* width of the cells is 9 characters, but if you want to key in longish pieces of text, or big numbers, you can alter the width setting to suit yourself. With numbers that are too big for the cell, SuperCalc automatically converts them to scientific notation; it does not extend into the next column.

5 Move the spreadsheet cursor **UP** three more lines, **RIGHT** two columns and finally **DOWN** one line to cell D8. (This manoeuvre has set the cursor movement to downwards.)

Your spreadsheet (or 'cell') cursor should now be in cell D8, with the cursor direction set to downwards.

6 Key in the number **75** and tap **[RETURN]**.

Now we shall try entering a formula.

7 Tap the **[RETURN]** key once more to move down a line and key in, **75*52** (75 multiplied by 52). Keep an eye on the empty highlighted cell and tap **[RETURN]**.

The answer appears almost before you have finished tapping the [RETURN] key. That is quite a simple formula, let's now see one of the most useful features of a spreadsheet - the ability to write formulae which incorporate data from other cells.

8 Tap **[RETURN]** once more to skip another line and key in, **D8*C4** (or **d8*c4**) **[RETURN]**.

This is really saying to SuperCalc, take the numerical value (the result of the formula) in cell D8 and multiply it by the numerical value of cell C4 (which in this case happens to be a number you have keyed in). But it is perfectly possible to carry out any mathematical activity on two (or more) cells which all contain formulae, as we shall see on the next page.

253

■ SECTION 10-3
Putting Information Onto The Spreadsheet

Let's start by creating another cell with a formula in it.

9 Move the cells cursor to cell A14. Then key in, "**annual income** and tap **[RETURN]**. Move the cell cursor to cell D14 and key in **c4*250** and tap **[RETURN]**.

This is a fairly simple example, but it is only the principle which concerns us for the moment, so bear with us.

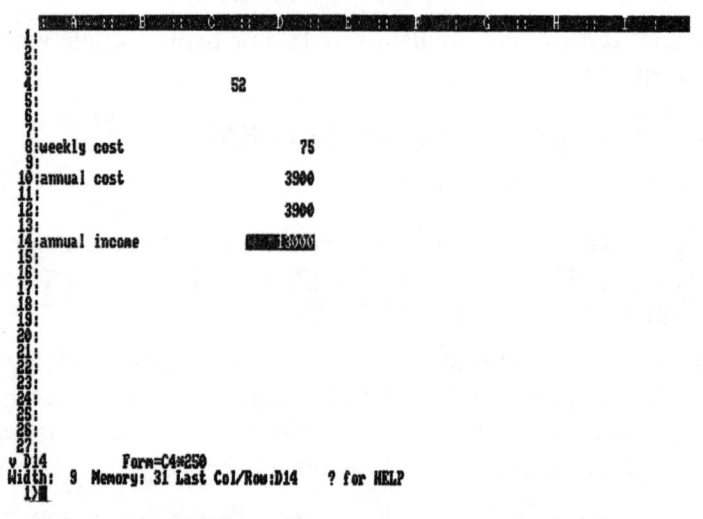

```
        A      B      C      D      E      F      G      H      I
 1:
 2:
 3:
 4:                          52
 5:
 6:
 7:
 8: weekly cost              75
 9:
10: annual cost             3900
11:
12:                         3900
13:
14: annual income           13000
15:
16:
...
27:
 v D14        Form=C4*250
Width:  9  Memory: 31 Last Col/Row:D14    ? for HELP
```

Fig. 1: The spreadsheet showing formula entry.

So now we have some cells which contain formulae, we can demonstrate that you can use a formula which incorporates only the addresses of other cells which contain formulae - (if you see what we mean). We want you to put some text in cell A20, but before you move the cursor there with the arrow keys, let me show you a quick way to *'Goto'* a specific cell.

■ SECTION 10-3
Putting Information Onto The Spreadsheet

1 Tap the **equals sign** key (=). The status line prompts you to *'Enter cell to jump to'*. Key in **a20[RETURN]** and watch the cursor go straight to the cell you specified.

Note: After this exercise, you can try keying in, **=bk254[RETURN]** to see the bottom right hand corner of the SuperCalc spreadsheet. Then key in, **=a1[RETURN]** to get back to the top left hand corner.

2 Key in, "**Profit[RETURN]**, then move the cells cursor to **D20**. Now key in the formula, **d14-d10[RETURN]** to get your answer immediately.

Now all this is pretty straightforward, but let me show you one of the things that make spreadsheet programmes so useful - the ability to answer *'what if'* questions. For example, what if the weekly cost went up to 150? what effect would that have on the figures?

1 Tap **=d8[RETURN]**. When the cursor is in position on cell D8, key in **150** and, keeping an eye on the screen, tap **[RETURN]**.

Nothing changes except that cell and one other (D12). Now let's make a more wide reaching change.

2 **Goto** cell **d10** and change the contents of the cell to **d8*c4**, watch the screen again and tap **[RETURN]**.

This time all the cells which use D8 directly or indirectly change at the same time. Try changing D8 again to see how quickly you can answer *what if* questions.

SECTION 10-4
Commands - Saving Your Work

When you are working with any computer program you must get into the habit of saving your work regularly and frequently. Fairly obviously you will have to key in a command of some kind, but the keyboard seems to be dedicated to inputting data at the moment, so how do you say to SuperCalc, *'Hold on a moment, I want to instruct you to do something else'*? There must be a key somewhere which acts as a switch to turn data inputting off and *command* inputting on. Yes there is, it is the *'slash'* key (/). When you tap the slash key it tells SuperCalc that the next key stroke is going to represent one of its command words.

1 Tap the **slash key** (/) and you'll see a row of 20 letters and a question mark appear. Those twenty letters are the initials of SuperCalc command words. Tap the **?** key to get a help screen which lists their meanings. When you have read the screen, tap the **[SPACEBAR]** to get back to your spreadsheet.

```
SuperCalc2    AnswerScreen Slash Commands:
  A(rrange)--- Sorts cells in ascending or descending order.
  B(lank)----- Removes (empties) contents of cells.
  C(opy)------ Duplicates contents and display format of cells.
  D(elete)---- Erases entire rows or columns.
  E(dit)------ Allows editing of cell contents.
  F(ormat)---- Sets display format at Entry, Row, Column, or Global levels.
  G(lobal)---- Changes global display or calculation options.
  I(nsert)---- Adds empty rows or columns.
  L(oad)------ Reads spreadsheet (or portion) from disk into the workspace.
  M(ove)------ Inserts existing rows or columns at new positions.
  O(utput)---- Sends display or cell contents to printer, screen or disk.
  P(rotect)--- Prevents future alteration of cells.
  Q(uit)------ Ends the SuperCalc2 program.
  R(eplicate)- Reproduces contents of partial rows or columns.
  S(ave)------ Stores the current spreadsheet on disk.
  T(itle)----- Locks upper rows or left-hand columns from scrolling.
  U(nprotect)- Allows alteration of protected cells.
  W(indow)---- Splits the screen display.
  X(eXecute)-- Accepts commands and data from an .XQT file.
  Z(ap)------- Erases spreadsheet and format settings from workspace.




  Press any key to continue ▌
```

Fig. 2: SuperCalc commands.

SECTION 10-4
Commands - Saving Your Work

Notice that the slash symbol you keyed in is still in the entry line.

2   You will have noticed that the command you want is Save, so tap the letter **[S]**. SuperCalc now prompts you to key in a name for the spreadsheet file it will create. Key in **A:CF1[RETURN]** (to ensure that the file is saved on a floppy disc rather than the memory disc). After a burp from the disc drive, SuperCalc asks you if you want to save All of the spreadsheet - save everything as you have set it, or save just the Values - the current values of the formulae, not the formulae themselves, or save only Part of the spreadsheet. Tap the letter **[A]** to save all your work.

SuperCalc writes your file to disc. If, later on, you save the file again under the same name (A:CF1) SuperCalc will burp again and then tell you that a file with that name exists on the disc and it will give you the choice of either Overwriting the old file, creating a Backup or Changing the name.

SECTION 10-5
Commands - Cancelling And Quitting

Say that half way through keying in a command you decide to change your mind and do something else first. How do you cancel what you have keyed in? Then again, let's say you are keying some data in and you realise that the cursor is on the wrong cell. You can't move the cursor until you have cleared the entry line, but how do you do that? Very easily. As we have already seen:

1 Hold down the [ALT] key and then tap the letter [Z]. This clears the entry line and allows you to start again. Remember this works for commands and for data.

So that's how you get rid of an entry, but how do you get rid of the spreadsheet? Well it depends what you want to do.

If you want to carry on working with SuperCalc - say, to create another spreadsheet *'model'* , then:

1 Tap the command switch key, /, then tap the letter [Z] to *'zap'* the spreadsheet. SuperCalc seems to be incredulous: *'Zap - ENTIRE - Worksheet?'* it says and it offers you three options: Yes, go ahead - No, don't do it - and yes, but just erase the contents of the spreadsheet. For now, just tap [N].

And how about if you want to stop working with SuperCalc? It's simple. In fact too simple! If you have forgotten to save the latest version of your work you will lose it. So always double check when you use this command. So, to quit:

1 *Make sure you have saved your work*, then tap / followed by the letter [Q]. Once again SuperCalc offers three options: Exit from SuperCalc back to CP/M, Yes or No, or exit from SuperCalc to some other program. Tap the letter [Y] to get back to the system prompt.

SECTION 10-6
Starting Up And Loading A File

1 Start up SuperCalc in the usual way. When you get the copyright screen, tap the **[RETURN]** key to get SuperCalc's empty worksheet.

Now you have the choice of either creating a brand new spreadsheet model, or of loading one which already exists. We shall load the one you have been working on so far,

2 Key in, /L (for, *'command load'*). SuperCalc asks you to key in a file name, or - if you can't remember the name, to tap [RETURN] to look at the directory. Tap **[RETURN]**, to get a list of four options:

- Tap [C] to Choose another disc drive - in other words *'log-on'* to another drive
- Tap [D] to get a directory of all the files on the Disk *(sic)*
- Tap [S] to get a directory of just the SuperCalc format files
- Tap [E] to key in the name of the file you want to load

3 Tap **[C]**, then the letter **[A]** (to log to drive A:). Next tap **[S]** to get a list of the SuperCalc files.

Notice that all the file names (in capitals) end with *.CAL*, including your one (the last on the list), even though you only gave it the name *CF1*. The *.CAL* tells you that the files are SuperCalc Spreadsheet (or worksheet) files. Notice also that the first four files on the list have a line of text below the filename which gives a short description of what's in the file. How do you get SuperCalc to do that for your file?

4 Tap the **[SPACEBAR]** to clear the directory from the screen and then tap **[E]** to enter a file name. This gets you back to the empty spreadsheet. Key in **A:CF1** and tap **[RETURN]** to begin loading your file, then tap **[A]** for all of the file.

SECTION 10-6
Starting Up And Loading A File

When you spreadsheet is back on screen, notice that the cells cursor is where you left it when you closed down.

Now to create that line of text which describes what's in this file. The thing to remember is that SuperCalc uses any text which appears in cell A1 as the descriptive label for the file. So,

1 Move the cells cursor to cell A1 *(remember =A1)*. Now key in **"my first spreadsheet [RETURN]**.

2 Now we need to save the amended file. Tap /[S] and key in **A:CF1[RETURN]**, then after a pause, tap in **[O]** to overwrite the existing file, and tap **[A]** to save all of the file.

Now we need to get another directory to check that we have our descriptive line.

3 Tap /[L], tap **[RETURN]**, Tap **[C]** followed by **[A]**, then tap **[S]**. When SuperCalc has listed the files you'll see your descriptive line of text.

This is one of those occasions when we want to change our mind half way through putting in a series of commands.

4 Hold down the **[ALT]** key and tap the letter **[Z]** to cancel the activity. (Remember, *ALT-Z* cancels an entry, while /Z *'zaps'* the whole spreadsheet.)

■ SECTION 10-7
Getting Rid Of Unwanted Items - Blank

As we construct spreadsheet models we often end up with items which don't actually contribute much to the *'story line'*. Even on our simple model we have one cell which is not really doing much, cell D12. It is left over from an example we worked through earlier and now it's just flapping about doing nothing.

1 Move down to cell **D12**. Let's erase the contents of this cell, or in SuperCalc terminology, let's *'blank'* it out. We need the 'Blank' command, so tap /[**B**]. SuperCalc asks you to enter the range of cells you want to blank out (which tells you that you can blank out several cells in one go if you want to). Here we want to blank out the cell where the cursor is, so tap [**RETURN**] and SuperCalc clears it immediately.

In this case, blanking the cell had no effect on the rest of the spreadsheet, but if you blank out a cell which is used by other cells (in formulae), then you might cause problems. e.g.

2 Move to cell **C4**. Now repeat the blank command sequence - /[**B**][**RETURN**]. You will see that most of the other entries now show a zero result. That's because - either directly or indirectly - they use the figure in cell C4 in their calculations. So, key in the figure **52** and tap [**RETURN**] to restore the situation.

SECTION 10-7
Getting Rid Of Unwanted Items - Delete

Now we have blanked out cell D12 we have spoiled the nice tidy layout of our spreadsheet. We now have three blank lines after line 10 rather than one. We need to delete two lines to smarten things up.

Note: By the way, don't forget to save your work regularly. If you haven't saved since you started up, do so now.

1 Just for the sake of this exercise, move your cells cursor to cell **A1**.

(You don't *have* to do this to delete something, I just want to demonstrate that you can carry out most of SuperCalc's commands wherever your cursor is.)

2 Tap **/[D]** (for the delete command). SuperCalc asks you whether you want to delete a Row, a Column, or a File.

(*JC:* I always used to get confused between rows and columns. I could never remember which way they went. I know I'm a bit simple, but the only way I could get myself to remember was to think of *'rowing across the water'* and *'holding buildings up with columns'*. Daft innit!? Still you don't want to know my problems, so...)

3 Tap the letter **[R]** and then, in answer to SuperCalc's prompt for a range, key in **12:13** (rows or lines 12 *to* 13) and tap **[RETURN]**. The screen redraws and there you are with a new layout.

Note: Whenever you specify a range, you key it in as we did here - where it begins, then a colon, then where it ends.

4 Save this amended version of your spreadsheet now. (Don't forget to put *A:* at the beginning of the file name.)

SECTION 10-8
Printing A Copy Of The Spreadsheet

When you decide that you want a 'hard copy' of your work, you have to remember that (in the jargon) you are asking SuperCalc to *'output'* information. So the command you want is *'Output'*.

1   Tap /[O]. SuperCalc asks if you want to *'output'* the display (what you can see on screen), or whether you want it to output a *'contents report'* (a detailed description of how you have set up the spreadsheet). We want a printout of what is on screen, so tap [D].

Next, SuperCalc asks you to specify how much of the spreadsheet you want to print (you don't *have* to print it all).

2   Key in the word **ALL** and tap **[RETURN]**.

At this point you might expect the printer to burst into action, but no. SuperCalc offers you still more options for outputting the information. You can send it to the printer, or you can pause for a moment and check that the printer is set up properly, or you can send the information to the screen (the console), or you can write the information to a file on disc.

3   Tap the letter **[C]** to send it to the screen. SuperCalc prints, on screen, only what it will print on paper, so this gives you a chance to see what you'll get. When you have had a look at the screen display, tap the **[SPACE BAR]**.

4   But we do want a print out on paper so, Tap /[O] then [D] then **ALL[RETURN]** then check that you have paper in the printer, and tap **[P]**.

After a few moments you will have your hard copy of the work you have done. Impressive stuff, eh!? Well alright, but this *is* only an introduction. (Tap any key to clear the print routine.)

263

■ SECTION 10-9
Inserting Extra Rows And Columns

Let's say that after looking at our print out of the spreadsheet we decide that we really ought to have an underline below line 10 to separate cost from income. And let's also say that we want the *'annual income'* line to move down a line to accommodate the line of underlining. We could, in this instance, make those adjustments in any order. But on many occasions, when you want to *insert* a new line or column of information you have to make room for it first. This is how you do it (it is the same procedure for lines and columns).

1 Just for interest's sake, move the cells cursor to the 'Profit' total, cell D18 and have a look in the first line of the control information, at the contents of that cell. The line should read, '∨ *D18   Form=D12-D10'* (assuming that the down arrow was the last one you tapped). We shall see what happens when we change the layout.

2 Tap /[I]. Select Row, by tapping [R]. Then for 'Range' key in the number of the line where you want the new line to be put - in this case **11** - and tap [RETURN]. SuperCalc re-draws the screen.

Row 11 and everything below it shifts down one line. Notice the cursor is still in cell D18, but there's nothing there any more.

3 Move the cells cursor down to cell D19 and you will see that SuperCalc has automatically changed the formula in the cell to allow for the new positions of the cells. The contents of the cell now reads, *'Form=D13-D10'*. So you can add lines or delete them without worrying about changing all the subsequent entries.

Now we are ready to put in our line of underlining.

■ SECTION 10-10
Replicating Entries

1 Move your cells cursor to cell **A11**. Now key in "========= (nine equals signs) and tap **[RETURN]**.

Note: Unless you alter the setting, SuperCalc cells are 9 characters wide.

We want this underlining to extend right across from the left margin to the far side of column D, but there are separate cells involved, so the most effective way of getting things right is to ensure that all the cells have the same information in them. We need to replicate the entry in cell A11.

2 Tap **/[R]**. Key in **A11** for the range and tap **[RETURN]**. Now we want these equals signs to be replicated in cells B11, C11 and D11, so key in the start and finish cells of the to (or destination) range. i.e. key in **B11:D11** and tap **[RETURN]** to see the underlining right the way across the spreadsheet.

Now we probably want a similar line of underlining in line 15, so:

3 Key in **/[R]** then **A11[RETURN]** then **A15:D15[RETURN]**.

Well that's fine for replicating one cell, but can we replicate a whole line in one go?

4 Key in **/[R]** then **A15:D15[RETURN]**, then the destination **A20**. (You don't need to put any more than the start point for the destination, SuperCalc can work out the rest.)

5 Time to save again.

SECTION 10-11
Some Closing Words

There are many more commands and activities we could examine, but in this quick overview we have merely been trying to give you the *'feel'* of working with SuperCalc.

We use SuperCalc for many different kinds of jobs, for example, producing cashflow projections and business plans for the bank - yes, we write fiction too (some might even say fantasy).

The main thing is, it is simple to use for everyday mundane jobs and yet, if you want to get into the heady heights of advanced mathematics and statistics, the facilities are there. It is really up to you how you use it. Only you know your true needs of a spreadsheet program. But we think it's pretty safe to say, that whatever your needs for processing numbers, SuperCalc should fit the bill for most of them.

Happy counting!

Make sure you've saved your work and then close down with the Quit command.

Chapter Eleven
Integrated Software mini Office Professional

SECTION 11-1
Introduction

mini Office Professional is produced by Mandarin/Database Software.

At first sight, mini Office Professional appears a little crude on screen. It might remind you of some of the old BBC software used in schools, but don't be put off by initial impressions, this is a very useful and easy to use *'integrated'* office package which will give, particularly the small business, access to a range of facilities, without spending a great deal of time learning the ins and outs of wildly different software packages. So what is an integrated software package. Put simply it is a single software system that incorporates a range of programs which do different jobs, but they do those jobs in such a way that information can be swapped (exported and imported) between the programs. For example, you can use database files, or spreadsheet files in your word processor.

The standard package includes a word processor, database, spreadsheet, communications, graphics and disc utilities. To obtain the spelling checker and Thesaurus you have to place a separate order and return your disc 1 master disc, which is a bit of a bind, so if you think you'll need these, (and who doesn't these days!) you'd be better off going for the upgraded package, *mini Office Professional Plus*, from the start.

■ SECTION 11-2
Getting mini Office Started

The User Guide and Quick Reference Card that come with the software are very easy to follow and give comprehensive instructions for starting up and for all the features. Like so many manuals or user guides, though, they are more concerned with the software features than with the use you might want to make of them. What we shall attempt to do in this section, (as we have with other software included in this book) is to introduce you to mini Office, as we think you might want to approach it. We shall begin by looking briefly at each of the facilities and then concentrate on how you integrate the use of them.

1 The current version of mini Office, as we go to press, is in 8000 format and so to create a working copy of the programs, you will need to use your 8000COPY facility. Follow the instructions given in the section headed *'Copying A Disc From 8000 Format'* (Section 8-8) to make a working copy of the Master discs.

You should make your working copy of mini Office Professional bootable, i.e. load CP/M automatically when you switch on and insert the disc. You can also, if you choose, get it to load straight into mini Office as described in Section 8-9.

2 To start using your working disc, switch on your PCW9512 and insert the disc. If mini Office does not load automatically, at the system prompt, key in **'office'** (in either capitals or lower case) and tap **[ENTER]**. The mini Office Main Menu appears, with Word Processor highlighted.

See the next page.

SECTION 11-2
Getting mini Office Started

```
         Mini Office Professional
         Mini Office Main Menu

              Word processor
              Database
              Spreadsheet
              Graphics
              Communications
              Disc utilities
              Setup system
              Exit to CP/M

       Use ↓ and ↑ to select, then ENTER

            © Database Software 1989
```

Fig. 1:   mini Office main menu.

3   To set up mini Office for your system, use the arrow keys to move the cursor down to **'Setup system'**, near the bottom of the list and tap **[ENTER]**.

Note: You can use either the [RETURN] or the [ENTER] key with mini Office, they both do the same job. We shall simply refer to [ENTER] for the sake of simplicity. Another way of making a selection is to tap the [+] key and the initial letter of the function you want.

If you are just starting you may want to leave the settings as they are for the moment, but if you wish to make changes, with a twin drive machine you can toggle between drive A and drive B from here. If you have more than one user and wish to separate their work, you can allocate up to sixteen user numbers, 0-15.

SECTION 11-2
Getting mini Office Started

Where you have set up another printer, and you will have to use a dot matrix printer if you wish to print out graphics, you can tell mini Office, and if need be set up new printer codes. You can save the new settings you have made and load them up again next time you need them.

mini Office gives you access to a number of disc utilities which you can use from the Main Menu or while using a program. We shall come to these later. Let's get started with Word processing.

SECTION 11-3
Word Processing

1   Tap **[EXIT]** to leave the Setup system Menu and return to the Main menu. Tap **[+] W** and the Word processor loads and the Menu appears.

2   To start keying in a document, tap **[ENTER]** for *'Edit document'*. You now have the editing screen on which you will enter your work.

The screen has two parts. The *'Status block'* at the top which tells you various things about the state of the computer and shows the function key menus. A ruler, showing margins and tabs, separates this from the *'Work Page'* where you can see the Start and End points of your work indicated.

3   Start keying in your document. Words will automatically wrap around onto the next line when one line is full. You can use [RETURN] or [ENTER] to start a new line. Use the [DEL] keys in the usual way. (If you don't have a document that you want to create yet, try keying in the next four paragraphs, without the highlighting and typesetting features.)

4   Save as you go along. Tap the **[f1]** key and the *'Save menu'* appears. (If you forget to save, mini Office will remind you automatically after a quarter of an hour or so and you have the option to save or tap [EXIT] to continue editing without saving.) Delete the filename mini Office offers you and key in a new name (only the name, not the drive letter or suffix .DOC), then tap **[ENTER]**, followed by **[EXIT]**.

There are some very useful features available to you while you are editing. If you just wish to save a block of text you define the block as you would if you were going to move, copy or delete it and tap [f2].

SECTION 11-3
Word Processing

5 Go to the start of the opening paragraph of your text, tap **[CUT]** or **[EXTRA][M]** then move to the end of the paragraph and repeat this. Dim square brackets will mark where your block begins and ends. You can only define one block on screen at a time.

6 To copy the block, make sure the cursor is outside the block and tap **[COPY]** or **[EXTRA][C]**. (To move the block you use **[PASTE]** or **[EXTRA][T]** and to delete the block, **[SHIFT/ALT/DEL]** or **[EXTRA][D]**.)

Note: There are some other refinements to these procedures as shown in the Word processing section of the User Guide.

7 To save the block, perhaps to use in another document, tap **[f2]** (SHIFT + F1) and a menu appears. Move the cursor to the name that the menu offers you and delete it with **[DEL>]**, then key in a name for the new block and tap **[ENTER]**.

8 Once you have saved the block, mini Office returns you automatically to the Save Block menu, tap **[EXIT]** and you are back at your document.

In addition to identifying blocks of text for processing, as above, you may want to pick out sections to alter the layout or add printing enhancements. As with blocks, the markers you put in the text will usually be in pairs showing where the feature should start and end.

You can alter the layout of parts of text by inserting justification commands, left, right and full; centring blocks or single lines; inserting a new ruler.

There are several printing enhancements such as underlining, bold, italics etc.. And you can alter the line spacing; add headers and footers and page numbers.

SECTION 11-3
Word Processing

Once you enter the codes for these you will see the codes on screen, (provided you have not tapped [f6] to remove codes), but the changes will not be apparent on screen. To see the effect, you need to go into *'Page Mode'* by tapping [f3]. You tap [f3] again to return to normal editing mode.

The full list of keystrokes you need is given in your User Guide. You probably can't hope to remember them all, but that doesn't matter. You'll soon learn the ones you use most often, and you have the Reference Card supplied with the software to help you when you need it.

What we shall do now is look briefly at how you set up these layout changes and enhancements, not the details of each individual feature.

1 Move back to the beginning of your document using **[EXTRA]** and the **[Up Arrow]**. If your document doesn't have a heading, key one in now. To centre this heading, with the cursor on the heading line, hold down **[ALT]** and tap **[M]**. A dim star symbol appears beside the heading.

When you start keying in text from scratch, mini Office automatically justifies it to the left margin, this is its default setting. If text contains tab settings you cannot justify to the right any lines which contain tabs. Such lines will be left as they are and all other lines right justified.

2 Move the cursor down to the start of the first paragraph of text. Hold down **[ALT] [SHIFT]** and tap **[J]**.

3 Move the cursor down to the start of the third paragraph and hold down **[ALT] [SHIFT]** and tap **[J]**. You have now set full justification on for the first two paragraphs.

SECTION 11-3
Word Processing

4 To see the effect of what you have done, tap the **[f3] 'Page Mode'** key and the paragraphs appear with the new settings. Tap **[f3]** again to return to the Edit screen. To return to left justification, you use **[ALT]** and **[<]**.

In addition to altering the horizontal alignment of text, you can vary the line spacing and set up joined phrases as shown in the User Guide section, 'Line spacing commands'.

It may well be that you want a section of text to stand out by giving it narrower margin settings. To do this you need to create a new ruler just for that section of text. In doing this, you will also see how to set up a new ruler to change the margin and tab settings for your whole document.

1 Move the cursor to the start of paragraph four of your document, hold down **[EXTRA]** and tap **[R]**. A copy of the current ruler appears just above the paragraph.

2 To edit this ruler, move the cursor onto the ruler line and use **[<DEL]** and **[DEL>]** to move the margins in. (To move the right margin (>) to the right, put the cursor *in the ruler line* and tap the spacebar. To move the left margin (<) to the left, with the cursor *on the left margin marker,* tap [<DEL].)

3 To alter the tab settings, delete any tabs you do not want by tapping **[DEL>]** or **[<DEL]**, move the cursor to the new position and tap **[T]** or the **[TAB]** key. To adjust the text to the new margins, tap **[RELAY]** and all the remaining text will be adjusted.

SECTION 11-3
Word Processing

4 To return to the original ruler setting for the subsequent paragraphs, move the cursor down to the beginning of the next paragraph, hold down **[EXTRA]** and tap **[R]**. The original ruler appears above the paragraph and the remaining text is automatically realigned to it.

Other ways of emphasising text are to enhance them by emboldening, underlining, italics etc. You use these in much the same way as we have seen previously, except that the commands work in pairs usually, with one command at the beginning of the text you want to highlight and another at the end to cancel the highlighting, as follows.

1 Move the cursor back to the beginning of the document ([ALT/DOC]). To underline the heading, hold down **[SHIFT] [ALT]** and tap **[U]**. Move to the end of the heading and turn the underlining off with **[ALT] [U]**. (A dim U appears where the underlining starts and a dim u where it ends.)

The same method sets all enhancements on and off. The reference card that came with your software will give you the relevant key combinations for each.

If you wish to have a look at the effect of the kind of refinements we have been talking about, you can see them in a file called *'DEMO.DOC'*.

If you wish to save your document,

1 Tap **[f1]** and follow the save procedures we described earlier, changing the name you are offered to one that relates to your document. At the Load/Save menu, select **'Load Document'** and load *'DEMO.DOC'*.

SECTION 11-3
Word Processing

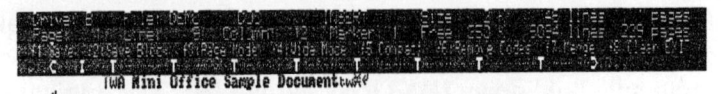

Fig. 2: mini Office document with 'dim' codes.

2   With the first part of the document on screen, tap **[f3]** to see the version that would appear if you printed the document off. (You might like to take a printout, but unless you have a dot matrix printer attached, you will not see the full effect.)

3   Tap **[f3]** again to return to the Edit screen and work through the document calling up Page Mode in the same way until you have seen all the enhancements and finishing back at the Edit screen.

The Word Processor has a number of other very useful features which we shall mention just in passing and which you can explore, when you have need of them, by referring to the User Guide. For example, you can add Headers and Footers to your pages and set up Page Numbering.

SECTION 11-3
Word Processing

When you are Editing a document the on screen menu also allows you to alter the width of the screen display ([f4]) to 40 characters; to Compact ([f5]) a document to remove unnecessary gaps and speed up editing; to Remove Codes ([f6]), the dim markers you have embedded, so that mini Office can read documents created in other word processing programs; to Merge ([f7]) documents to build up larger documents; and Clear EXIT ([f8]). This takes you to the Yes/No option which checks 'Are you sure?' you want to exit, as all that you have entered will be erased if not already saved.

As with many word processing programs, mini Office Word Processor gives you the option to work in Insert Mode (the default) or Overwrite Mode. In overwrite mode, the text is overwritten, but embedded codes are not. If you try to change a code, the word processor changes temporarily to Insert Mode and beeps to warn you.

You can toggle between the two modes by using [EXTRA][O] 'O' for 'Overwrite'.

One of the most annoying mistakes that you can make when keying in text is using the wrong case. You set Shift Lock on to key in a heading and then forget to switch it off again and find that the subsequent text has lower case letters where you wanted upper case and vice versa. mini Office is sympathetic to our forgetfulness and gives us a quick and easy way to change the case of letters.

[EXTRA][U] changes the letter to upper case, [EXTRA][L] changes the letter to lower case and [EXTRA][S] changes the current case. So if you forgot to put capital letters at the beginning of the words in your heading you could quickly remedy this by moving to the first letter of the first word and holding down [EXTRA] and tapping [U], then [SHIFT] [WORD/CHAR] to move to the beginning of the second word and [EXTRA][U] again and so on.

SECTION 11-3
Word Processing

Tabs work in the usual way. When you tap the tab key, the cursor or text moves across to the next tab marker to the right. If there are no tab markers to the right, the tab key acts like the spacebar. To start a new line you use the [RETURN] key and mini Office also has a facility for marking an automatic indent on the first line of a new paragraph. To set this up you edit the ruler as we saw earlier, and key in 'I' where you want the indent to start. When keying in or editing your text, you tap [ALT/RETURN] or [SHIFT/ALT/RETURN] and the first line of text moves across to the marker position.

Finally, just in case you need to keep an eye on how many words you've written, mini Office will do a word count for you. [EXTRA][A] (for 'Add up'?) will display the number of words in your document, at the bottom of the screen and as with many other tasks you perform, [EXIT] returns you to normal edit mode.

■ SECTION 11-4
The Word Processor Menu

We have used the Word processor Menu several times already, when starting to edit a document, saving a block and loading/saving a document. Editing and loading we accessed from this menu direct, but for saving we used the on-screen function key options to get to the Load/Save menu.

We'll have a look now at the other options on this menu, which you can reach either directly on loading the Word Processor or from a document by tapping [EXIT]. 'Edit document' we've already looked at in some detail.

'Search' and 'Search and Replace' allow you to find a particular word or group of characters (a *'string'* of characters) in a document. With the latter you can identify an alternative to replace the string.

1   To Search, first load a document or create one through edit document. Tap **[EXIT]** to return to the menu and select **Search**. The Search menu appears and you can specify whether the string should be case dependent (the default is yes) and if the search should ignore control codes or not. (To toggle between each of these options, you move the cursor onto the option and tap [RETURN].)

2   To begin the search, select **'Search for'** and enter the search string (the word or group of characters you want to find). Tap **[RETURN]** and the search will begin and stop at the first occurrence of the string. You can then edit the string if you wish and tap **[FIND]** or **[EXTRA][F]** to proceed to the next occurrence.

3   Tap **[EXIT]** to return to the Search Menu and **[EXIT]** again to return to the Word Processor Menu.

SECTION 11-4
The Word Processor Menu

To search and replace you select this option from the menu and key in the string you want to find followed by [RETURN]. Then key in the replacement string and tap return again and the process starts. One word of caution with this process. If you specify a string e.g a word like 'and', this will be replaced even where the combination 'and' appears in a longer word 'hand', 'expand' etc. The way to avoid this is to include the spaces at the beginning and end of your string if you want only whole words to be changed. You also need to be at the beginning of your document as the search goes forwards from the cursor position.

'Database' is an option we'll come to in a minute, but it is the quick way to access your data records to check details or include them in your document.

'Clear document' will remove all text from the word processor and, because of this, you are asked to confirm your selection before the text is cleared.

'Load/Save' we've seen, so I don't want to say much more, except that you can merge mini Office .DOC files from here and Save ASCII files for transmission to a different word processor or via a communications module and you can switch off the beep associated with the save prompt.

'Disc Utilities' are common to all mini Office modules, so we shall deal with these later.

Let's look now at the *'Print'* Menu.

SECTION 11-5
The Word Processor Menu - Printing

If you do not have a document loaded, load one now then return to the Word Processor Menu.

1 Select **'Print'** from the menu.

You now have a range of options.

'Preview' works like the Page Mode option and shows you, on screen, how the printed document will look, except that it scrolls through the whole document. You can stop scrolling by tapping **[STOP]** and continue by tapping any key. Tap **[EXIT]** to return to the menu.

'Preview page(s)' allows you to specify particular parts of the document for preview.

'Print' will print the whole document in line with the *'Set Up Printer'* Option, but you can specify certain pages only for printing with *'Print Page(s)'*.

1 To **'Set Up Printer'**, select this option. To alter the number of copies key in the new number. Move the cursor down to **'Page format'** and tap **[RETURN]**.

2 To change a setting, highlight the option and key in the new number. To change **'Paper type'** highlight the option and tap **[RETURN]**. Tap **[EXIT]**.

3 Select **'Default settings'** and highlight **'Printer type'**. To change this, if you have a parallel printer attached to your PCW, tap **[RETURN]**. Do the same with **'Justify spacing'** to select *'Daisy wheel'* if necessary also.

SECTION 11-5
The Word Processor Menu - Printing

4 When all settings are correct, tap **[EXIT]** to return to the Print Menu and select **'Print'** to print your document. When printing has finished, tap **[EXIT]** to return to the Word Processor menu.

We've gone in to quite some detail about how you use the mini Office Word Processor, because it is different from other word processors you might have used. It is quite straightforward and simple to use but the main strength is in how it integrates with other word processing software and the other components of mini Office and we shall move on to these now.

■ SECTION 11-6
Spell Checker And Thesaurus

If you have mini Office Professional Plus, you will have the Spell Checker and Thesaurus as part of the package. If you do not, you will have to return your disc 1 master disc as indicated on the 'Additional Information' sheet.

You can access the Spellchecker Menu directly from the Main Menu or by tapping [f2] while editing a document. In either case you should have a document open by loading or editing. You then exit from the document and the word processing module.

1 From the Main Menu, select **'Spell Checker'** and the menu appears. Select **'Spell Check'** from here and the spelling of your document will be checked.

Note: The Spell Check moves forward through your document, so the cursor should be at the beginning if you want to check all the text.

As Spell Checker works through your document it compares words with its own or the user dictionaries, if there are any. If it finds a word it does not know you then have several options; to *'Skip'* and the word will be ignored; to make a *'Manual correction'*; to *'Add to user dictionary'*; to *'Display suggestions'*.

To check spelling while you're working in a document, you tap [f2]. The options are then as follows: *'Thesaurus'* will present you with synonyms for the word the cursor is on, or you will be asked to key a word in if the cursor is not on one and when you tap [RETURN] a list will appear. The parts of speech are also shown. You use the arrow keys and [RETURN] to select the word you want and then tap [EXIT] to go back to the editing screen: *'Document'* checks the spelling from the current cursor position and you then have the same options as we described above when working from the Main Menu: *'Word'* checks the spelling of the word you are currently on with, again, the same options as above: *'Lookup'* allows you to key in a word and then check it against the dictionaries.

SECTION 11-6
Spell Checker And Thesaurus

With the Thesaurus option from the Spellchecker Menu, you type in the word and when you tap [RETURN], the screen clears and a list of synonyms appears. These will be divided between different parts of speech where appropriate. You use the arrow keys and [RETURN] to select the one you want and then Exit to return to the Spell Checker Menu.

You can set up User Dictionaries with the *'Create'* option in the Dictionary Menu and peruse and edit them with the *'Edit'* option. Changes, alterations, additions and deletions can then be saved and will be available for your next spelling check.

■ SECTION 11-7
Database Module

As your business grows or you wish to extend your use of the computer, you will quite likely want to keep records of such things as your customers, suppliers, clients etc. Whether or not you have used a database before, you might like to start by referring to the beginning of the Database section of your User Guide where you'll find a brief step by step introduction.

This database is designed for easy access and dynamic record keeping, where individual records can be sorted under different index headings and simple mathematical operations can be performed on the data. The example they give for instance would allow you to prepare an alphabetical list of members, a summary of full-paying and discounted members and a list of who still owes their subscription.

We'll have a look at how you set up your own datafile and then how you can use this in conjunction with the Word Processing module to merge data with text.

1 If you are not already at the mini Office Main Menu, tap **[EXIT]** until you are back there. Select **'Database'** and the Database Menu appears.

2 To create a new datafile, select **'Alter structure'**. A message appears telling you there is no structure defined. At the bottom of the screen are several options, the one we want is *'(A)dd'* so tap **[A]**.

The *'Alter structure'* screen is divided into columns into which you will put the different fields of your record structure and details of the size and type of information for each.

SECTION 11-7
Database Module

The number of the field, in this case 001, is shown in the first column and mini Office Database is waiting for you to fill in the other details.

1 Below the main columns the cursor is beside the instruction *'Enter field name'*. Enter the **title** of the first field (e.g. Name), followed by **[RETURN]**. This then appears in dim type in the column next to the number 001 and the word *'Alpha'* appears in column three.

This column identifies the type of information the field will contain. If the field is simply text, then it will be Alpha, so in this case we can leave it as it is. If the entry is a number, like a telephone number, which is only a reference, then that also can be Alpha. If, however, you want to process a numerical entry in some way then you will have to change the entry type to Date, Number or Formula as appropriate.

2 You select the relevant type by using the arrow keys, but for the moment, just tap **[RETURN]**. You now select the size, style and position of the entry. Move the cursor onto the **'Size'** icon, using the arrow keys, and scroll through the range using the **[RETURN]** key. When you see the one you want, leave it on screen and move the cursor to **'Normal'**.

3 Again, use the **[RETURN]** key to select the style of character you want. You can select normal weight or dim printing from 'Norm' in the same way, provided your printer is able to respond.

4 Move the cursor onto **'Place'** and tap **[RETURN]**. Use the arrow keys to position the start of the field entry. Tap **[RETURN]** and use the arrow keys to define the size of the field.

SECTION 11-7
Database Module

You will see a counter at the top showing how many characters you have allocated. You can define more than one line by using the up and down arrows. The size should be sufficient to cope with what you anticipate the largest entry to be. Don't be too generous, however, because you cannot overlap fields and you still have to get all your information into the fixed space you have defined. The maximum size for an Alpha field is 72 characters.

5 Tap **[RETURN]** to go back to the alter structure screen and then **[A]** to add the second field. This time we'll include a date (e.g. date of birth), so enter **'DOB'** for the name of field and tap the **'Down arrow'** twice, for UK date, followed by **[RETURN]**.

Note: Once again you can vary the size and style of the entry and you can define its position as before, but the number of characters is fixed (00/00/0000).

Using the same technique as above you can add an age entry as number. Once you select number you are asked how many decimal points, which lead character and which separator character you want. (For a price in the U.K. you would want two decimal places, the £ as lead character and commas as separators, for example.) The number of characters allocated is once again fixed, (at twenty) and, when you start to edit, the first number will be at the end of the allocated space.

1 At the *'Alter structure'* screen, tap **[A]** for Add and key in **'Age'**. Tap **[RETURN]** and select **'Number'** and tap **[RETURN]**. We do not need decimal places, lead character or separators here, so tap **[RETURN]** three times and position the field alongside that for date of birth. Tap **[RETURN]** to go back to the Alter structure screen.

The last type of field is Formula, which allows you to prescribe calculations or conditions related to number entries.

SECTION 11-7
Database Module

The mini Office User Guide gives full details of the types of formulae available, but following our example, if we wanted to define a condition applicable to say all those people aged 25 and over, say for car insurance, we could create a formula which related to that field as 003 or as 'Age'.

1 At the *'Alter structure'* screen, tap **[A]** and key in **'Class'** for field name. Then select **'Formula'** for the field type. Tap **[RETURN]** three times then enter the formula **IF([Age]<25,1,2)** then **[RETURN]**. (Both square and round brackets must be included in the formula and notice there should be no space between *'IF'* and the rest.)

Thus we have a quite simple formula, if the age is less than 25 i.e. the 'if' condition is true, the class is 1, if not (i.e. the 'if' condition is not true and the age is greater than 25) the class is 2. (Commas must separate the first condition from the second.)

Once you have made a division into categories using such a formula, you can then process the results quite readily, by using 'Class' as a sort indicator.

1 If you want to add text to your fields to remind you what they are, at the *'Alter structure'* screen, tap **[T]** for Text. (The blocks you have identified for your fields are shown in dim highlighting.) You can make the same alterations to style and size as before, and you can toggle between underlining off and on.

2 Highlight the **'Text'** option, tap **[RETURN]** and key in the title you want to give to the first field, then move the cursor down alongside the appropriate field block and tap **[RETURN]**. (The title does not have to be the same as the field name.) Repeat this for the other fields.

SECTION 11-7
Database Module

3 To save your structure, tap **[EXIT]** three times to get back to the Database Menu. Select **'Load/Save'** and then **'Save all records'**. Key in a name for the file that relates to the data you will be recording and tap **[RETURN]**.

4 Now, if you wish to proceed to enter data, tap **[EXIT]**, select **'Edit data'** and you are presented with a blank record card. Tap **[N]** for 'New' and the cursor flashes on the first field. Key in the name and tap **[RETURN]**. Continue until each of the fields you have data for is completed. Where you are keying in a date you must key in the full date and the (/) separators, e.g. 21/03/1950.

Note: Once the age is entered in field 003, the class field adjusts automatically in response to the formula.

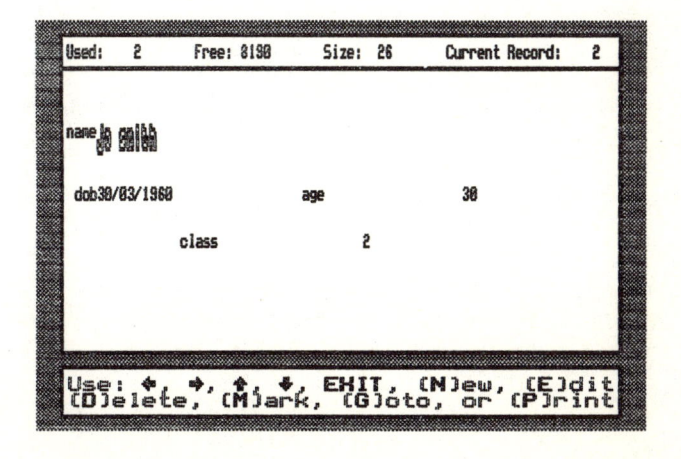

Fig. 3: A Sample Record Card.

SECTION 11-7
Database Module

5 Tap **[N]** to proceed to the next record and repeat the process. Continue until your records are up to date and then tap **[EXIT]** and repeat the *'Save'* routine using the same datafile name as before.

You can set up as many datafiles as you need, provided you have the space to store them. Try to organise your work so that data you are likely to process en bloc fits on a single disc and remember to give your files names that remind you what they contain.

Once your file is complete you can then proceed to sort the data.

SECTION 11-8
Processing Data

You sort data by field names. When you access the Sort Data menu from the Database menu, having first opened a datafile, you are presented with a list of the field names and types. The options from here are to sort, specify Ascending or Descending order or Clear any settings.

With the cursor on the field of your choice, specify whether the sort should be ascending or descending and then tap 'S' and the sort will begin. You can specify more than one sort field, primary and secondary, and the sort will take them in the order you selected them.

You can search for specific data using the *'Search and Mark Data'* option from the Database menu, once you have opened a datafile. This option calls up the list of field names and types. Using the arrow keys, you identify the field you want, key in the parameters for the search (string or number), add the 'Operator' (less than, equal to etc.) and tap 'S' to start the search.

Once the search is complete, you can display the marked records and, if you wish, print them out. You can then perform a sort on the marked records.

The *'Calculations'* option in the Database Menu allows you to perform simple mathematical operations on your records. For instance, you could total all the subscriptions shown or marked in the sample file *'MEMBERS2.DBS'* (field 005). You could then use *'Alter all records'* to change the subscription, and the Database would automatically calculate the new discounts and amounts payable.

The full procedures for processing your records are described in your User Guide. Accessing options from menus is done in the same way we described in previous sections and so we haven't repeated them here. The tasks you can perform from each option are shown on screen.

SECTION 11-9
Printing The Results

Once you have tried out each of these features, you will begin to see that by working out in advance which fields you want, and the formulae you want to include, you can perform some quite complex analytical processes on your data.

We'll come to Disc Utilities later, as they are common to all mini Office modules, so for now we'll just summarise the printing facilities that the Database offers you.

The first four items in the Print Menu deal with the attributes of your system and the style of printing. mini Office assumes that you have a PCW printer. To change this (assuming you have another printer attached to your system), you highlight the option and tap the [RETURN] key to toggle between that and Parallel. The other three options work in the same way.

To print all the records in your datafile to the specification you have made, you move the cursor down to *'Print all records'* and tap [RETURN]. You are given a Yes/No option to pause between records and whichever one you choose starts the print routine. *'Print marked records'* will print those records you marked during a search.

To set up a different print format for your data, you use *'Edit report/label format'*. With this menu you can specify general layout parameters such as width and depth, number of records across the page or sheet of labels and how to divide records. You can also design the layout of the fields within your records. If, for instance, you wish to print out labels which only contain names and addresses, in a standard layout, you select 'Edit report/label and using the arrow keys to position the cursor, you tap the [PASTE] key followed by the number of the field.

■ SECTION 11-9
Printing The Results

To *'Test print'* or *'Print report/labels'* you exit from the Edit Menu and return to the Print Menu and make the appropriate selection. If you want to leave a space between fields on the printout, you will need to leave a space between the field numbers. You can also add punctuation and any constant messages (e.g. First Class Post) at the editing stage.

As well as saving your datafiles and marked records for future reference, you can save the information in report or label format by selecting *'Save Report/Label Format'* from the Load/Save Menu. You can also save files containing, for example, name and address information as a Mail Merge file so that it can be read by the Word Processor module, as we shall see now.

SECTION 11-10
Using Database Files For Mailmerging

Mail Merge is a facility which allows you to take information from a database and insert it into a standard letter, thus personalising it. It will be individually addressed and could contain particular information like the class of insurance or the individual subscription amount for each person in turn.

To set up the standard letter you will need to know which fields you want where. For instance the name might be fields one and two, so where you want the 'pigeonholes' for these to appear in the letter, you hold down the [ALT] key and tap [D] (for *data*, I suppose). A dim letter 'D' appears and while still holding down the [ALT] key, you add the field number.

Then, when you select the *'Database'* option from the Word Processor Menu, you can load your data file, which will have the extension .MRG. Before you print your document, you will need to assign the fields to the appropriate string, and you do this through the *'Assign strings'* option in the Database Menu.

Once you select *'Print'*, one copy of the document will print out for each record in your datafile. To save the set-up for future use, you select the *'Load/Save Set Up'* option from the Word Processor menu.

If you need further details to help with the process of setting up merge documents and preparing your datafile for merging, you will find step by step instructions in the User Guide.

■ SECTION 11-11
Spreadsheet Module

1 To explain what this spreadsheet is like, you'd best have it on screen, so select the **'Spreadsheet'** option from the mini Office Main Menu and then tap **[RETURN]** for *'Edit Data'*.

The main part of the screen contains the top left corner of a very large sheet which is marked out in rows and columns. It's very similar to SuperCalc^2, if you have already looked at that. The cursor, a blank rectangle, sits over one of the intersections of these rows and columns, in this case 'A001', which is called a 'cell'.

In these cells you can enter text, data or formulae which you can use to deal with many kinds of situations involving calculations. You can use the sheet, which has 99 rows and 99 columns, to undertake quite complex financial operations. You can set up expenditure records, economic forecasting and explore profit margins and pricing policies.

2 To move around the sheet you use the arrow keys. Try this now and then return to cell 'A001' the 'home cell' by tapping **[key 2 on number pad]** (possibly marked SP.CHK).

Before you start to set up your own spreadsheet, it may be as well to have a look at one of the samples that mini Office 'prepared earlier'.

1 Tap **[EXIT]** to leave the blank sheet and select **'Load/Save'** from the Spreadsheet Menu. Select **'Load Data'** and then the file **'SPEND.SPR'**. Tap **[EXIT]** then select **'Edit Data'** and you have the spreadsheet on screen. (See overleaf.)

Before we look at this in any detail, just a word about the top of the screen. In the top left hand corner is the amount of space you still have free to work with and in the top right hand corner is the name of the file you are working on.

SECTION 11-11
Spreadsheet Module

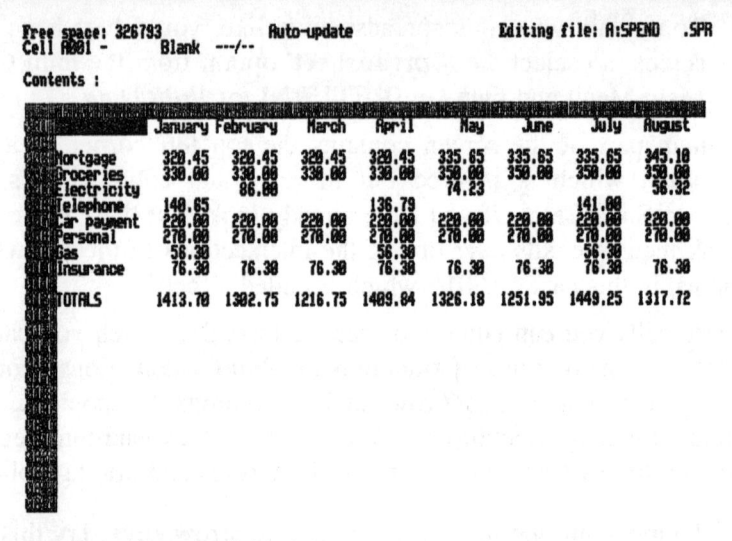

```
Free space: 326793           Auto-update              Editing file: A:SPEND  .SPR
Cell A001 -      Blank  ---/--
Contents :
```

	January	February	March	April	May	June	July	August
Mortgage	320.45	320.45	320.45	320.45	335.65	335.65	335.65	345.10
Groceries	330.00	330.00	330.00	330.00	350.00	350.00	350.00	350.00
Electricity			86.00			74.23		56.32
Telephone	140.65			136.79			141.00	
Car payment	220.00	220.00	220.00	220.00	220.00	220.00	220.00	220.00
Personal	270.00	270.00	270.00	270.00	270.00	270.00	270.00	270.00
Gas	56.30			56.30			56.30	
Insurance	76.30	76.30	76.30	76.30	76.30	76.30	76.30	76.30
TOTALS	1413.70	1302.75	1216.75	1409.84	1326.18	1251.95	1449.25	1317.72

Fig. 4: A Sample spreadsheet.

Auto-update shows that any additions or changes you make will be automatically implemented once entered. You can switch this off and go to manual update by tapping [ALT/U] and then using [f3] to speed up data entry if for instance you are making a number of changes.

The cell that the cursor is on and a summary of its contents are shown in lines two and three. As you move the cursor around the sheet you will see this line change.

1 Try this now and move across to see the data not currently on screen. Use the 'SP.CHK' or 'GRID' key to get back to cell 'A001'.

298

SECTION 11-11
Spreadsheet Module

To change an entry, you simply move the cursor to the cell and key in the new value. If Auto-update is on, when you tap [RETURN], the new value will appear. If the entry involves a formula, then all the related data will be updated too (just as in SuperCalc).

When you start to set up a spreadsheet for your own data, it is very important that you plan it out carefully in advance. You need to decide what each column and row is going to contain. Very often, the columns will represent progressive time slots, months or quarters for example, but the rows will need to contain all the basic data and all the calculations you want to make from these. If you can, keep a manual record, initially, to double check that you are getting the correct information out.

You can insert text into your spreadsheet, either as titles or as a description of data. As such, mini Office Spreadsheet knows that these cells do not contain data which needs to be processed. If your *text* entry begins with a number or mathematical symbol *(e.g. '3rd Qtr Sales')*, you should enter a single quote mark before it to identify it as text (again, this is similar to the procedure you saw in the chapter about SuperCalc^2).

If the text you have is too long to fit into the cell, tap [ALT/S] first and the space will expand to fit. You can alter the width of a column from the standard 7 characters in a similar way by tapping [ALT/W].

To enter numbers, you move the cursor to the appropriate cell and key in the number. Numbers can start with a mathematical symbol or decimal point. By default, numbers have two decimal places, as used in money entries. You can alter this by tapping [ALT/D] and following the on-screen instructions before making your entry.

SECTION 11-11
Spreadsheet Module

Formulae involve using the data of a number of cells to produce a calculation, the result of which will appear in the new cell. These can be quite straightforward operations involving operators like plus, minus, multiply, divide, raise to the power, less than, greater than, equal to or not equal to, which are represented by the symbols shown in your Reference Card.

They can also include more advanced functions such as logical operators, text functions, arithmetic functions, statistical functions and spreadsheet functions. Once again you can refer to the Reference Card to see how to enter these. Remember these can be a bit confusing if you don't take the trouble to plan out in advance exactly what you want to do with your data. Once you know what information you want, then it is much simpler to decide which functions you need.

Perhaps now is the time to get started with setting up your own spreadsheet. Begin by planning out on paper what information you want to include and what calculations are needed. Try laying this all out on a large sheet similar to the layout you will use on the computer and once you are happy with this start creating your own spreadsheet.

1 Tap **[EXIT]** twice to return to mini Office Main Menu, and when you are ready to begin, select **'Spreadsheet'**, then **'Edit data'** and you're ready to go.

Once you feel you are ready to progress, your User Guide will show you how to launch into more complex processes such as protecting data, looking up tables, using windows and preparing graphics windows.

Just before we leave the spreadsheet, however, make sure you save your work regularly, with a name that makes it clear to you what the spreadsheet contains.

SECTION 11-12
Graphics Module

The graphics module enables you to produce bar charts, pie charts and line graphs on-screen which you can save and print with a dot matrix printer. You can key in data direct or import it from the spreadsheet module. Unfortunately, you cannot import these graphs and charts into any other module.

Once again, the module uses the same structure of menus and options we have seen in other modules, with the addition of some icons for selecting types of graph and details of final presentation.

The graphics module handles numerical data, including formulae as we saw with spreadsheets. You can also add text and process all or sets of the data. Although the presentation is not sophisticated, either on screen or on paper, the ability to represent your data graphically can be very valuable, both in clarifying situations for yourself, and in illustrating your projections for others.

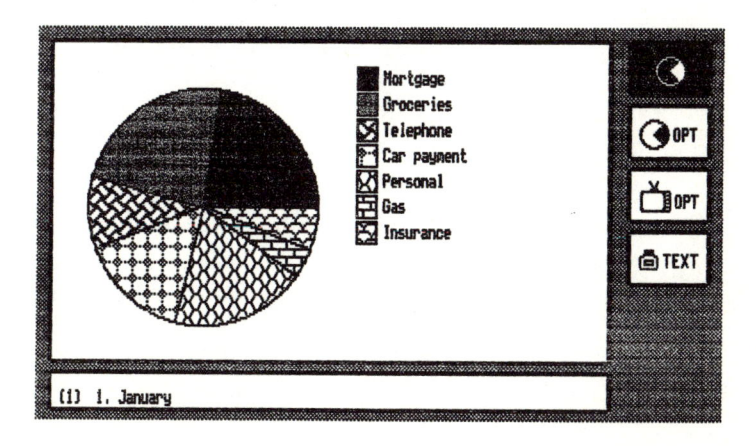

Fig. 5:   Sample Pie Chart.

SECTION 11-13
Communications Module

Through the Communications module, you can link your PCW, with the aid of a modem and telephone line, to a range of outside facilities. These include other computers, with or without a modem and telephone link, electronic mail and information services such as Prestel and bulletin boards of various sorts.

Those of you who (like us) are located in a rather remote region, or who find difficulty in getting out and about, will find this extends your possibilities no end. You can now enjoy rapid transmission of data.

Before you can make use of this facility, however, you will need to buy a serial/parallel interface and a modem which you then attach to the serial port of your PCW.

Once you are set up, you can save information from an outside source to an ASCII file on your computer, transmit information from your computer, call up information on screen from an outside source and use a 'Phonebook' to dial numbers automatically.

■ SECTION 11-14
Disc Utilities

We have referred to Disc Utilities several times in this chapter, but since they are common to all modules it seemed sensible to deal with them only once. Now that you are familiar with the facilities the modules have to offer and, hopefully have some idea how you can integrate their use to make your business more efficient, we shall conclude this mini Office chapter by briefly outlining the Disc Utilities. The procedures are very straightforward.

Basically, what the Disc utilities are designed to do is to help you organise your work. To sort files, erase files which are no longer needed and rename files, either from the Main Menu or within a module.

'Catalogue disc' shows you a list of all the files on the disc in the selected drive (in other words a directory of the disc). For single drive machines this will always be drive A:, or drive M:, but for twin drive machines you can get a directory for drives A:, B: and M:. If you change the disc, say, in drive A:, you simply tap A, or [ENTER], and the new catalogue appears.

If you are the only user, there will only be one user number, probably zero, and so *'Catalogue disc'* will show you all files. If files created by more than one user are on a disc, only those of the selected user will show.

The list of files will be displayed alphabetically by name, but it is possible to change this to 'Type' by toggling on the *'Sort file by'* line.

One way in which you can help to organise your work without the aid of the 'Disc Utilities' option is to create separate data discs and save related files to that disc. For example, if you have a datafile which you use for mailmerging, you could keep the word processed merge document on the same disc.

303

SECTION 11-14
Disc Utilities

Try not to hang on to files that you really have finished with. Copy any information that you do wish to keep into a new file where appropriate and then erase the original. You can use wild card symbols to erase groups of files, but you can only rename one file at a time.

Some Closing Words

■ Some Closing Words
Applications We Have Not Explored

There are, of course, many more types of application than we have had space to examine in this book. Just to give you an idea of what's possible, here's a short list of applications for the PCW which we haven't covered:

- Time management
- Typing tutors
- Graphics
- Programming languages
- Payroll
- Stock control
- Computer based learning
- Stocks and shares management
- Financial planning
- Financial controls
- Invoicing
- Credit control
- Estimating
- Pricing
- Production control
- Process control
- Labelling
- Printing controls

And so on. In short, if you have a task that's repetitive, or requires a great deal of accuracy, or simply requires that a lot of data has to be handled quickly, then there's a fair chance you'll find software to do it on your PCW.

Some Closing Words
Applications We Have Not Explored

The applications we have explored in this book have always been the most popular ones - along with book-keeping and accounts.

But there is a problem with accounting packages, which has made us chary of including them in this book: accountancy practice is highly regulated, yet, paradoxically, accounting software systems tend to be more varied than any of the types we have examined. We find it very difficult to choose a 'typical' example - one that might be used by an overwhelming number of PCW users.

For example, at one end of the scale might be a system from a large software publisher, like SageSoft, who's accounting systems, are very thorough and very systematic in the way they work - which makes them useful for, say, medium sized companies.

But quite often the *'one man band'* doesn't want (or need?) accounting software which dots every 'i' and crosses every 't' in a double entry bookkeeping system. He and his accountant need a system which does nothing much more than keep track of daily transactions and work out the VAT. So for him, the VQAL *(Vat Quarters Accounts Ledgers)* system from a small software house, Honeysett Computers of Preston on Wye, Herefordshire, might be an adequate solution (particularly as it can be integrated with a till and stock control sytem). So the best piece of advice we can give where accounting software is concerned is, talk to your accountant to find out what you need and then keep an eye on the adverts in the computer comics.

As people become more used to using computers every day, other types of software will come into favour. For example, many people are already moving away from simple word processing and into DTP *(Desk Top Publishing)*. DTP packages enable you to produce typeset masters on your own computers. This means that you can produce your own letterheads, brochures, newsletters and the like. And you can get quite professional looking results - providing you know a bit about graphic design.

■ Some Closing Words
Applications We Have Not Explored

The actual quality of output depends on the quality of the printer you are using. You see, you can't use a daisywheel printer with a DTP system, because daisywheels cannot form the shapes of the typeset letters. This immediately means that you will have to buy at least a dot matrix printer (instead of, or as well as your daisywheel printer). And for the best results you really need a laser printer. So there are costs over and above the straight cost of the software you will have to be aware of.

But everything costs money, so there's no reason to let it discourage you. We hope that this book has gone some way to showing you how versatile your computer is. The plain and simple fact is that your PCW *is* a general purpose computer.

So why not exploit its potential..?

Index

Index

Index

!

8000copy	163

A

Abandoning your work, LocoScript	26
Accounting packages	308
Ambiguous file names	174
Applications, possible	307
Applications, general introduction to	145

B

Booting and rebooting the system	153
Booting Direct into a program	166

C

COPY key, LocoScript	36
CP/M, commands	
file name masks	182
general points	181
structure	181
CP/M, function	149
Creating a document with LocoScript	19
CUT key	25

D

Data disc creating	169
Data file, definitions	129
Databases, functions	195
Databases, general points	195
dBase II	
adding records	239
append command	239
browse command	241
browse command, editing controls	241
browse command, using selectively	242

Index

dBase II (continued)		
command file	246	
create a new database	237	
data fields, types	238	
DISPLAY command	243	
DISPLAY command, using selectively	244	
DO command	246	
ERASE command	244	
examine and alter records, browse	241	
examining records, display (list)	243	
functions	233	
GOTO command	243	
introduction	233	
LIST command, using selectively	244	
programming with	246	
record sorting	245	
saving data	240	
SORT command	245	
starting up	234	
USE command	239,	240
WELCOME program	235	
Deleting (erasing) a file	178	
Directories	155	
Disc drives	12	
Disc drives, general	14	
Disc drives, memory drive (M:)	12	
Disc management screen, general	14	
DISCKIT	160	
formatting with	170	
using	161	
Discs and drives	150	
Discs		
care of	151	
checking the available space	158	
copying	160	
copying with 8000COPY	163	
formatting	169	
Document set-up, LocoScript	33	

Index

Drive M:, The memory drive	12
DTP	308

E

ERA command	178
Erasing (deleting) a file	178

F

File name masks	174
File names	172
File names, ambiguous	174
File type extensions, ones to avoid	173
Files	
care of	151
copying	176
erasing (deleting)	178
naming and storing	172
protecting	188
renaming	180
setting passwords	190
Function keys	
setting to issue commands	187
setting up	184

H

Housekeeping	152

I

Inserting text, LocoScript	27
Installing software, general points	191
Integrated software, definition	269

K

Keying in text	20

Index

L

LocoFile
adapting a database file	214
altering records	208
an introduction	197
capabilities	202
datafile, setting up your own	226
datafile setup	220
deleting (erasing) a record	212
exchanging data with LocoMail	230
extract items	224
finding a specific record	205
goto menu	205
index, changing	220, 223
index key, changing	206
installing	198
moving through the records	204
pattern card, setting up	228
record card	203
record card, moving around	203
running	202
squashing files	212

LocoMail
creating the pigeonholes for data	120
exchanging data with LocoFile	230
fill and merge	118
mailshot run, the	134
master letter, creating	119
master letter, merge	125
merge data file	128
printing, fill	123

LocoScript
abandoning your work	26
assembling large documents	32
automatic exchange, caution	54
blank page display	20
blocks of text, handling	55

Index

LocoScript (continued)
- character & line spacing — 81
- character pitch — 82
- clear menu — 67
- closing down — 13
- copy a file — 49, 52
- copy key — 36
- creating a document — 16
- cut and copy — 55
- cut and paste — 56
- deleting a sentence at a time — 51
- deleting text — 23
- disc management display — 11
- document set-up — 33, 104
- editing a document — 16
- emboldening — 101
- files cursor — 15
- find — 49
- find and replace — 52
- finishing work on a document — 21
- forced page break — 79
- group cursor — 15
- inserting block of text — 46
- inserting text — 27
- layout, saving a — 75
- line spacing — 82
- mailmerging, background — 117
- margins, changing — 68
- margins, changing temporarily — 69
- marking sections of text — 35
- page length, setting — 79
- page options — 106
- paper sizes and types — 104
- paper type option — 80
- pasting in text — 30
- printers, using others — 107
- printing — 40

Index

LocoScript (continued)
- printing part of a document — 44
- re-laying the text — 24
- save and print — 22
- search — 51
- set and clear codes, keystrokes — 65
- set and clear menus, using — 64
- set menu — 66
- standard phrases — 57
- standard phrases, saving — 59
- standard printer settings — 40
- standard template, creating — 89
- starting up — 9, 10
- stock layouts, creating & using — 77
- tables, setting up — 74
- tabs — 71
- tabs, types of — 72
- text, centring — 87
- text, justifying — 83
- text, right aligning — 87
- the CUT key — 25
- underlining — 98

LocoSpell
- checking your spelling — 141
- introduction — 139

M

mini Office Professional — 269
- auto update - ss module — 298
- calculations - db module — 293
- case change - wp module — 279
- cells, adjusting the size - ss module — 299
- cells - ss module — 297
- changing an entry - ss module — 299
- communications module — 302
- create new datafile - db module — 287
- database module, introduction — 287
- datafiles and mailmerging — 296

Index

mini Office Professional (continued)

defining a block - wp module	274
dim codes - wp module	278
disc utilities	303
editing the ruler - wp module	276
entering text - ss module	299
field size - db module	289
field types - db module	288
formulae - db module	290
formulae - ss module	300
general introduction	269
graphics module	301
handling blocks - wp module	274
housekeeping	303
insert & overwrite - wp module	279
justifying text - wp module	275
keying in text - wp module	273
label format - db module	295
mailmerge standard letter	296
main menu	271
margins and spacings - wp module	276
moving around the worksheet - ss module	297
planning the layout - ss module	299
preparing the system for your computer	270
print enhancements - wp module	274, 277
print format - db module	294
printer set up - wp module	283
printing - wp module	283
printing results - db module	294
saving your work - db module	291
saving your work - wp module	273
screen display width - wp module	279
search & replace - wp module	282
search - wp module	281
search for specific data - db module	293
set up	271
sorting data - db module	293

Index

mini Office Professional (continued)

spell checker & thesaurus	285
spell checker, user dictionaries	286
spreadsheet module	297, 299
status block	273
tab settings - wp module	276
word count - wp module	280
word processing module	273
word processor menu	282

O

Operating system	149

P

Passwords, modes of protection	190
Passwords, setting up	190
Pasting in text, LocoScript	30
PIP.COM	176
PIP.COM, parameters	177
Print wheel, changing	111

Printer

control mode	43
loading paper	42
paper release lever	42
platen	42
ribbon, changing	113
tractor feed, removing	41
types	107
Printers, parallel, adding	183
Printing with LocoScript	40
PROFILE.SUB	166, 183
Protecting files	188

R

Renaming a file	180
Resetting the system	153
RPED	167

Index

S

Saving your work, The memory drive (M:)	13
SuperCalc^2	250
automatic update of formulae	264
BLANK command	261
cancelling an entry ([ALT][Z])	258
cell	250
cell coordinates	251
cell position, formulae auto update	264
cells default width	253
clearing the spreadsheet (/ZAP)	258
command signal key (/)	256
command switch key (/)	256
commands, position of the cursor	262
data types	252
DELETE command, the	262
directory, getting	259
duplicating the contents of a cell	265
erasing the contents of a cell (or cells)	261
file, descriptive label (cell A1)	260
files, loading	259
formula entries	253
GOTO command	254
inputting commands	256
INSERT command	264
keying in data	251
labelling a file	260
loading a file	259
OUTPUT command, (printing)	263
printing a spreadsheet, output command	263
printing on the screen	263
putting information on the worksheet	252
QUIT command	258
range, entering	265
range, specifying one	262
REPLICATE command	265

Index

SuperCalc² (continued)
    SAVE command — 256, 257
    spreadsheet control information — 251
    spreadsheet cursor — 250
    spreadsheet cursor, moving — 250
    spreadsheet cursor direction — 251
    starting up — 250
    text entries — 252
    what if questions — 255
    worksheet — 250
    ZAP command, the — 258
Setting a password — 190
Spreadsheets, general introduction to — 249
Starting a document — 15
SUBMIT RPED — 167
SUBMIT.COM — 166